ALEXANDER OF APHRODISIAS

On Aristotle

On Coming-to-Be

and Perishing 2.2-5

ALEXANDER OF APHRODISIAS

On Aristotle On Coming-to-Be and Perishing 2.2-5

Translated by
Emma Gannagé

Guest editor: Peter Adamson

Duckworth

Ancient Commentators on Aristotle
General editor: Richard Sorabji

First published in 2005 by
Gerald Duckworth & Co. Ltd.
90-93 Cowcross Street, London EC1M 6BF
Tel: 020 7490 7300
Fax: 020 7490 0080
inquiries@duckworth-publishers.co.uk
www.ducknet.co.uk

A catalogue record for this book is available from the British Library

ISBN 0 7156 3303 1

Acknowledgments

The present translations have been made possible by generous and imaginative funding from the following sources: the National Endowment for the Humanities, Division of Research Programs, an independent federal agency of the USA; the Leverhulme Trust; the British Academy; the Jowett Copyright Trustees; the Royal Society (UK); Centro Internazionale A. Beltrame di Storia dello Spazio e del Tempo (Padua); Mario Mignucci; Liverpool University; the Leventis Foundation; the Arts and Humanities Research Board of the British Academy; the Esmée Fairbairn Charitable Trust; the Henry Brown Trust; Mr and Mrs N. Egon; the Netherlands Organisation for Scientific Research (NWO/GW), Dr Victoria Solomonides, the Cultural Attaché of the Greek Embassy in London. The editor wishes to thank the Council of Gresham College for a special grant for the preparation of this volume for press, Peter Adamson, Inna Kupreeva, and Stephen Menn for their comments, Peter Adamson, Inna Kupreeva and John Sellars for preparing the volume for press, and Deborah Blake who has been Duckworth's editor for all volumes in this series since the beginning.

Printed and bound in Great Britain by
Biddles Ltd, Kings Lynn, Norfolk

Contents

Guest Editor's preface vii
Author's preface ix
Introduction 1
  Alexander of Aphrodisias 2
  Alexander's commentary *On Aristotle On Coming-to-Be and Perishing* 6
  Jābir b. Ḥayyān, *Book of Morphology* 10
  I: The authenticity of Alexander's commentary in Jābir's *Book of Morphology*, and the theory of elements 14
    A: Four explicit references 15
    B: Ya'qūb b. Isḥāq al-Isrā'īlī as confirmation of the commentary's authenticity 21
    C: Elements in the proper sense, and the primary perceptible bodies 43
  II: Prime matter and elemental hylomorphism 56
    A: Alexander and the tradition 57
    B: Elemental change and prime matter 60
  Conclusion 81

Translation 83

Appendix: Treatise of Ya'qūb b. Isḥāq al-Isrā'īlī al-Maḥallī 127
Bibliography 131
English-Arabic Glossary 139
Arabic-English Index 146
Subject Index 161

A Jean-Pierre Osier
pour m'avoir appris l'essentiel

Guest Editor's Preface

This volume is an unusual addition to the Ancient Commentators series. Although it does render into English a Greek commentary on Aristotle, what Emma Gannagé has provided is in fact a translation of a translation. Alexander's commentary on *On Coming-to-Be and Perishing* (which in this volume will be called *On Generation and Corruption*, or *GC* for short) is lost in Greek and had been thought lost in Arabic as well. But in the introduction to this volume, Gannagé shows that fragments found in an early Arabic alchemical work ascribed to Jābir b. Ḥayyān constitute an Arabic translation of Alexander's commentary on *GC* II.2-5. These fragments are thus an important piece of evidence for the transmission of Greek philosophy and science into Arabic. Those interested in the Arabic translation movement will be especially grateful to Gannagé for her thorough index of Arabic terms, at the end of this volume. The translation is also of considerable philosophical importance, as the introduction to this volume shows. It adds to our understanding not only of late ancient chemistry, but also of how ancient authors viewed Aristotle's cosmology and his theory of matter and the elements. In this commentary we see Alexander attempting nothing less than a unified theory of Aristotle's physics and chemistry.

Of great assistance for the editing of this volume were Inna Kupreeva, who helped to edit the translation and prepare the introduction, and John Sellars, who helped put the volume into camera ready copy. I am also grateful for the support of the Leverhulme Foundation, which allowed me to give this volume the attention it deserved.

Peter Adamson

Author's Preface

The present volume is a revised version of a part of my PhD thesis, 'Le commentaire d'Alexandre d'Aphrodise *In De generatione et corruptione*, perdu en grec retrouvé en arabe dans Jābir b. Ḥayyān, *Kitāb al-Taṣrīf* (Université Panthéon-Sorbonne, Paris I, décembre 1998). Thanks are due to my dissertation supervisor Prof Remi Brague and to the members of the Jury, particularly Dr Fritz Zimmermann for his constant and valuable support.

This research was initiated, at the Warburg Institute, at the instigation of Dr Silvia Fazzo, during a short stay at the autumn 1995-1996 thanks to a Henry Franckfort Fellowship. The fantastic atmosphere of the Warburg Institute and the great resources of its library were decisive at the beginning of this work. I am very grateful to all the members of the Institute then and in particular to Prof Charles Burnett who welcomed this research in his seminar.

The French Institute in Teheran (Institut Français de recherche en Iran) supported my trip to Teheran and welcomed me during the time necessary to my research. My thanks to the Director at that time, Dr Remy Boucharlat and to all the scholars who were present for their warm welcome. Iran will always be associated in my mind with Dr Asghar Mahdawi, who very kindly put his collection of manuscripts at my disposal. I have wonderful memories of the long hours spent working in his fantastic place and of the conversations we sometimes had. For all that I am very grateful to him.

I am indebted to Prof George Saliba and Prof Maroun Aouad for stimulating and very fruitful discussions of my views, as well as to Prof Dimitri Gutas for providing me with valuable advice concerning the translation.

I am grateful to the readers for the Ancient Commentators series and in particular to Dr Steven Menn for his useful comments.

My thanks are also due to Nicole Stephan and Lara Challita, who contributed to the translation of this work into English.

I wish to thank the editorial board of the Ancient Commentators series and especially Dr Inna Kupreeva and Dr John Sellars for their assistance in the preparation of this volume. In its final form, this book is very much indebted to Dr Peter Adamson: he put it into readable English, and his remarks led me to clarify my thoughts on some issues. I am deeply grateful to him for his zeal and his endless patience.

Finally there are no words to express my gratitude to Richard Sorabji. Crossing his path is determining in a scholar's life: I have benefited from his intellectual generosity, his constant enthusiasm and support, and his outstanding scholarship.

Emma Gannagé
Beirut, July 2005

Introduction

The discovery of important fragments of an ancient commentary on Aristotle's *De Generatione et Corruptione* (hereafter *GC*) in an Arabic alchemical treatise may seem surprising in two respects. First, it casts doubt on the thesis that it was Book 4 of the *Meteorologica* that was the inspiration for the theory of elements and their transformation, as we find it in the alchemists.[1] Second, the existence of such extensive philosophical extracts in an alchemical text sheds light on the theoretical foundations of Arabic alchemy, defined as the art of transforming metals, and especially transforming common metals into precious ones.[2]

The surprise may be lessened somewhat, if we consider the texts in question, namely Alexander of Aphrodisias' commentary *in GC* and the *Book of Morphology* (*Kitāb al-Taṣrīf*) by Jābir b. Ḥayyān. What we find in Jābir, whose immense corpus includes collections of philosophical treatises, is nothing other than an early philosophical form of alchemy.[3] Also, the philosophical

[1] See P. Kraus (1986), 30; for a contrary view see M. Ullmann, '*al-kīmiyā*", in H.A.R. Gibb (1960-), vol. 5, 110-15. For Ullmann *Meteor.* 4 is neither a work of chemistry in the modern sense, nor a point of departure for alchemy.

[2] See Ibn al-Nadīm, *al-Fihrist*, ed. G. Flügel (1872), 351.

[3] In the early period of Arabic philosophy the line between the 'philosophical' and 'alchemical' traditions was rather blurry. Alchemy's claim to discover the secret of producing gold was a long-running controversy amongst philosophers; yet on the other hand, the Arabic alchemical tradition was distinctive in its solid theoretical foundation. M. Ullmann has indicated the unique status of alchemy which, given its theoretical foundations, must be distinguished from minerology, the art of chemistry used by the craftsman, and pharmacology. 'As a whole it was a natural philosophy which aimed not only at teaching the transmutation of the metals, but also at the whole connection the world' (Ullmann, '*al-kīmiyā*", in H.A.R. Gibb (1960-), vol. 5, 112). The philosophical tradition included opponents of alchemy, but also supporters of, at least, its theoretical possibility. Amongst the latter should be counted especially Abū Bakr al-Rāzī (864-925), author of one of the most important medieval works on alchemy, *Sirr al-asrār* (*Secretum secretorum*); but we may also include al-Fārābī, who believed the transmutation of metals to be possible. On detractors of alchemy, see for instance al-Mas'ūdī, *Murūj al-dhabab wa ma'ādin al-jawhar*, ed. S. Pilla (1965), §3312, reporting that the philosopher al-Kindī composed a treatise against alchemy, attempting to disprove the claims of its adherents. This is confirmed by Ibn al-Nadīm, who in the *Fihrist* tells us that al-Kindī composed a work entitled *R. fī 'l-tanbīh 'alā khidā' al-kīmiyā'iyyīn* (*Warning Against the*

digressions scattered through his works are very numerous, and references to Aristotle and the Greek commentators (especially Alexander) are also frequent. And the philosophical alchemy elaborated by Jābir is fundamentally grounded in the theory of the elements, their combination, and their reduction to the elementary qualities. Seen in this light, it is not *Meteorologica* 4, which deals with the formation of primary compound bodies – that is, homoiomers, and not elements – that would have provided the theoretical foundations of Jābir's physical theory, but rather *GC* Book 2, and especially chapters 2-5, which study the number of the elements and their mutual transformations.

Jābir's as yet unedited *Book of Morphology* contains a literal Arabic translation of a commentary on Aristotle's *GC* 2.2-5. This commentary, otherwise lost, takes the form of *lemmata* from Aristotle accompanied by explanatory remarks. In four places Jābir refers explicitly to Alexander of Aphrodisias. In this introduction, I show that the preserved translation is in fact to be ascribed to Alexander in its entirety. Some points of philosophical interest to be found in the commentary will also be discussed.

Alexander of Aphrodisias

What we know about Alexander of Aphrodisias comes first from the dedication of *De Fato* to the Emperors Severus VII and Antonius Caracalla, in which Alexander thanks the emperors for a recommendation that allowed him to become a professor of Aristotelian philosophy. The text can thus be dated between 198 AD, the year Septimus began to share power with his son Antonius, and 209, the year Geta, Antonius' brother, was designated as Augustus.[4] It is probable that Alexander was referring to an imperial chair in Aristotelian philosophy in Athens. As a professor of philosophy at the turn of the century, he must have been born in the beginning of the second half of the second century.[5] Although many cities were referred to as 'Aphrodisias', P. Thillet maintains that 'at this time, Aphrodisias of Carie was without doubt the only city important enough to be included as part of someone's name without ambiguity'.[6] An inscription recently discovered at Aphrodisias,[7] on a statue base set up by Alexander for his father, gives the complete name of the philosopher,

Deceits of the Alchemists). Al-Mas'ūdī goes on to say, however, that the philosopher al-Rāzī attacked al-Kindī, and defended the possibility of alchemy. (I owe this reference to the kindness of Dr Peter Adamson.) In addition it is worth mentioning the position of Ibn Sīnā in the *Shifā'*: he condemns alchemy for its vain pretension to be able to transmute metals (see Ibn Sīnā, *Al-Shifā', al-Ṭabī'īyyāt*, vol. 5: *al-ma'ādin wa al-āthār al-'ulwiyya*, ed. A. Muntasar (1965), 22). For a survey of attitudes towards alchemy among medieval Arabic philosophers and scientists, see M. Ullmann, 'al-kīmiyā'', 113-15.

[4] See R.B. Todd (1976), 1, n. 3.

[5] See R. Goulet and M. Aouad (1989), 126.

[6] See P. Thillet (1984), viii.

[7] See A. Chaniotis (2004a), 388-9; reference taken from R. Goulet's addition to S. Fazzo (2003), 61. See also A. Chaniotis (2004b). I am very grateful to Maroun Aouad and Richard Sorabji for these references.

Titus Aurelius Alexandros, and states that he was *diadokhos* at Athens, which means one of the heads of the philosophical Schools in Athens in succession to Plato, Aristotle, Zeno, and Epicurus.[8] Moreover it informs us that Alexander's father was a philosopher and thus might have been his first teacher in philosophy. Herminus and Sosigenes[9] are explicitly cited as Alexander's teachers, though we do not know where or when he studied with them.[10] Alexander often refers to them in his work. Aristotle of Mytilene[11] may also be added to this group. Arabic bibliographers duly mention Alexander of Aphrodisias; however, several confuse him with Alexander of Damascus, so that he is frequently said to have had stormy relations with Galen.[12]

The only commentaries by Alexander extant in Greek are those on the *An. Pr.*, *Top.*, *Meteor.*, and *Metaph.* 2-5. We know however that he wrote commentaries on all the logical writings of Aristotle except the *Sophistical Refutations*, as well as on the four treatises dealing with physics and *De Anima* (hereafter *DA*).[13] Alexander also wrote independent treatises (*suggrammata*) aimed at a more general audience, in order to present either controversial opinions (as in his *De Anima*) or themes that Aristotle himself had not developed, and that Alexander attempted to treat from an Aristotelian perspective. For example, *De Fato* and *De Providentia* attempted to integrate Aristotelian cosmology with a theory of providence. These two treatises reflect the philosophical preoccupations of Alexander's time, and in particular show him responding to the Christian criticism that Aristotle's system lacked any theory of divine providence. These independent treatises all have a markedly polemical character, directed variously against the Christians, the Platonists, and the Stoics (principally Chrysippus). *De Mixtione*, for instance, is directed against the Stoics' theory of the *krasis di' holou*.

Finally, there are two large collections of short treatises that are probably not directly by Alexander, yet reflect the activity of his school.[14] The first, a set of

[8] See J.H. Oliver (1977).

[9] Alexander refers to him as his teacher, *ho didaskalos hêmôn*; see *in Meteor.* 143,13. Sosigenes had interests in logic and is reported (by Alexander, *in Meteor.* 143,14) to have written a treatise on vision (*Peri Opseôs*) in eight books. See R.B. Todd (1976), 11.

[10] See P. Thillet (1984), viii.

[11] On the identity of this philosopher mentioned by several sources as a teacher of Alexander of Aphrodisias and called Aristotle, see the entry by R. Goulet, 'Aristote de Mytilène', in R. Goulet (1989), 412 and references given there. Aristotle of Mytilene is mentioned by Galen as one of the best contemporary Peripatetic philosophers. Galen refers to him as one of the head figures in the Peripatetic school (*anêr prôteusas en têi Peripatêtikêi theôriai*); see R.B. Todd (1976), 11. See R.W. Sharples (1990a), 86-9 and 89-95, for Alexander's relations with his contemporaries and direct predecessors.

[12] On the origin of this confusion, see M. Aouad and R. Goulet (1989), 126-7, and P. Thillet (1984), xxxiii-xlix. For the argument that the dispute between Alexander and Galen is reported only in the Arabic tradition, see S. Fazzo (2002).

[13] R.B. Todd (1976), 14-15, notes that he was the first Peripatetic to work on Aristotle's psychological treatises.

[14] For an analysis of the way in which the short treatises attributed to Alexander can inform us about the activity of his 'school', see Sharples (1990a), esp. 104 ff.

texts gathered by Bruns under the title *De Anima libri Mantissa*, is related to Alexander's *De Anima*, and must have constituted its second book.[15] The second collection is a set of *Quaestiones* arranged in four books. The three first books, brought together under the title: *Phusikai skholikai aporiai kai luseis*,[16] include a variety of texts on diverse topics, ranging from physics to psychology by way of metaphysics and logic. R.B. Todd distinguishes within these collections two sets of questions devoted roughly to a single general topic, which he describes as 'notes', on *DA* and *GC* respectively.[17] Sharples adds a third series related to the *Physics*.[18] The fourth book, titled 'Problems on Ethics' deals, as his title shows, with ethical problems.[19]

A complete bibliography of Alexander's writings, which also takes into consideration the Arabic tradition, has been provided by Sharples in his *Bericht* and supplemented by the article 'Alexandros of Aphrodisias' co-written by R. Goulet and M. Aouad and published in the *Dictionnaire des Philosophes Antiques*.[20] A few recent discoveries on the subject of the transmission of Alexander's writings may be added:

(1) Fragments of Alexander's lost commentary on *Phys.* 4-8 were recently discovered in the margins of a manuscript in the National Library, Parisinus sup. Gr. 643.[21]

(2) A short treatise attributed to Alexander and entitled *A Treatise by Alexander of Aphrodisias that every separate cause is in all things and in none according to the opinion of Aristotle*[22] (D29), preserved only in its Arabic

[15] See *CAG* Suppl. 2.1 (ed. I. Bruns), 101-86. For a brief description of its contents, see Todd (1976), 18; for the details of the treatises which it contains and for the problem of the authenticity of many of them, see M. Aouad and R. Goulet (1989), 134.

[16] Edited by I. Bruns, *CAG* Suppl. 2.2, 1-116, and translated in R.W. Sharples (1992) and (1994). For the description of these collections and the character of the treatises they contain, see Sharples' introductions to the two volumes mentioned above.

[17] See R.B. Todd (1976), 19, nn. 89 and 90.

[18] See R.B. Todd (1976), 19 and R.W. Sharples (1992), 3.

[19] Edited by I. Bruns, *CAG* Suppl. 2.2, 117-63 and translated in R.W. Sharples (1990).

[20] See R.W. Sharples (1987), 1176-243, M. Aouad and R. Goulet (1989), 125-39, along with S. Fazzo (2003), 61-70. See also the introduction in P. Thillet (1984), lii-lxxiii. For the Arabic tradition see A. Dietrich (1964); J. van Ess (1965); H. Gätje (1966), and F.W. Zimmermann and H.V. Brown (1973).

[21] See M. Rashed (1995); E. Giannakis (1996) has collected the citations from Alexander in the scholia, dated to the tenth to eleventh centuries, found in the margins of the school edition of the Arabic translation by Isḥāq b. Ḥunayn (d. 910/911) of Aristotle's *Physics* in the MS Leiden Or. 583; these citations would have been excerpted from Philoponus' commentary ad loc.

[22] Edited and translated by F.W. Zimmermann (1994a), 48-51 and 10-13, whose translation I reproduce. The number of the treatise is the one it has in the list of Alexander's works in Arabic in Dietrich (1964) cited above, whose numeration I use henceforth.

version, is in fact an extended version of the Kindī circle's translation of Proclus, *Elements of Theology* 98.[23]

(3) *Discourse of Alexander: that form is the completion and perfection of motion. According to the view of Aristotle*[24] (D8) is a version adapted from *Quaest.* 1.21, and takes its place alongside the version that we already have (D2b).[25]

(4) *Discourse of Alexander: that actuality is more general than motion, according to the opinion of Aristotle*[26] (D9) is in fact an adapted version of *De Aeternitate mundi contra Proclum* 4. 4-6 by John Philoponus.[27]

(5) *Discourse of Alexander of Aphrodisias: How to prove wrong the claim that one thing will always come to be from another, and to establish that it is from nothing that everything comes to be*[28] (D 16) is an adapted version of *Aet.* 9.11 by Philoponus.[29]

(6) *On coming-to-be* (D27g),[30] long considered to be a copy of D16, is in fact falsely attributed to Alexander. This treatise also originates at least partially in *Aet.*[31]

[23] This has been discovered by F.W. Zimmermann (1994a). He has also shown that a certain number of Arabic translations of Alexander's *Quaestiones* have been revised in the circle of al-Kindī where they were subjected to modifications post-dating their translation. The majority of these treatises, if not all of them, formed at some point part of a collection combining works by Proclus and Alexander; see ibid.

[24] Edited by A. Badawī (1947), 289-90, and translated by him in Badawī (1987), 165-6. English title from F.W. Zimmermann (1994a), 25.

[25] F.W. Zimmermann and A. Hasnawi have independently arrived at this discovery, see F.W. Zimmermann (1994a), 25-9 and A. Hasnawi (1994), 55-68. Another translation of this treatise has been already recognised and published by H. Gätje (1966), 262, who has detached the translation of *Quaest.* 1.21, from the ensemble of three treatises transmitted as one under the title: *kalām al-Iskandar al-Afrūdīsī, naql Sa'īd b. Ya'qūb al-Dimashqī* [Discourse of Alexander of Aphrodisias, translation of Sa'īd b. Ya'qūb al-Dimashqī] (D 2) edited by A. Badawī (1947), 278-80.

[26] Edited by A. Badawī (1947), 293-4; English title from F.W. Zimmermann (1994a), 22. A. Hasnawi (1994), 68, n. 32, notes that this treatise is not mentioned by the Arabic bibliographers.

[27] This discovery, as well as the following one, concerning D 16, has been made by A. Hasnawi (1994), 68-75.

[28] S. Fazzo and H. Wiesner (1993), at 138 n. 47, were the first to signal the inauthenticity of the attribution of this treatise to Alexander.

[29] See A. Hasnawi (1994), 76-92, who points out that apart from the introductory passage originating from *De Aeternitate Mundi contra Proclum* 9.8, the rest of D 16 corresponds, with the exception of a few lacunae, to *Aet.* 9.11, 345,4-355,27.

[30] This classification has been proposed by F.W. Zimmermann (1994a), 15-16, in order to distinguish the seven treatises transmitted together in the MS. Istanbul, Carullah 1279 under the heading, 'Extracted by Alexander from Aristotle's *Theologia*' (D 27), which contains in fact the Arabic translation of 20 propositions of Proclus' *Elements of Theology* and five treatises explicitly attributed to Alexander of Aphrodisias.

[31] S. Fazzo was the first to question the authenticity of D27g and to point out the discrepancies between D16 and D27g which had previously been considered as two identical versions of the same lost Greek original. But she has not seen their origin in

(7) More light has been shed on a Syriac version of the *Treatise of Alexander of Aphrodisias on the discourse concerning the principles of the universe, according to the opinion of Aristotle the philosopher* (D1):[32] it is a treatise by Sergius of Resh'aynā, also entitled *On the principles of the universe.*[33] It is still unedited but was translated by Furlani based on a London manuscript.[34] C. Genequand observes that 'it corresponds very closely to the Arabic version, particularly at the beginning and has the same conclusion. But it is noteworthy that the whole section on the intellect and the self-thought of the First is missing'.[35] On the one hand this comparison confirms the authenticity of the treatise, which has long been doubted,[36] but on the other, it reinforces the suspicion that the Arabic version may be a combination of different texts mixed with the original Arabic version of Alexander's treatise.[37]

(8) The treatise *On the celestial sphere* (D26) is in fact composed of three extracts from *On the principles of the universe* (D1).[38]

(9) It is now established that *The book of Poetic Gleanings by Aristotle the philosopher* (D30), whose authenticity was questioned by F. Zimmermann, is an Arabic pseudo-epigraph based on an epitome of Aristotle's *Top.* and the Arabic version of the *Rhetoric.*[39]

To this short list of new elements concerning the survival of Alexander's works we may now add the extracts of the Arabic version of his commentary on Aristotle's *GC* 2.2-5 found in the first ten folios of Jābir b. Ḥayyān's *Book of Morphology.*

Alexander's commentary *On Aristotle On Generation and Corruption*

Alexander's commentary on Aristotle's *GC* was previously considered lost. There are however several lengthy extracts reproduced in the commentary on this text by John Philoponus.[40] Todd remarks that *Mixt.* is, in places, quite

Philoponus; see S. Fazzo (1997). Concerning the origin of D27g, see Hasnawi (1994), 101-6, who finds and analyses parallels in *Aet.*

[32] Edited by A. Badawī (1947), 253-77 and translated by A. Badawī (1987), 135-53. See the recent edition based on several manuscripts, with parallel English translation, in C. Genequand (2001). See also on the subject of this treatise, M. Aouad and R. Goulet (1987), 135 and S. Fazzo (2003), 67.

[33] C. Genequand (1997), 271-6, has made this discovery.

[34] G. Furlani (1923).

[35] See C. Genequand (2001), 34.

[36] See S. Pines (1986c) and D. Gutas (1988), 217.

[37] See C. Genequand (1997), 272.

[38] As shown in C. Genequand (2001), 28.

[39] See F.W. Zimmermann (1994b), whose English translation of the title I reproduce.

[40] See the *Index Nominum* to Philoponus *in GC* (*CAG* vol. 14), under *Alexandros.*

similar to Alexander's commentary on *GC* and could serve as a guideline to determine the authenticity of citations of Alexander in Philoponus' text.[41]

Some of the *Quaestiones* also develop themes very close to those dealt with in *GC* and could serve, to a certain extent, as an indication of Alexander's approach in his commentary. For example, the subject of *Quaest.* 1.5 (*That growth is only in the form and not in the matter*) concerns *GC* 1.5, 321b19 ff. This subject, also taken up in the last chapter of *Mixt.*,[42] is also found in Philoponus' commentary *in GC ad loc.*[43] It is also possible to look in the *Quaestiones* for solutions to certain problems raised by *GC*, though in the context of the *Quaestiones* Alexander might be expected to give his own opinions rather than straight exegesis of Aristotle. *Quaest.* 1.6 for instance examines the problem of water's being cold rather than moist, but his handling of the problem there differs from what we find in the extracts presented in this volume. Other *Quaestiones* reproduce or summarise passages from *GC*. For example *Quaest.* 3.5 takes up a point from *GC* 2.11, 338a4-b5, and gives it an orthodox presentation. By contrast *Quaest.* 2.22[44] presents a solution quite different from that found in Alexander's commentary, on *GC* 2.11, 337b25 ff.

In the Arabic tradition, the bibliographers all refer to an Arabic translation of Alexander's commentary on *GC*, ascribing it to Abū Bishr Mattā.[45] It was previously considered lost, as is the Arabic version of the *GC* itself.[46] There are

[41] See R.B. Todd (1976), 14, who notes (244) that chapters 13-15 of the *De Mixtione* are most certainly related to Alexander's commentary *in GC*. In Philoponus' commentary *in GC* 1.5, 102,31-108,17, Alexander's demonstration is found in the same form in which it appears in *De Mixtione*, ch. 13-15: all Alexander's arguments are re-stated in the same order.

[42] See *Mixt.* 235,14-236,5.

[43] See Philoponus, *in GC* 106,3-11.

[44] See R.W. Sharples (1994), 26-8, and the beginning of the title: 'Explanation of a passage from the second [book] of Aristotle's "On Coming-to-Be and Passing-Away", differing from that in the commentary on it'.

[45] Ibn al-Nadīm (ed. G. Flügel [1872], 251) tells us that Alexander's commentary was translated into Arabic by Abū Bishr Mattā b. Yūnus (d. 940). The first book was also translated by Qusṭā b. Lūqā. Mattā's translation was revised by Yaḥyā b. 'Adī. Ibn al-Nadīm also mentions a commentary by Olympiodorus translated by Asṭāth, two commentaries by Themistius, a long and a short one, as well as a commentary of John Philoponus translated into Syriac and Arabic. This information is to some extent corroborated by later bibliographers. See for example al-Qifṭī, *Ta'rīkh al-Ḥukamā'*, ed. J. Lippert (1903), 30. An isolated report by Ibn Abī Uṣaybi'a is worth mentioning since it may help to identify a probable copy of the Arabic version of Alexander's commentary in circulation. He remarks that a doctor in Egypt, Bilamẓafar (b-l-m-ẓ-f-r) Naṣr b. Maḥmūd b. al-Mu'arraf, has copied Alexander's commentary and that he himself saw his name in the colophon of the copy dated 534H/1140, see Ibn Abī Uṣaybi'a, *'Uyūn al-anbā' fī ṭabaqāt al-aṭṭibā'*, ed. A. Müller (1884), vol. 2, 108.

[46] Arabic biobibliographers mention concerning Aristotle's *GC* a single translation from Greek into Syriac and at least two independent Arabic versions. Ibn al-Nadīm (ed. G. Flügel (1872), 251), reports that Ḥunayn b. Isḥāq translated *GC* from Greek into Syriac. Apart from that, he mentions two translations from Syriac into Arabic: one by Isḥāq b. Ḥunayn (d. 910/911) and one by Abū 'Uthmān al-Dimashqī (fl. *ca* 900). A third

however some previously known extant sections of the commentary: two fragments conserved in ms. Chester Beatty 3702, and the theses ascribed to Alexander by Ibn Rushd (Averroes), in the latter's *Epitome* and *Middle Commentary* on *GC*.[47]

The extant fragments in ms. Chester Beatty 3702, fol. 168b are citations that appear in the *K. al-sa'āda wa al-is'ād* of Abū al-Ḥasan Muḥammad b. Abī Dharr Yūsuf al-'Āmirī.[48] One fragment seems of dubious authenticity,[49] but nothing casts doubt on the authenticity of the other: 'Alexander says, in his commentary on *GC*, "nature is able to dissolve all the components of matter from which life comes. For this reason eternity [of matter] takes place, because what is dissolved is renewed, and this goes on for ever" '.[50]

The references given in Ibn Rushd's *Middle Commentary* and *Epitome*[51] are rather more substantial. We can distinguish three clusters of citations in the *Middle Commentary*. (1) With reference to *GC* 1.5, 321b32-322a4, Alexander is cited three times[52] demonstrating, against Aristotle, that growth is not only in the form but also in the matter. (2) The citation of Alexander regarding *GC* 2.2 330a24-9[53] is confirmed by Philoponus,[54] who reproduces it almost literally (see below). (3) A third citation is given regarding *GC* 2.3 330b25-30.[55] Ibn Rushd also refers twice to Alexander in his *Epitome*. As in the *Middle Commentary* he cites Alexander's demonstration that growth is in matter as well as form (on *GC* 1.5, 322a14-16).[56] The second citation deals with the preservation of species due to the eternity of celestial motion, *GC* 2.11, 338a17.[57]

translation is attributed to Ibn Bakkūs (Ibrāhīm b. Bakkūsh [possibly Bakkūsh or Bakkūs] Abū Isḥāq al-'Ushshāri): but the information is second-hand, based on oral reports. No copies of any of the mentioned versions have been recovered so far. For the Arabic version of Isḥāq b. Ḥunayn see G. Serra (1973) and (1997); A. Tessier (1979) and (1984). For a complete review and recent update of the Arabic tradition of the *GC* see M. Rashed (2003), 314.

[47] See R.W. Sharples (1987), 1176-243 and M. Aouad and R. Goulet (1987).

[48] Edited and translated by A.A. Ghorab (1972), 81-2.

[49] See A.A. Ghorab (1972), 81, who himself seems to doubt the authenticity of this quotation (87 no. 2): 'Alexander said: things noble by nature are like [the following examples]: to revere and glorify God, to do justice, not to do injustice to anybody, to respect people and to be decent to them. Things noble by convention are like [the following example]: not to eat in the market-place'.

[50] English translation by A.A. Ghorab (1972), 82.

[51] Ed. J. al-'Alawī (1995), with index of proper names under *al-Iskandar*; and ed. A.W. al-Taftazānī and S. Zāyid (1994). For an English translation based on Latin and Hebrew versions see S. Kurland (1958). For an edition of the Latin version see F.H. Fobes (1956), 105 ff.

[52] See al-'Alawī (1994), 50-1, 53; and S. Kurland (1958) 34, 35, 37. See also *Quaest.* 1.5 and D 19.

[53] See J. al-'Alawī (1994), 95, and S. Kurland (1958), 74, 23 ff.

[54] See Philoponus *in GC* 214,23-4; 223,10-12.

[55] See J. al-'Alawī (1994), 97-8 and S. Kurland (1958), 76-7. Kurland assumes, wrongly, that this is an extract from Alexander's commentary *in Meteorology*.

[56] See A.W. al-Taftazānī, and S. Zāyid (1994), 13, and S. Kurland (1958), 117.

[57] See A.W. al-Taftazānī, and S. Zāyid (1994), 35, and S. Kurland (1958), 137.

Finally, P. Kraus first noted[58] the existence of 'an almost complete literal translation of chapters 2 to 5 of the second book of *GC*' in an unedited treatise by Jābir b. Ḥayyān, entitled *Book of Morphology*. Kraus pointed out that this was accompanied by a 'long commentary that has its sources in Antiquity. A quick comparison demonstrates that it is not John Philoponus' commentary, the only one thought to be extant. [...] At several points Jābir refers to Alexander of Aphrodisias; thus everything leads us to believe that he had Alexander's commentary in front of him'. Indeed, the ten first folios of the text basically reproduce *in extenso GC* 2.2-5, along with an extensive commentary. The expression '*qāla al-Iskandar*' (Alexander said) appears four times, following *lemmata* introduced by '*qāla Arisṭūṭālīs*' (Aristotle said). Are only the four fragments prefaced by '*qāla al-Iskandar*' to be attributed to Alexander, or is he the author of the entire commentary? Though he denied that the commentary was that of Philoponus, Kraus remarked that Jābir's commentary is, at several points, very close to Philoponus',[59] and further that: 'Extracts of Alexander's commentary were probably included in all later Greek commentaries. We must therefore consider the possibility that Jābir knew Alexander's commentary only indirectly'. Recall that the Arabic bibliographers mention Arabic translations of commentaries by Olympiodorus and Themistius, in addition to those of Philoponus and Alexander.

In addition to identifying the extracts of the ancient commentary preserved in the *Book of Morphology*, we must also consider Jābir's work itself. The nature, the requirements and the scope of the treatise account for his choice to transmit this text, as well as for the selection of these extracts rather than others. The narrow and punctual identification of the commentary and its author must be understood within a wider frame 'in terms of inherent variance within the manuscript matrix'.[60] The gaps in the transmitted commentary show a deliberate choice on Jābir's part. Analysis of the terminology of the text, and identification of the author of the translation that Jābir is here quoting, will have consequences on the dating of the *Book of Morphology* and thereby of the Jābirian corpus. All these factors, as well as Jābir's unusual compositional strategy, determined the reception of this text. The textual situation is further complicated by the hazards of transmission, a strongly corrupted text that is cut off in the middle of a sentence, and the annotations and revisions of the copyist.

[58] P. Kraus (1986), 322.
[59] ibid.
[60] See K.C. Ryding (1990). She suggests a re-evaluation of the study of the Jābirian corpus 'through the application of postmodern textual criticism within the framework of what is termed "the new medievalism". In this analytical approach [...] variance and fluidity of discourse are in fact considered the foremost characteristics of the medieval manuscript matrix'.

Jābir b. Ḥayyān, *Book of Morphology*

Jābir b. Ḥayyān b. ʻAbdallāh al-Kūfī al-Ṣūfī Abū ʻAbdallāh or Abū Mūsā was an alchemist who would have lived in Baghdad in the eighth century in the Imāmite *milieu.* Tradition sees him as a disciple of Imām Jaʻfar al-Ṣādiq (d. 765), who is said to have initiated him into alchemy. An immense scientific and philosophical corpus is attributed to Jābir; Kraus counts some three thousand titles.[61] The historicity of Jābir himself and the authenticity of the works attributed to him are matters of controversy. But in any case the corpus is divided into collections of treatises, which are explicitly mentioned in the treatises themselves: either by notes mentioning the collection to which the treatise belongs, or by references directing the reader to other collections of treatises for further information.[62]

The collection of 144 Books called *Kutub al-Mawāzīn* (*Books of Balances*), to which the *Book of Morphology* belongs, is dedicated to the exposition of the balance theory at the base of Jābir's system.[63] This theory 'has as its goal to reduce all natural phenomena and in general all human knowledge to a system of quantity and measure', thereby conferring upon them a precise scientific character.[64] In the physical world all things are composed of four elements, which are themselves composed of four elementary qualities or 'natures' (*ṭabā'iʻ*). This makes it possible to calculate the degree of intensity of the qualities of each constituent, so as to establish the quantitative structure of a thing. Hence one may produce new bodies, and in particular the elixir that can influence metals. The collection of *Kutub al-Mawāzīn* has as its ultimate aim the production of the 'supreme elixir' which is able to bring about all the transmutations, but along the way it delves deeply into cosmology and physics in general.

The balance theory is thus a method intended to establish a quantitative system for the natural sciences. Jābir firstly applies it to the three kingdoms of the *sublunary* world, giving mathematical laws that govern the transformation, generation and corruption of all things. 'All things fall under <the principle> of the balance', and thus become comprehensible.[65] The practice of alchemy is then based on the reduction of bodies to their elements, and on the modification of the elementary qualities. Jābir's balance theory gives this practice its most systematic structure. For, by measuring the constitutive natures of a body, the

[61] See P. Kraus (1943). With regard to the problem of authorship, Kraus concludes that these treatises are apocryphal writings composed by a shīʻite school of alchemists ca. late ninth to early tenth century, xvii-xxv; xxxiii-xl; lvii-lviii. P. Lory (1996), 51-2, points out that a large number of these treatises are opuscles that cover only two or three folios, so that the corpus is not so enormous as it might seem.

[62] The most comprehensive classification to date is still the one by P. Kraus (1943), 3-171.

[63] It would originally have been composed of 144 treatises listed by P. Kraus (1943), 75-99; 44 have been preserved.

[64] See P. Kraus (1986), ix and 187.

[65] See ibid., 187 ff.

alchemist can precisely establish their exact proportions, and thereby change the constitution of the body through the alteration of the quantities or the intensities of the natures; it is even possible to create new bodies. Thus Jābir can aspire to a quantitative theory of the elements. He classifies the intensities of the natures following a complex arithmetical system inspired by Galen, which he improved. However, the arithmetical data, despite their precision, remain empirical if they are not supplemented by the theory of the 'balance of letters', which is the most precise system for determining the intensity of the natures in a body. This theory is grounded on a fundamental identity between the natures that constitute a body and the letters that compose the body's name. The name expresses the essence of the thing it designates, and manifests its true nature. The analysis of words thus allows us to establish the qualitative and quantitative structure of the things that those words express. Jābir divides the twenty-eight letters of the Arabic alphabet into four groups of seven letters, each group corresponding to one of the four elementary qualities. Thus the twenty-eight letters correspond to the twenty-eight possible intensities (four degrees of intensity and seven subdivisions for each degree). There is a corresponding table of numerical values for the four degrees of intensities of the four elementary qualities, which obey the progression 1, 3, 5, 8. The position of a letter in a word determines the intensity of the quality that it 'represents'.

The application of this theory is the purpose of the third part of the *Morphology*, where it is analysed in terms of the rules of Arabic grammar. However, letters only represent the manifest nature of a thing; the 'latent' part eludes our perception. Hence the need for the balance theory, which completes the values obtained from the analysis of the letters, yielding a total of seventeen parts, each body having an identical structure regulated by the number seventeen.[66] The transmutation of bodies is made possible by the dual structure of all bodies: the 'interior' part of the body is the counterpart of the 'manifest' part, which is expressed by the letters in its name. Thus the alchemist is able, through the analysis of letters, to find the relationship between the interior and the exterior of a body. This allows him not only to bring the body into equilibrium, by completing the values of those natures that are lacking, but also to transmute one body into another. He does this by changing the relationship between its internal parts and its manifest parts, while maintaining the equilibrium of its parts. The letters, then, do not merely *represent* the elementary qualities; they *are* the qualities, they embody them.

All of this is reflected in the title *K. al- Taṣrīf,* which plays on a double meaning, physical and grammatical. The word *taṣrīf* is derived from the root *ṣ-r-f*, which means *to change direction, divert, derive*. But it can also mean *to transmute*, *transform, inflect,*[67] in other words to make a thing change from one state or condition to another. It may also refer to the explication or interpretation of a text. In grammar *'ilm al-taṣrīf* 'is the science that studies the alterations of

[66] This number is the sum of 1, 3, 5, and 8, which constitute an arithmetical progression that describes the four degrees of intensity of the elementary qualities.
[67] See W. Lane (1893), 1680.

words, excluding the declensional endings (*i'rāb*)'.[68] Thus it is equivalent to morphology. This is why, in translations from Greek, *taṣrīf* invariably renders *ptôsis* (inflection), so that it is strictly confined to a grammatical usage.[69] But inflection has essentially to do with meaning: it is the *modulation* of the basic meaning of a term according to strict rules.[70] The double meaning of *taṣrīf*, then, corresponds to the alchemical and linguistic parallelism of the theory of balances: the 'derivation' of a word from its basic root, on the one hand, and the 'derivation' of a body from its basic qualities, on the other.

The first part of the *Morphology* (§§10-111), the one translated in the present volume, is dedicated to reproducing the translation of a Greek commentary on *GC* 2.2-5. But Jābir undertakes this only to establish the theoretical framework for his physical theory, and to delineate the fundamental doctrine of the balance theory. In what follows, he will apply this theory to the artificial production of beings belonging to the three sublunary kingdoms: animal, vegetable, and mineral (§§112-48). Next is Jābir's clearly Neoplatonic cosmology (§§150-67), which depicts the world as a set of concentric circles, in which the four elementary qualities or natures constitute the last hypostatic circle at the limit of

[68] See, C.H.M. Versteegh, '*Taṣrīf*, in H.A.R. Gibb (1960-) vol. 10, 360-1; A. Elamrani-Jamal (1983), 29-30 and P. Kraus (1986), 241. Kraus suggests that *taṣrīf* corresponds, for philosophers, to the Greek *sumplokê* which originally means 'interweaving', 'connexion'. It is found with this meaning in *Cael.* 3.4, 303a7, referring to the combination of the primary magnitudes out of which all things are generated, according to the atomists. The term *sumplokê* is also used in grammar and logic to designate a combination of letters in words, or of words in sentences (see Plato *Sophist* 262C). However, the Arabic translators never use *taṣrīf* to render *sumplokê*, which is regularly translated by *ta'līf* or *tarkīb*. For *ta'līf*, see *Cat.* 1a16; 1b25; 2a8; 13b10-13 and A. Badawī (1948), vol. 1, 4, 6, 45; *Int.* 21a5 and A. Badawī (1948), vol. 1, 84; *Cael.*, 303a7 ff. and A. Badawī (1961), 329. For *tarkīb*, see *DA*, 428a25; 432a11 and A. Badawī (1980), 70, 79; *Top.* 112b27-30; 113a1 and A. Badawī (1948), vol. 2, 518-19.

[69] For the definition of *ptôsis* (which properly signifies a 'fall') see *Poet.* 1457a18-23 and A. Badawī 1953, 128. See also *Cat.* 1a15 and K. Georr (1948), 319, 372; *Int.* 16b1 and A. Badawī (1948), vol. 1, 61. Versteegh notes that while *i'rāb* designates, in grammar, nominal declensions and must render the Greek *ptôsis*, the terms *ṣarf* and *taṣrīf* are used in philosophical circles for all morphological changes of nouns and verbs, but this term is not found until after the first Greek translations. Now, the declension designated by *i'rāb* is not merely phonetic, but also semantic, since it entails a change in the signification of the word and so a change of referent (cf. Fakhruddīn al-Rāzī, *Mafātīḥ al-ghayb* (ed. 'A. Muḥammad (n.d.), vol. 1, 48, and Dionysios of Thrace, *Scholia*, 230, 34-5 cited by the author). He himself thinks that the word *ṣarf* is connected to the Greek *klisis*, although he fails to establish clearly the exact relation between the two terms. See C.H.M. Versteegh (1977), 63-7 and for the opposite opinion A. Elamrani-Jamal (1983), 29-30. In Aristotle, *ptôsis* or inflexion is a general term which covers any kind of modification or variation of a basic form; it is thus common to noun and verb; whereas the Stoics limit *ptôsis* to nouns only.

[70] See A. J.-L. Delamarre, (1980). See also M. Frede (1994), esp. 122 ff. Frede points out that the Stoics could identify the 'case' with the constitutive qualities of an object, insofar as the concept signified by the case belongs to a true assertion. The truth of the assertion would thus entail the existence of the quality signified by the case.

the material world. Jābir calls the Aristotelian elementary qualities 'natures' and endows them with a concrete and independent existence. This is followed by a section on the balance of letters (§§169-84), as described above. The treatise concludes with a critique of reasoning by analogy, as used in *kalām* (§§185-203). The relationship between this final section and the rest of the work is difficult to determine.[71]

Within this larger work, the extracts of our commentary begin abruptly at *GC* 2.2, 329b32, after the second chapter has already begun, and subsequent to the statement of the premises Aristotle will use in the following demonstration. Aristotle's goal in this section is to determine which are the primary, tangible qualities that enter into the composition of perceptible elementary bodies. In order to combine together, the qualities must be reciprocally active and passive and must therefore be contrary. The qualities must therefore be tangible, in order to permit reciprocal action and passion, as only sensible bodies can be affected (*pathêtika*). Among tangible qualities, the hot, cold, dry and moist are primary, because only they are reciprocally active and passive through themselves, and not through anything else. All other tangible qualities are therefore derived from these four primary qualities.[72] In the fragments here extant, we proceed directly to the characteristics of the moist and its derivatives. This lacuna, like those later on, shows Jābir's deliberate choice of which extracts to reproduce. *K. al-Taṣrīf* simply assumes the context of the first tangible qualities, and Jābir is uninterested in the demonstration of the primacy of these qualities. He is rather concerned with the reciprocal transformation of simple bodies, due to the combination and interaction of the elementary qualities that constitute them. He clearly indicates this interest in his prologue: 'In our present book, we will describe, by way of instruction, the morphology of the Natures, their states and quantities, and the aspects of their union, this way our book will be accomplished' (§8). Jābir wants to establish the theoretical grounds of the transmutation of simple bodies: the commentary serves as the doctrinal foundation for his alchemical theory. For this reason he prunes the text so as to keep only what deals directly and concretely with the reciprocal transformation of elements. Thus he reproduces almost in its entirety (with the exception of 331b21-4) the fourth chapter, which describes the mechanics of elementary transformation, and most of chapter 5, from which he omits the logical demonstration that no element can be the matter for another.[73] In the second chapter, however, he limits himself to the reduction of the tangible qualities to dry and moist (329b34-330a14; 20 and 24). And he omits most of the third

[71] Though K.C. Ryding (1990), 119, notes that the use of analogical reasoning (*qiyās*) characterises both grammar and alchemy. 'In Arabic grammar it serves as a basis for regularisation of morphological and syntactic phenomena, and in alchemy it has similarly powerful applications, as in the mathematical correlation between the phonemes that constitute a lexical item and the actual quantitative structure of the item itself'.

[72] See *GC* 2.2, 329b6-25.

[73] He omits the following passages: *GC* 332a4-6; 8-10; 13-23; 23-6; 332b5-7; 10-14; 333a2-7.

chapter, leaving out the logical deduction of the constitution of the elements, based on the possible combinations of elementary qualities in pairs, as well as the doxographical exposition (330a30-330b25 and 33-4). In this chapter he retains only the determination of each element by its proper quality, the discussion of where elements are placed in the cosmos, and the description of the maximal intensification of the elements' constitutive qualities and its consequences. In short, everything of a demonstrative nature or of philosophical interest is eliminated in favour of physical, even materialist, descriptions of the characteristics of the four elemental qualities and their derivatives, and of the transformation of simple bodies into one another by means of these qualities.

I: The authenticity of Alexander's commentary in Jābir's *Book of Morphology*, and the theory of elements

A prologue, which is clearly distinct in style and terminology, precedes the commentary preserved by Jābir. The latter bears all the distinctive signs of an ancient Greek commentary: the Aristotelian text is explained sequentially, reproduced in the form of *lemmata* of varying length, followed by a literal exegesis.[74] Phrases from Aristotle's text often reappear in the exegetical sections. The explanation of the lemma is usually introduced by a general exposition, which reminds the reader of what has come before and prepares him for what will follow. These introductory passages are distinguished by their logical structure.[75] It is characteristic of Alexander's method in his commentaries to explain not only individual passages, but also the train of thought that runs through the passages.[76] Our commentary frequently considers different interpretations for a given passage, phrase, or particularly difficult expression. This too is characteristic of Alexander, as can be seen from his *Quaestiones* as well as his exegetical writings.[77] Similarly, he does not hesitate to draw parallels with other philosophical schools.[78]

Nevertheless, as we have seen the commentary reproduced by Jābir does not represent the entirety of Alexander's commentary in *GC* 2.2-5, but consists rather of extracts. Here one might worry that the commentary is not only incomplete, but also only a free paraphrase of the original. Might Jābir have summarised Alexander's text, while modifying the style and including original developments? Or, again, might he have drawn from other commentators?

[74] See R.W. Sharples (1990a), 95-6; R. Sorabji (1990b); A.J. Festugière (1971), 551, 555. R.B. Todd (1976), 15, distinguishes three characteristic elements in Alexander's commentaries: at the beginning, the first general exposition of the text; then a longer paraphrase of the passages with a problematic meaning; and finally, parallels with other philosophical schools.

[75] See the translation in this volume (hereafter *Morphology*), §§68-70.

[76] See P. Moraux (1979), 53.

[77] See P. Moraux (1979), 102, who points out that, in problematic cases, Alexander does not hesitate to provide a series of interpretations that differ but are in his view equally plausible.

[78] See for instance *Morphology* §94 and R.B. Todd (1976), 15.

Towards answering these questions, we must first determine whether only the four passages prefaced by explicit references to Alexander are to be ascribed to him. In this case the extracts would in fact be from a later commentary that refers to Alexander's. Unfortunately the only ancient commentary on *GC* now extant is that of Philoponus, preserved in the original Greek. As mentioned above, P. Kraus has already pointed out that this is not the basis of our text: 'the choice of *lemmata* is often different, and Jābir's explanations are almost always more detailed'.[79] Yet in several places Jābir's commentary is very close to that of Philoponus. I will therefore begin by comparing the four explicit references to Alexander with the parallel texts in Philoponus; this will lay to rest the hypothesis that our extracts are based on Philoponus (section **A**). In section **B** below, I will establish Alexander's authorship of the entire commentary reproduced in the *Morphology* via a comparison with an unedited treatise by the physician Ya'qūb b. Isḥāq al-Isrā'īlī al-Maḥallī (*fl.* 1202), who also preserves extracts from the same commentary.

A: Four explicit references

The first of these explicit references to Alexander to appear in the text will require the most in-depth discussion, which I postpone to the end of this section (**Ad**). Let us begin, then, with the second:

Aa: *Morphology* §§68-72

> Then [Aristotle said]: that all [the elements] are generated out of all and the way in which their change into one another takes place, has now been stated. Moreover, we have to examine them in this way (*GC* 2.4-5, 331b36-332a3). By saying that, Aristotle started talking about things previously discussed. Those who use other methods and other arguments have also discussed these things. He first explained that none of the primary bodies is matter or principle and also [that matter] is not the intermediate body among these bodies. But, matter is something else, other than a sensible body insofar as it is not a body. Nevertheless, it is not something separated from bodies and it cannot subsist in isolation (*GC* 2.5, 332a33-5). Then he explained that the elements, I mean the primary bodies, are four and that their change takes place from all into all (*GC* 2.5, 332b1-30). In this chapter, he explained that the change of the elements does not go on to infinity, but their change does in a circle among them (*GC* 2.5, 332b30-333a15). As to the reason why he explained that the transformation of the elements in a straight line does not go on to infinity and he did not explain that the elements are not more than four, we say that, given that this had already been said when he explained that, since the sensible contrarieties by which bodies are given a form and affected by a nature are four, it was impossible that there exist more than the four

[79] P. Kraus (1986), 322-3.

primary bodies. He furthermore said: for matter is not one of the natural bodies, either one or two or more (*GC* 2.5, 332a5-6). Alexander said: Aristotle has explained here that it is impossible that any one of the four simple bodies become matter, nor any other, or two or more according to the opinion of the *phusikoi* (*al-ṭabī'iyyūn*). Then Aristotle said: nevertheless, they cannot all be one element, like for instance that they all be water or air or fire or earth, since change in general only belongs to contraries (*GC* 2.5, 332a6-8). We say that it is impossible that one of the primary bodies becomes matter for the rest.

Context: transition between chapters 4 and 5. It has already been demonstrated that there exist four simple bodies, with an underlying, incorporeal matter. Each of the simple bodies is constituted by a pair of primary tangible qualities, which allows them to transform from one into another. Here the same point is demonstrated from a different starting-point (*Morphology* §68). The extract is situated at the beginning of chapter 5, which first shows that none of the simple bodies can be the principle for all the others, nor can they be the matter for natural bodies. All are derived and transformable (*GC* 332a4-332b5). The second part of the chapter demonstrates that the elements transform cyclically, not in an infinite straight line (*GC* 332b5-333a15).

Aa situates the argument against the background of what has preceded, and concisely summarises the plan of the chapter by dividing it into three parts: (1) None of the primary bodies is matter or principle, nor can there be an intermediate body between them. But there is no separate matter (*Morphology* §69,1-8). (2) The elements are four in number and transform reciprocally (*Morphology* §69,9-10). (3) The elements transform in a cycle (*Morphology* §69,11-12).

Aa refers to the brevity of Aristotle's review of the demonstration of the number of elements; lest the reader think that such a demonstration is missing from the present context, the commentary points out that Aristotle has already demonstrated it in 2.3, 330b1-3 (*Morphology* §69,13-19). In short, then, **Aa** is an introductory section typical of ancient commentaries: it indicates the beginning of the linear explanation and introduce the first lines of the chapter (*Morphology* §68).

The parallel section of Philoponus *in GC* is noticeably different.[80] First, in its choice of lemma: the lemma in Aa includes the conclusion to chapter 4 and the first sentence of chapter 5, whereas Philoponus begins at the start of chapter 5. Also, Philoponus' introduction lacks the concision and lucidity of our text. He proposes two different interpretations of the goal of the chapter, which both in fact have to do with the first part. This is followed by a fastidious and exhaustive list of arguments for determining the number of principles. Finally, at no point does he cite the name of Alexander, and his interpretation is quite

[80] cf. Philoponus *in GC* 237,4-238,28.

different from what we find in Jābir. Thus it is clear that Jābir makes no use of Philoponus' commentary here.

Ab: *Morphology* §§95-6

Aristotle said: let the earth be indicated by *A* and water by *M*, air by *P* and fire by *R*. Then, if *P* changes into *M* and *R*, there will be a contrariety for *PR*. Let this contrariety be whiteness and blackness. Also, owing to the fact that *P* changes into *M*, there will be another contrariety, for *M* and *R* are not identical. Let this contrariety be dryness and moisture. Let dryness be indicated by *I* and moisture by *L*. If then whiteness remains, water will be white and moist, and if it does not, water will be black, for the change only takes place into contraries. It follows then necessarily that water be either white or black. Let it then be *J* [black] first; similarly *I* will then belong to *R* – I mean the dryness – so that the change will then occur also to *R* – I mean fire – into water, for they are contraries, since fire was first black and then dry, and water was first moist and then white. (*GC* 2.5, 332b14-27)

Alexander said: he wanted to show that change does not take place only from the middle to the two extremes, but that change takes place for the last two extremes also, into one another. For the change of all [the elements] into all annuls [the possibility] that either one of them be their principle. It is believed in this regard that what [Aristotle] explained is not that both extremes change into those that are between them, though he did indeed admit this. Yet this is not so, rather this [sc. that both extremes change into those that are between them] was also shown, *modo continuo* and according to the necessity of the change of all into all, through which both extremes change also into one another. It is possible that he [sc. Aristotle] might have meant by 'the extremes' that there are very many contrarieties in between them, as for water and fire, air and earth. If someone who believes that it is evident that by 'the extremes', he [sc. Aristotle] meant 'those which are on both sides of the middle which has been posited as the principle', observes that these [change] into one another and do not change only into all of what is between them, then he annuls the principle that has been posited and that we just stated. For he makes clear that fire changes into water and not only into air, which was posited as a principle.

Preliminary remark: the lemma is unusually long for the usage in ancient commentaries. Perhaps Jābir had direct access to Aristotle's text as well as the commentary; or, more likely, he could have assembled the *lexeis* within the commentary to form a seamless text. A different problem is determining the extent of the extract cited here; the beginning is marked clearly by the reference to Alexander, but unlike **Aa** there is no obvious marker for the end of the fragment.

Context: Here Aristotle demonstrates that no intermediate element can be the principle for the others, because of the reciprocal transformation of elements. Aristotle builds his own theory on the refutation of those Presocratics[81] who posited one of the elements as a principle (air for Anaximenes, water for Thales). He argues that it is absurd to say, for instance, that air and water transform into their adjacent elements, while the extreme elements earth and fire do not: this would make the cyclical transformation of elements impossible.

Ab highlights an important point in Aristotle's demonstration: he is not concerned to show that the intermediates transform into the extremes, but rather that the extremes can transform into one another (*Morphology* §96). For, if we suppose that the extremes can only be reached from the intermediates, then the transformation remains rectilinear, even if the movement is reciprocal. The transformation of the two extremes into one another presupposes cyclical transformation, and this eliminates the possibility that any one element is the principle for the others.

Formally considered, **Ab** first clearly states the problem, then lays out the stages of the demonstration. This uses the assumption of an intermediary element or principle to show that no element can be principle for the others: for the transformation of the intermediates into the extremes entails the transformation of the extremes into the intermediates.

Now, Philoponus reproduces an extract of Alexander's commentary on the same passage.[82] This extract is quite similar to **Ab**, though not wholly identical:

> Alexander inquires how it could be that having proposed to prove that the extremes change into one another, he apparently has not proved *that*; but rather has demonstrated instead that contraries change into one another. And he says: 'Perhaps in the beginning too he referred by 'extremes' to contraries; and after that, as is also more adequate, he proved from the terms set down that all [elements] have contrariety in relation to one another. And if this is the case, it is clear that all will change into each other too'. It is manifest that he has proved the extremes, viz. earth and fire, to have contrariety in relation to one another, since he has assumed fire to be black and dry, and earth black and moist. So by this argument earth changes into fire in respect of the moist and the dry. Accordingly, from what has been proven, we have that not only none of the intermediates is the principle, but that none of the extremes is, either. For if the extremes and generally all [the elements] alike change into each other, there will be no more reason for any one to be the principle than for any other. (trans. I. Kupreeva)

[81] At the end of the section, summarising his exposition, the commentator identifies those who hold the view refuted by Aristotle: Anaximenes, Diogenes and Thales (*Book of Morphology*, end of §99).
[82] See Philoponus *in GC* 249,18-30.

Philoponus' extract is not as fully articulated as **Ab**. Its context is different, as it is given at the end of Philoponus' exegesis and is used merely to corroborate a previous demonstration. Thus Philoponus is not the source for **Ab**: his extract is given as the conclusion to a demonstration, while Jābir's begins one – in the *Morphology* the explication of the Aristotelian diagram described in the lemma immediately follows the theoretical introduction contained in **Ab**.

Ac: *Morphology* §102,9-105,4

> Aristotle said: for they change into one another (*GC* 2.5, 332b30-333a1). To understand that this [new contrariety] comes from adding one more thing, it is evident and manifest that if *D* changes into another thing, another contrariety will belong to *D* and *R*, I mean fire. Thus, the first [element] will have a contrariety, when this is added to it. So, if those [added elements] are infinite in number, the contrarieties in the [first element] will be infinite in number. If that is so, it will be impossible to define any thing, or for any thing to be generated. For if it is generated <out of> something else, it will need to pass and cross through as many as these contrarieties, indeed through even more (*GC* 2.5, 333a7-10). Alexander said: he repeats what has been already concluded, as I said, as if it had not yet been explained. For the fact that all [the elements] change into one another has been explained already, in the manner we have mentioned (see *GC* 2.5, 333a3).

This extract has no equivalent in Philoponus' commentary. Its purpose is merely to point out that Aristotle has already demonstrated the same point elsewhere; Aristotle speaks 'as if he had not already demonstrated this (*ka'annahu lam yubayyin ba'd hādhā*)', though he in fact has, at 322b12-30.

Ad: *Morphology* §§23-4

> Aristotle said: manifestly then all the other *stoikheia* (*al-aḥruf*) can be reduced to the four kinds (*GC* 2.2, 330a24-5). You should know that the matter is as Alexander said: one must enquire why roughness and smoothness are subsumed under dryness and moisture. In answer to that, we say that roughness derives from dryness, for what is rough is solid while the smooth derives from moist, for the smooth is something fluid and liquid. Or, it would be better and more appropriate [to say] that neither of these qualities are active or passive, just like heaviness and lightness are not that either. Manifestly, then, all the other remaining genera and tangible differences that [Aristotle] names contrarieties, are reduced to the first four that we have previously described, namely: heat, coldness, dryness and moisture.

This is addressed to the conclusion of Book 2, chapter 2, and its demonstration of the reduction of all tangible qualities to the four primary ones. Aristotle enumerates seven pairs of tangible qualities at 329b16 ff., with a view to determining which ones are constitutive of the primary bodies. He demonstrates how all of these pairs, apart from rough and smooth, may be subsumed under one of the two primary pairs of contraries (warm and cold, dry and moist). By aligning rough and smooth with heavy and light as equally incapable of action and passion, Alexander points out their different nature:[83] unlike all the other qualities that have been mentioned, rough and smooth, and heavy and light, are incapable of action and passion. Thus they cannot be combined to form homeomerous substances. Their anomalous nature explains Aristotle's omission.[84]

The attribution of this passage to Alexander is confirmed by Philoponus, who reproduces **Ad** with a few minor differences, following the same lemma (*GC* 2.2, 330a24):[85]

> Alexander, however, raises a difficulty: how is smoothness reduced to wetness and roughness to dryness? Is it because roughness would appear (*doxeien*) to belong to solidity and dryness (for you can see the boundaries at which its parts are connected) and smoothness to wetness (for what is wet is something uniform, with its surface always smooth, because its parts settle down together with each other)? Or better, he says, to say that these contrarieties are neither active nor passive, since in origin they are not even qualities. For rough and smooth, as he says in the *Categories*,[86]

[83] In fact, Aristotle sets lightness and weight apart from other tangible contrarieties from the very beginning; not only are they not among the first tangible contrarieties, but they are not even derived from these. The concluding sentence of the demonstration is eloquent enough in this respect: *dêlon toinun hoti pasai hai allai diaphorai anagontai eis tas prôtas tettaras* (330a24-5): all the others, *except* the heavy and the light. See on this H.H. Joachim (1922), 204.

[84] Note the shift in meaning between the question and the answer. Whereas the question regards the justification for the reduction of smooth and rough to dry and moist (the reduction itself being considered as an established fact), the answer expands the field of investigation by querying the status of the two qualities: the fact that they are inactive and impassive does not explain their reduction to dry and moist, but accounts for their natural difference from the other qualities that are on the same list.

[85] See Philoponus *in GC* 223,9-17. In his commentary *ad* 329b20, H.H. Joachim (1922), 204, refers to Philoponus' explanation of the omission of a detailed description of the way in which smooth and rough are subsumed under moist and dry. But he refers only to Philoponus' commentary ad loc. where rough and smooth are aligned with light and heavy as equally incapable of acting and being acted upon by themselves. Following Joachim, F. Solmsen (1960), 337, n. 7, judges that the commentator here only reproduces Aristotle's explanation. He concludes from this that the text of *GC* that we have is corrupt. But neither of them notice that Philoponus repeats the same question at the end of the chapter and that he attributes the explanation to Alexander of Aphrodisias. This weakens the hypothesis that Aristotle's text in this place is corrupt; if so, then it was already corrupt in Alexander's time.

[86] cf. *Cat.* 8, 10a16 ff. and Simplicius *in Cat.* 262,32-264,4, who, discussing this point, mentions two opinions of interest for our subject. The first is that of Andronicus, who suggests a fifth kind of quality in which he includes rare and dense, heavy and light, and

consist in a certain arrangement of the parts. But if they are not qualities, they are neither passive nor active. (trans. C.J.F. Williams)

Note the usage of the optative *doxeien* in setting out the first alternative; this suggests that it is a hypothesis that will be ruled out in what follows. This is further supported by the wording of the second alternative (*ê ameinon*). Moreover, where Jābir's text is very similar to that of Philoponus, as it is here, to the point that even the structure of Alexander's sentences has been loyally reproduced, the two versions may nevertheless be clearly distinguished:

(1) **Ad** subsumes the smooth under the moist, like a species under a genus, on the basis that they share a generic nature (namely fluidity). Conversely, Philoponus' extract characterises the genus by the constitutive differences of the two species.

(2) **Ad** aligns the rough and the smooth with the light and the heavy, as incapable of action and passion, while Alexander apud Philoponus simply denies that the rough and the smooth are qualities, without mentioning the heavy or the light.

This confirms, of course, that Philoponus is not Jābir's source. However, it also raises the problem of authenticity. Even if we assume that the variant version of the first alternative is Philoponus and not Alexander, it remains to be determined whether the apodosis ('they are not even qualities'), with its reference to the *Categories*, is derived from Alexander. In short, we must ask which solution to the problem – that presented in **Ad** or that in Philoponus – is genuinely Alexander's. Happily, the Arabic tradition provides us with a second piece of evidence, which will allow us not only to determine the authenticity of **Ad**, but also prove that the entire commentary found in Jābir, and not just the four passages just studied, is that of Alexander.

B: Ya'qūb b. Isḥāq al-Isrā'īlī as confirmation of the commentary's authenticity

We find the decisive proof of the authenticity of our extracts in their entirety in an unedited treatise by the physician Ya'qūb b. Isḥāq al-Isrā'īlī al-Maḥallī As'aduldīn,[87] discovered in a thirteenth-century manuscript (Istanbul,

thick and fine (263,19-26). The second is that of the students of Achaicus, who classify the qualities that were 'in the *GC* joined with hot and cold, dry and moist', namely heavy and light, hard and soft, rough and smooth, thick and fine, in a fourth kind as all being derived from rare and dense (263,28-31). It is worth noting that although these pairs of contraries (heavy and light, thick and fine, hard and soft) were never considered by Aristotle as falling under the genus of quality (he does not mention them in *Cat.* 8), several commentators tried to describe them as a kind of quality.

[87] The author is a Jewish doctor from al-Maḥalla in Egypt, as is clear from his *nisba*. Fairly little is known about him, apart from the fact that he lived in Cairo and that he

Nuruosmaniye 3589).[88] The author is extremely interested in the theory of elements, and devotes another treatise to the topic.[89] He knows and cites the work of numerous philosophers on this subject.[90] Of particular interest to us is the prologue of the treatise, where he cites directly from Alexander's commentary.[91]

At this point **Ad** is reproduced in its entirety. There is also another extract from Alexander's commentary, which appears identically in the *Morphology* without an explicit reference to the author. The following pages provide a comparison of the relevant passages from the *Morphology* (§§36-40 and §24) to those from Ya'qūb b. Isḥāq. For a translation see the Appendix at the end of this volume.

made a trip to Damascus in 1202 (598 H). He also visited Morocco where he took up pharmacology and became, besides, a student of Ibn Tūmart. He wrote medical treatises and one treatise on the climate of Damascus. His doctrine of elements, which he expounded in several short philosophical treatises, was vigorously attacked. See Ibn Abī Uṣaybi'a, *'Uyūn al-anbā' fī ṭabaqāt al-aṭṭibā'*, ed. A. Müller (1884), vol. 2, 118, and A. Dietrich (1966), 174.

[88] The manuscript is a *majmū'a* dated 1260/70, and contains twelve treatises. Ten (n° 2 to 12) are attributed to Ya'qūb b. Isḥāq al-Isrā'īlī. According to A. Dietrich, Ya'qūb b. Isḥāq is also the author of those not bearing his name. Of the ten treatises attributed to Ya'qūb b. Isḥāq al-Isrā'īlī, seven have to do with the doctrine of the elements and the refutation of the criticisms it aroused. I plan, with the preliminary agreement of Prof A. Dietrich, to publish all the treatises of the *majmū'a*. It is the excellent article by M. Aouad and R. Goulet (1989), 130, signalling a fragment of this commentary reproduced in Dietrich's catalogue, that put me on the track.

[89] Quoted in the other treatises of Ya'qūb, *K. al-usṭuqussāt* is unknown to us, unless it is identical with the second *Maqāla* of the treatise no. 2 of the *majmū'a*, entitled: *al-maqālatu al-thāniyatu fī al-usṭuqussāti wa taḥqīqi al-qawli fīhā*; See A. Dietrich (1966), 175.

[90] In different treatises of our *majmū'a*, Ya'qūb b. Isḥāq cites and reproduces excerpts from Aristotle's *GC*, and from 'the commentator (*mufassir*)' of this book (fols 26b-27a), from the *Categories* and *De Interpretatione* (e.g. fol. 27b), and from Themistius' commentary on the *Physics* (fols 26b and 27b). In our treatise, apart from the excerpts from the *GC* accompanied by the commentary of Alexander of Aphrodisias, he reproduces an excerpt from Olympiodorus' now lost commentary ad loc. See the Appendix below and A. Dietrich (1966), 177.

[91] See Nuruosmaniye 3589, fol. 47b15-16: *Fa-ḥassaltuhu* (sc. *kalāmu al-Iskandari*) *fī tilka al-laylati wa ṭāla'tuhu,* [...] *wa hādhā naṣṣu kalāmihi* (I obtained them [sc. the words of Alexander] that very night and perused them [...] this is the wording of what he said).

Morphology §§36-40

§36 *Wa qāla: innahu lammā kānati al-ajsāmu al-basīṭatu arba'atan, fa-inna ithnayni ithnayni minhumā humā min kulli wāḥidin mina al-ithnayni al-awwalayni.* (*GC*, 2.3, 330b30-2)

§37 *Wa dhālika an yanqasima al-tanāsuba alladhī yūjadu lahā 'inda al-amākini, wa huwa alladhī min ajlihi thaqīlatun wa khafīfatun, wa dhālika lammā kānati al-amākinu makānayni, a'nī al-fawqa wa huwa alladhī yalī al-jisma al-akhīra, wa al-asfala wa huwa alladhī yalī al-jisma al-wasaṭa. Fa-al-ithnāni min al-usṭuqussāti hiyā munāsibatun li-makāni al-fawqi, a'nī al-nāra wa al-hawā'a, wa al-akhīrāni munāsibāni li-al-asfali, a'nī al-mā'a wa al-arḍa. Fa-li-dhālika ṣāra al-ithnāni al-awwalāni khafīfayni, wa al-akhīrāni thaqīlayni.*

§38 *Wa qawluhu 'min kulli wāḥidin min dhaynika al-awwalayni' ya'nī al-usṭuqussayni alladhayni fawqa ka-al-usṭuqussayni alladhayni asfala lahumā munāsabatun ilā makānayni ākharayni, ammā dhaynika fa-ilā fawqi, wa ammā hādhā fa-ilā asfali. Wa dhālika anna al-makānayni al-akhīrayni wa al-awwalayni humā wāḥidatun bi-a'yāniha wa humā al-fawqu wa al-asfalu.*

§39 *Thumma qāla: inna al-nāra wa al-hawā'a humā yasmuwāni ilā al-nihāyati wa al-ḥaddi. Wa ammā al-arḍu wa al-mā'u fa-humā yaṣīrani ilā al-wasaṭi.* (*GC*, II 3, 330b32-3)

Istanbul, Nuruosmaniye 3589, fol. 47b16-48a7[92]

Qāla Arisṭū: wa lammā kānat al-ajsāmu **[17]** *al-basīṭatu arba'atan, fa-inna ithnayni ithnayni minhumā humā min kulli wāḥidin mina al-ithnayni al-awwalayni.* (*GC* 2.3, 330b30-2)

Qāla al-Iskandaru: **[18]** *innahu yaqsimu al-tanāsuba alladhī yūjadu lahā 'inda al-amākini, wa huwa alladhī min ajlihi hiya thaqīlatun wa khafīfatun.*

[92] In this column I reproduce excerpts from the treatise which I was able to read from the copies of the folios of the manuscript kindly provided by Prof A. Dietrich, whose courtesy is here gratefully acknowledged. For a translation of the whole treatise see the Appendix below. The manuscript is described in A. Dietrich (1966), 174. The script, a *naskhī*, is of a very bad quality, with inconsistent diacritical punctuation.

§40 *Ya'nī anna al-nāra wa al-hawā'a humā min al-jismi al-khafīfi wa taḥta hādhā maḥṣūrānī. Wa dhālika huwa alladhī yaṣīru ilā al-ḥaddi, fa-innahu yusammā al-nihāyata wa al-ṭarafa al-akhīra jiddan, wa hādhā huwa ḥawla al-'ālami. Wa al-'ālamu wa al-mā'u humā min al-jismi alladhī yaṣīru al-wasaṭa, ya'nī annahumā min al-jismi al-thaqīli.*

[19] *i'lam waffaqaka Allahu, annaka idhā ta'ammalta hādhā al-kalāma, ra'ayta annahu yushīru ilā al-sababi al-fā'ili li-al-khiffati* **[20]** *wa al-thiqli, lā <ilā> al-khiffati wa al-thiqli. Wa dhālika annahu qāla 'innahu yaqsimu al-tanāsuba alladhī yūjadu lahā 'inda* **[21]** *al-amākini, wa huwa alladhī min ajlihi hiya thaqīlatun wa khafīfatun'. Fa-kāna qaṣduhu al-sababa al-fā'ila li-al-khiffati* **[22]** *wa al-thiqli, lā al-khiffata wa al-thiqla.*

Fa-qad yajūzu idhan an yakūna qawluhu 'min dhaynika al-awwalayni' lamā naqalahu fī al-amākini al-akhīrati, lākin qālahu fī al-khafīfi wa al-thaqīli min ḥaythu yushabbihuhā ka-al-jinsayni.

Fa-yanbaghī idhan an yuṭlaba al-tanāsuba alladhī min ajlihi takūnu al-khiffatu wa al-thiqlu **[23]** *li-annahu qad tabayyana min kalāmihi anna isma 'al-awwali' wāqi'un 'alayhi wa huwa al-sababu.*

Thumma yaqūlu qabla hādha al-faṣli: **[24]** *inna al-ḥarārata hiya fā'ilatun li-al-takhalkhuli wa al-khiffati, wa al-burūdata hiya fā'ilatun li-al-takāthufi wa al-thiqli.*

§24 *Fa-yanbaghī an ta'lama anna al-amra kamā qāla al-Iskandaru: innahu qad yajibu an yaṭluba al-insānu lima ṣāra al-khushūnatu wa al-malāsatu taḥta al-yubūsati wa al-ruṭūbati maḥṣūratayni.*[...]

Thumma qāla fī faṣlin **[25]** *qabla hadha ayḍan, 'inda kalāmihi fī al-khushūnati wa al-malāsati:*

aw yakūnu al-awwlā wa al-aḥrā anna hātayni al-kayfiyyatayni laysatā lā fā'ilatun wa lā munfa'ilatun, kamā annahu wa lā al-thiqla wa lā al-khiffata. Fa-ẓāhirun idhan anna jamī'a al-ajnāsi wa al-fuṣūli al-malmūsati al-bāqiyati, wa huwa yusammīhā al-mutaḍāddāti, qad tartaqī ilā hādhihi al-arba'ati al-ūlā al-mutaqaddimi waṣfuhā, wa hiyā al-ḥarāratu wa al-burūdatu wa al-yubūsatu wa al-ruṭūbatu.

aw yakūnu al-aḥrā wa al-awwlā an yuqāla **[48a1]** *anna hātayni al-kayfiyyatayni laysatā lā fā'ilatun wa lā munfa'ilatun, kamā annahu wa lā al-thiqla wa lā al-khiffata. Fa-ẓāhirun* **[2]** *idhan anna jamī'a al-fuṣūli*[v] *al-malmūsati al-bāqiyati, wa hiya allatī yusammīhā al-mutaḍāddāti, qad tartaqī ilā* **[3]** *hādhihi al-arba'ati al-ūlā allatī taqaddama waṣfuhā, wa hādhihi hiyā al-ḥarāratu wa al-burūdatu wa al-ruṭūbatu wa al-yubūsatu.*

[v] In the margin and in the text *al-aṣnāf.*

[4] *Fa-qad tabayyana anna al-kayfiyyāti al-uwwali hiya hādhihi al-arba'atu.*[...]

[48a25] *Wa yakūnu qawluhu 'al-tanāsubu alladhī yūjadu lahā* **[48b1]** *'inda al-amākini' ya'nī bi-dhālika anna munāsabata al-ḥārri al-basīṭi ilā fawqi, bi-ṭab'ihi, wa al-khiffatu* **[2]** *lāḥiqatun lahu; wa anna ḥarakata al-bāridi al-basīṭi ilā asfali bi-ṭab'ihi, wa al-thiqlu tābi'un lahu.*

[3] *Lammā qāla Arisṭū fī kitābi al-kawni wa al-fasādi inna al-kayfiyyāta al-uwwala li-sā'iri mā taḥta falaki al-qamari hiya al-ḥarāratu* **[4]** *wa al-burūdatu wa al-yubūsatu wa al-ruṭūbatu, thumma qāla 'al-ithnayni al-awwalayni minhum' fī qawlihi anna al-ḥarārata wa al-burūdata* **[5]** *aḥaqqu bi-al-awwaliyyati min hādhihi al-arba'ati li-annahumā al-fā'ilāni —wa ma'nā al-fā'ilayni annahumā yaf'alāni*[w] *akthara wa yanfa'ilān*[x] **[6]** *aqalla, wa al-yubūsata wa al-ruṭūbata munfa'ilāni li-annahuma yaf'alāni*[w] *aqalla wa yanfa'ilāni*[x] *akthara— wa anna al-takhalkhula wa al-takāthufa* **[7]** *wa al-khiffata wa al-thiqla min al-ḥarārati wa al-burūdati, fa-li-dhālika lā yuqālu 'an al-khiffati wa al-thiqli annahumā uwwalun.*

Note that Nuruosmaniye 3589, 47b-48a3, which is said to provide the exact wording of Alexander's discussion, reproduces exactly a portion of **Ad** (*Morphology* §24, though without the first part of Alexander's response). This leaves little room for doubt that it is the version in the *Morphology* that is authentic, and not that in Philoponus. It is also possible to determine that Jābir and Ya'qūb b. Isḥāq used two copies of an identical original, as will be shown in what follows.

[w] MS *yaf'alā.*
[x] MS *yanfa'ilā.*

Ba: Textual similarities

Nuruosmaniye 3589, 47b16-18, is a nearly exact parallel to *Morphology* §24; the only difference is that *qāla al-Iskandaru* ('Alexander said') is omitted in the *Morphology*. This parallel allows us conclude that Jābir's extracts are to be attributed to Alexander of Aphrodisias; even where Alexander's name is not explicitly mentioned, his commentary is Jābir's source.

Let us first consider the Aristotelian lemma (*GC* 2.3, 330b30-2): the reading by Ya'qūb b. Isḥāq is identical to that of the *Morphology*, notably concerning two respects in which the Aristotelian text is not definitively established: the partitive *hekateron* (or *hekatera*) and the choice of genitive (*prôton* or *topôn*). The translation of this lemma in the *Morphology*, as well as in Nuruosmaniye 3589, corresponds to the reading adopted by Philoponus[93] and Joachim[94] (*ontôn de terrarôn tôn haplôn sômatôn, hekatera toin duoin hekaterou tôn topôn estin*) the neutral plural *ekatera* having been translated by the dual *ithnayni, ithnayni minhumā*. The Loeb edition[95] (*...hekateron toin duoin hekaterou tôn topôn estin*) by contrast prefers the singular. The reading *hekatera* is more precise, insofar as it refers to the relation between the four primary bodies and the two natural places (up and down); *each of the two pairs* of elements occupies one of the nature places, 'up' in the case of fire and air, 'down' in the case of water and earth.

Our two texts preserve the reading *protôn*, translated as *al-awwalayni* ('the two first'), rather than *topôn*. Joachim (who, along with all modern editions of *GC*, retains *topôn*) reports[96] that this is the reading of mss. Parisiensis Regius 1853 (tenth century) and Vindobonensis, phil. Graec. 100 (early tenth century). These are the two oldest manuscripts of *GC*.[97] The same reading is found in one of the manuscripts of Philoponus' commentary (though the editor has not adopted it). This similarity regarding a reading of Aristotle's text which varies from version to version is a further piece of evidence for attributing the whole of Jābir's commentary to Alexander, since Ya'qūb b. Isḥāq mentions only Alexander's commentary in his prologue, without referring to any other version of the Aristotelian text. Moreover it is now clear that even when Alexander's name was not mentioned, it is his commentary which is reproduced.[98]

[93] cf. Philoponus *in GC* 229,12-14, who justifies his reading: *hekatera gar toin duoin, toutesti tôn duadôn tôn duo hekatera hekaterou tôn topôn, hê men tou anô hê de tou katô. hekatera gar eipen oudeterôs, oionei ta hekatera tôn duo*.

[94] cf. H.H. Joachim (1922), 42, 218.

[95] cf. *Aristotle on coming-to-be and passing away*, trans. E.S. Forster (1955), 276.

[96] It is Dr Silvia Fazzo who rightly draws my attention to this variant.

[97] H.H. Joachim (1922), 218, thinks that this could be a gloss explaining what kind of places (*topoi*) are at issue.

[98] On the basis of the excerpts from the *Book of Morphology* edited by P. Kraus (1935), 392-424, C. Baffioni has claimed (with some reservations pending the reading of the whole of *K. al-Taṣrīf*) that this has to do with Philoponus' *GC* commentary, interpreting the discrepancies between Philoponus' commentary and the fragments found in the excerpts edited by Kraus as a result of Jābir's manipulations on the text of Philoponus. Baffioni notably mentions as an additional indication in favour of this thesis al-Qifṭī's

This conclusion may be confirmed by examining Ya'qūb b. Isḥāq's use of Alexander in this passage. Ya'qūb in fact opposes Alexander's interpretation, which holds that the phrase '*al-awwalayn* (the two first)' refers not to the two natural places, up and down, but to two qualities, the light and the heavy (*Morphology* §§36-40). Thus he constructed his whole treatise to refute this interpretation.

Bb: Light and heavy as principles

Our passage (*Morphology* §§36-40) treats the end of *GC* 2.3. Aristotle has already deduced the number of elements from the four possible combinations between the four elementary qualities.[99] Even though fire, air, water, and earth 'appear to be simple', in fact 'each is mixed'. They are indeed the most simple and fundamental sublunary substances,[100] in that they are the first corporeal constituents of naturally composed bodies (*homoiomerê*). In other words, they cannot be decomposed into more primitive components.[101] Yet each is constituted from a pair of tangible qualities, which determine its 'form' as a perceptible body, and which Aristotle dignifies with the term *stoikheion* – an 'element' in the proper sense.[102] But the bodily elements we deal with are not even pure fire, earth, etc., but are always mixed together. The true elements are 'of the same nature as these, but not identical to them'. Elementary fire is *puroeidês*, 'has the form of fire', air is *aeroeidês*, and so on. Elements are pure to the degree that they are constituted only of a pair of primary qualities.

If the primary bodies we deal with are not elements strictly speaking, the latter must be located in the higher regions of the sublunary realm.[103] This is what justifies the cosmological classification of Aristotle's elements introduced here, in terms of the two places, up and down, since it is in these places that the

notice in *Ta'rīkh al-Ḥukamā'* which gives a certain preference to Philoponus' commentary. I think, however, that al-Qifṭī is content to repeat what previous bibliographers said with regard to Philoponus' *GC* commentary, viz. that the Syriac version is superior in quality to the Arabic one (cf. *Ta'rīkh al-Ḥukamā' li-Jamāladdīn Abī al-Ḥasan 'Alī b. Yūsuf al-Qifṭī*, ed. J. Lippert (1903), 40,21-41,2), which does not allow us to draw a conclusion about the overall superiority of Philoponus' commentary compared to other *GC* commentaries. See C. Baffioni (1986), 403-31, 408, and 421.

[99] In fact the four elemental qualities could be combined in six pairs, but two of these would be constituted by two contraries of the same kind (hot and cold, or dry and moist), which is logically impossible. See *GC* 2.3, 330a30-4.

[100] See *Cael.* 3.1, 298a29-32.

[101] See *GC* 2.1, 329a5 and 2.8, 334b31 ff., *PA* 646a12-17, and *Cael.* 3.3, 302a15-19.

[102] See *GC* 2.2, 329b10; 2.3, 330a30, 33; 330b1 ff. See also H.H. Joachim (1922), 189: 'Strictly speaking, *prôtê hulê* and the *enantiôseis* are the real "elements", i.e. the eternal elementary conditions of *genesis* and *phthora*. Earth, Air, Fire, and Water are "primary" and "simple" bodies'.

[103] Aristotle distinguishes in *Meteor.* 1.3, 340b23, the fire down here, which is an excess of heat, from the element that occupies the region above the air and below the heavenly sphere, and that 'we are accustomed to call fire, though it is not really fire' (trans. H.D.P. Lee); see also *Meteor.* 1.3, 340b15 f. and 1.4, 341b14 ff.

truly simple bodies are found. They are divided into two pairs: fire and air have the tendency to move 'up', i.e. towards the periphery of the cosmos, while water and earth tend to move 'down', towards its centre. This classification subdivides according to the 'purity' of the four elements: fire and earth, being 'extreme' elements, are the more pure, while water and air are intermediary and less pure.[104]

This cosmological classification is problematic in the context of *GC*, insofar as it appeals to qualities which have been excluded from the scope of the *GC*'s enquiry: lightness and heaviness have no explanatory power in discussions of mixture.[105] Conversely, there is no natural place assigned to the hot, cold, dry and moist as such. Thus commentators have tried to account for the coherence of the text and to explain how these two explanatory schemes, appealing to the two qualities of natural motion on the one hand, and the four tangible qualities on the other, could be reconciled.[106]

Appealing to the *De Caelo*, Alexander immediately establishes the relationship between the natural places and the heavy and light, which Aristotle has not explicitly mentioned in the text.[107] He also defines place with reference to the body that occupies it: 'up' refers to the outermost body, and 'down' to the most central body (*Morphology* §37: *al-fawqu wa huwa alladhī yalī al-jisma al-*

[104] Alexander completely neglected this second classification in his commentary. It is worth noting that the Stoics too divided the elements only into two groups, corresponding to the two cosmic places. See the Arabic version of the *Placita Philosophorum*, in H. Daiber (1980), 124 (Diels 311a). On Alexander's use of Stoic doctrines, see R.B. Todd (1976), 21-9, particularly on his assimilation of their theories to the extent that they sometimes become part of his own philosophical contribution.

[105] See H.H. Joachim (1922), 204; heavy and light bodies neither act nor are acted upon as such, unlike for instance cold and hot bodies which act upon a thing by making it partake of their own characteristics: a cold body chills whereas a light body does not lighten the adjacent body. See also Avicenna, *in GC*, who, enumerating the tangible qualities mentioned by Aristotle in 329b19-21, already grounds the distinction between the role of the elemental qualities and the role of weight and lightness in the distinction between the element *qua* element and the element *qua* part of the universe. He thus distinguishes clearly between the qualities operational in a cosmological account and those operational in a chemical one. Water, insofar as it is an element, must be characterised by active and passive qualities which will make possible mixture and the mutual transformation of the elements, but insofar as it is a constitutive part of the universe, weight and lightness are its more relevant qualities, particularly to the extent to which the order of the cosmos appears to be a result of natural movements accounted for by these qualities. See Ibn Sīnā, *Al-Shifā', al-Ṭabī'iyyāt, al-Kawn wa al-fasād*, ed. M. Qāsim and I. Madkour (1969), 149.

[106] F. Solmsen (1960), 397, doubts that the classification of the elements takes into account the distinction drawn in the preceding paragraph between the elements properly speaking and primary bodies which appear to us to be elements but in fact are not. He also thinks that the description of the true and real elements (330b21-30) is a later addition by Aristotle after the composition of the *Meteor.*, which could have inspired this passage, because even in *GC* Aristotle is essentially preoccupied by the case of fire.

[107] cf. *Cael.* 4.1, 308a29 ff.

akhīra, wa al-asfalu wa huwa alladhī yalī al-jisma al-wasaṭa).[108] Thus place is no longer external to body, but rather defined by the nature of body (*Morphology* §40: *Ya'nī anna al-nāra wa al-hawā'a humā min al-jismi al-khafīfi wa taḥta hādhā maḥṣūrān. Wa dhālika huwa alladhī yaṣīru ilā al-ḥaddi, fa-innahu yusammā al-nihāyata wa al-ṭarafa al-akhīra jiddan, wa hādhā huwa ḥawla al-'ālami* [...]).[109] By establishing an absolutely light body, which he identifies with the periphery of the universe, and an absolutely heavy body, with the centre of the universe, Alexander replaces an account in which natural *places* exercise causality with one that appeals to the *elements* that occupy those places. This is not a divergence from Aristotle; indeed it is based on passages in Aristotle that ascribe a certain causality to natural places.[110]

Alexander understands the natural movement of the elementary bodies in a cosmological context, the four elements being arranged in concentric circles,

[108] In *Cael.*, 4.1, 308a21-8, Aristotle defines 'up' in relation to the 'extremity of the world, which is both uppermost in position and primary in nature' (trans. Guthrie), and 'down' in relation to the centre. This definition could suggest that for Aristotle, physical place could exist prior to and independent from the object that occupies it. But this idea is denied by Aristotle himself, who, in *Phys.* 4.4, 212a24 ff., connects the three concepts as referring to the same reality: the upward direction, the periphery of the universe, and the body at the extreme boundary, and similarly with 'down', the centre of the universe and the body in the centre. Aristotle's physics does not include the concept of a geometrical, absolute and separate centre or periphery of the universe. See S. Waterlow (1982), 104 f. from which I draw.

[109] cf. *Cael.* 4.1, 308a29-31 and 4.3, 310b16-19.

[110] The problem of establishing the cause of the natural movement of the elements towards their natural places has received various interpretations in the course of the Aristotelian tradition, all striving, from the first commentators until modern critics, to solve the problem of the nature of the causality that links the element to its natural place. It is Aristotle's own ambiguity on this issue that gave rise to this problem. In fact the commentator must reconcile texts that attribute to the elements an intrinsic principle of movement, which is nothing else than their own nature (*Phys.* 8.4, 255a1-256a3 and 2.1, 192b20-2; *Cael.* 4.1, 308a14-15; 4.3, 310a31-b1; 310b24-6; 310b31-311a14), with other texts which seem to ascribe some kind of 'power' to place (*Phys.* 4.1, 208b8-25, though he goes on to deny it any causality some lines below, at 209a18-22). The complexity of the problem is well presented in the recent publications on the subject signalled to me by R.W. Sharples. See H. Lang (1992), 16, 98, 63-84, and 97-124, who does not recognise nature as an internal principle of motion but of being moved and thus maintains that natural places are the source of the elements' motion towards them, being the determinate actuality of what is moved. Thus elements are moved not *by* nature but *in conformity with nature*. K. Algra (1995), 192 ff. disagrees with this interpretation, arguing that the *telos* of the natural movement of the elements is not the natural place as such but 'being in a natural place' which corresponds to the full actualisation of the form; in this sense natural place is not by itself an independent final or formal cause, but a cause that is determined by the proper constitution of the elements, and belongs as such to their internal capacity of being moved. Thus 'it is part of the nature of each element to be in such-and-such place'. Finally, R. Sorabji (1988), 186-7, and briefly at 222, discusses natural place as a cause, and suggests that this might be compatible with the intrinsic nature of the body as the *efficient* cause of movement, if natural place is taken as *final* cause.

which constitute different regions within the sublunary realm. Thus, when air moves 'up', it does not submit to a 'power' exerted by place (*Phys*. 4.1, 208b10-11), but rather to the power of fire.[111] For, as Alexander duly emphasises, the body that moves towards the limit is the periphery, while the body that moves the furthest down is the centre (see *Morphology* §40: *al-jismu alladhī yaṣīru*[112] *al-wasaṭa*).[113] Thus the movement of the elementary body towards its proper place will be a movement towards what is similar to it, under the influence of the adjacent element, and in virtue of the reciprocal transformation of the elements, in which each element is 'like the form' of the one below it, which is considered to be 'like matter'.[114]

The natural movement of the elements towards their places is part and parcel of the elements' essential constitution, and is the realisation of their proper nature, at least insofar as they are heavy or light. For the natural place of each element is by definition linked to lightness or heaviness.[115] Thus there is an

[111] See V. Goldschmidt (1956), who in his analysis judiciously takes the source of causality to be the element present in its natural place rather than the place itself, since it is the adjacent element that is 'as a form'. He refers to *Phys*. 4.5, 212b29-213a2. See also *Cael*. 4.3, 310b8-15.

[112] *Ṣāra* 'to become', 'to come to', 'to get to' which conveys the idea of realisation and accomplishment (see W. Lane (1893), 1755). This term translates the Greek *tunkhanô* in the Arabic version of *Quaestio* 2.3, where the first bodies, by reaching their natural places, also reach their perfection. See *On the power coming from the motion of the sublime body towards the bodies that undergo coming-to-be and passing-away* (D 27f or vE 34) ms. Carullah 1279, fols. 64a 13-64b 19, fol. 64a 21: *wa bi-hādhihi al-ḥarakati* ***yaṣīru*** *kullu wāḥidin minhā ilā tamāmihi wa kamālihi* (through this motion each of them reaches its completion and perfection) and *Quaest*. 2.3, 48,10-11: *hê epi tous oikeious autois topous kinêsis ginetai, kath'hên hekaston autôn tês idias tunkhanei teleiotêtos* and R.W. Sharples (1992), 95, 3. Note the use of *maṣīr* in the same meaning in *Alexander of Aphrodisias' treatise on the discourse concerning the principles of the universe according to the opinion of Aristotle the philosopher* (D1), ed. in A. Badawī, *Arisṭū*, 253-77, 254, 8: *wa dhāka annahu 'alā hādhihi al-jihati yakūnu* ***maṣīru*** *kullu wāḥidin min al-ajsāmi ilā al-mawḍi'i al-ṭabī'ī alladhī yakhuṣṣuhu.*

[113] See *Phys*. 4.4, 212a24-7, and S. Waterlow (1982), 105, for whom the natural place is not a reality distinct from the element, but is determined by the element, which is moved by an internal principle of motion identical with its own nature: 'fire moves upward because by so doing it will form the physical periphery or spherical outer shell of the (sublunary) world. [...] Thus the earth tends towards the centre of the universe for no other reason than that it is the tendency of earth to make the centre of the universe by assuming the central position relative to the other elements'. The author also points out the way in which the natural motions of simple bodies illustrate the essential connexion between every process of change and its *terminus* which, for Aristotle, is the fundamental structure of all change in the sublunary world. The *terminus* is intrinsic to the movement and determines its direction.

[114] See *Phys*. 4.5, 212b29-213a1.

[115] See *Phys*. 8.4, 255b5-12, and 255b13-17: 'But the subject of our investigation is: on account of what are the light and heavy [bodies] moved to their proper places? The cause is that they are naturally disposed in a certain way, and this is what being light or heavy is, the former determined by the upwards, the latter by the downwards'. See also *Cael*. 4.3, 310a20-5 and 31-5 and 311a3-5; Alexander apud Simplicium *in Phys*. 1213,3-8

essential connection between the place and the nature of the natural body, since by reaching its natural place a body realises its form.[116] For a simple body, to become actually light is to become air or fire, and so to move up. For Alexander, the notion of actuality is thus linked to that of form:[117] the movement of a heavy or light body toward its proper place is its actualisation. The nature of fire is not only merely to move up, or even to be higher than other things, but *to be* the uppermost, i.e., to realise completely its nature as an absolutely light body.[118]

It is only in light of this complete identification of the nature of a body with the place it occupies that Alexander can propose another interpretation of the Aristotelian text ('simple bodies being four in number, every two of them belong to each of the first two', *Morphology* §36) by replacing the phrase 'the two first' – first considered as a gloss that explicates the nature of the two cosmic places – with the light and the heavy, which are designated as 'two *genera*' (*min ḥaythu yushabbihuhā ka-al-jinsayni, Morphology* §40). Alexander clearly alludes to *Cael.*, and its definition of the absolute light and heavy as determining the periphery and the centre of the universe.[119] More tentatively we

mentioned by K. Algra (1995), 214, n. 54, and F. Solmsen (1960), 122, 'The place of an element belongs to its *phusis* and cannot be as extrinsic to it as the "place" which Aristotle investigates in the *Physics*'.

[116] See *Cael.* 311a4-5. See also S. Pines (1986b), 234-5, who mentions a fragment of Alexander apud Simplicium *in Phys.* (1213,6-8) where Alexander defines the natural place of the first bodies as the actuality or perfection of these bodies, followed by a comment by Simplicius (ll. 8-17) who specifies that it is not the place itself that is the actuality, but the movement of a body towards its proper place that corresponds to its nature. I should also like to draw attention to the interesting position of R. Sokolowski (1970), 273, who questions Aristotle's theory that the motion of an element to its proper place is its movement to its proper form, on the grounds that it contradicts the concept of form in Aristotle's *Metaphysics*. Sokolowski is not unaware of the intrinsic dimension of this movement and its role in the constitution of the elements, but he still considers it as irrelevant to form in a strict metaphysical sense, which involves the realisation of a thing's essence itself, something the local motion does not do, in his view. From this perspective, the movement of the first bodies towards their proper places seems to him to be not so much an actualisation of potency as a relocation or re-arrangement of a body relative to the cosmos as a whole. It is an actualisation in a broad technical sense, but it is not the expression of substantial form.

[117] See S. Pines (1986b), 234-5.

[118] On the nature of simple bodies as an internal principle of movement in Alexander, see *Quaest.* 2.3, 48,9-12: 'For their movement to their proper places comes about in accordance with the primary nature that comes to be in each, according to which one is fire, another water, another earth; it is in accordance with this that each gains its individual perfection' (trans. R.W. Sharples (1992), 94-5), and *Quaest.* 2.18, 62,22-3: 'for they also have in themselves the principle of movement towards this' (trans. R.W. Sharples (1994), 15). Sharples notes (n. 65) that H. Lang (1992), 107-14, argues that it is a distortion to interpret the nature as an immanent principle of movement, as in Aristotle this is a principle of being moved (*Phys.* 2.1, 192b21) and rightly points out that the distortion, if indeed there is one, existed already in Alexander.

[119] See *Cael.* 4.4, 311a15: 'When I say "absolutely", I am thinking of the genus of the heavy or light as such, and excluding bodies which possess both weight and lightness

might refer to the *Timaeus*, and one aspect of Plato's theory that heaviness and lightness are linked to the natures of the primary bodies: they are a function of the triangles that compose them. Thus there is a correlation between heaviness and lightness, and a larger or smaller number of elementary triangles. Plato designates the elements as genera, referring to the types of regular solids that constitute them: each element is a genus of solid,[120] and the heaviness or lightness of the element is a function of the number of triangles in the solid.

At any rate, Alexander's interpretation would establish the relationship between this passage and the rest of the chapter, as being a classification of elements still based on tangible qualities. It identifies a consistent theme, namely the qualities that are constitutive of the elements' proper nature, whether these qualities are used to explain the movement of the elements, or their ability to interact with one another. In the context of this passage, their nature determines the place towards which they move. Alexander has thus raised the light and heavy to the status of separate qualities, irreducible to any other genus, and in this sense they may be called 'primary'.[121] In the wider context of *GC*, he gives them a status equal to that of the hot, cold, dry and moist; the natural movement of elements towards their places is however closely linked to their reciprocal transformation.

The denial that natural places explain the movement of the elements has been considered as a source for Philoponus' view, as he develops it in his commentary on the *Physics*. Here Philoponus explains such motion with reference to the arrangement of the parts of the cosmos relative to each other, while strenuously rejecting the idea of an attraction exerted by natural place.[122]

On this point it may be useful to quote Ibn Rushd's *Middle Commentary on GC* 2.3, 330b30 ff.[123] Ibn Rushd makes no mention of the cosmological division

(Guthrie trans. modified) and Simplicius *in Cael.* 4.4, 311a15 (707-9): 'when he [Aristotle] says "I am thinking of the genus", he means the *proper nature* by virtue of which a thing is such, and not compared to another thing'. The point of emphasis here is the nature of the light or heavy taken absolutely and as such and not in relation to another thing, i.e. that which is invariably carried upwards or downwards when not impeded.

120 See *Tim.* 55D.

121 Note that on two occasions Alexander calls tangible qualities 'genera'. Already in *Morphology* §24 he mentions 'all the other remaining genera (*ajnās*) and tangible differences'.

122 See the Preface by R. Sorabji in C.J.F. Williams (2000), vii-viii, and R. Sorabji (1988), 211-13, for an English translation of Philoponus *in Phys.* 581,18-31 and 632,4-634,2 and 202-4, where he suggests that Theophrastus does not consider Aristotle's natural places as a reality but as 'a way of talking about something else, namely, the physical parts of an organism and the arrangement of parts dictated by the nature of the organism'. Keimpe Algra considers that for Aristotle it is not place, but being in a place, that attracts each element, and that Theophrastus would accept this so long as natural place is, like place in general, construed as a relation instead of a surface. For a summary of the argument with bibliography, see R. Sorabji (2004), vol. 2, 13e.

123 This commentary (*Talkhīṣ al-kawn wa al-fasād*) which has been preserved in a Judeo-Arabic version, has been edited by J. al-'Alawī (1995). Before this edition became available to me, I have been able to consult this text in the manuscript Paris B.N. Hébreu

of the elements into their places, even when citing Aristotle. Instead he speaks only of a twofold division according to whether the elements have a heavy or light nature:

MS Hebrew 1009, fol. 29b16a ff. (J. al-'Alawī, ed., *Talkhīṣ al-kawn wa al-fasād*, Beirut 1995, p. 98,4-7):[124]

Wa lammā kānati al-ajsāmu al-basīṭatu arba'atan, kāna ithnāni minhumā 'an ṭabī'ati al-khafīfi, wa humā al-hawā'u wa al-nāru, wa ithnāni minhumā min ṭabī'ati al-thaqīli wa humā al-mā'u wa al-arḍu. Fa-al-khafīfu alladhī fī al-ghāyati huwa al-nāru, wa al-thaqīlu alladhī fī al-ghāyati huwa al-arḍu,	Since the simple bodies are four, two of them are of the nature of the light – namely air and fire – and two of them are of the nature of the heavy – namely water and earth. The extremely light is fire and extremely heavy is earth.
wa alladhāni baynahumā min ṭabī'ati al-mutawaṣṣiṭi.	The two <bodies> that are between them are of intermediate nature.

It is worth noting how static is Alexander's description of the elements. In *Morphology* §37 he uses the term *tanāsub* ('relation') and its derivatives four times, but never the term *ḥaraka* ('movement'); this term is only found once in our texts, but it is Ya'qūb b. Isḥāq who uses it (Nurosmaniye 3589, 48b2). Had Alexander been interested in the dynamic character of the relationship between simple bodies and natural places, we would have expected to encounter the word *mayl* (translating *rhopê*) – as it is used in Alexander's *Treatise answering Galen's attack on Aristotle's view that every mobile cannot move except by a mover*,[125] and in Alexander's *Treatise on the discourse concerning the principles*

1009 (fifteenth century) in the Bibliothèque Nationale of Paris, thanks to the efficient help of Mr. Michel Garel, hereby gratefully acknowledged. (For a description of this fine manuscript, see M. Garel (1991), 31; I have also consulted G. Vajda's *Index des manuscrits hébreux de la Bibliothèque Nationale*, at no 1402). The text that I submit here is my own transcription in Arabic characters of the Hebrew characters; I provide also references to the edition of al-'Alawī. There is an English translation of this text, annotated and compared with the Hebrew and Latin versions by S. Kurland (1958).

124 For the English translation, 77,3-8.

125 This treatise (D 28), lost in Greek, has been edited and translated in N. Rescher and M.E. Marmura (1965), 78 (trans., 17,20-7): 'He likewise made clear in the case of the bodies that move naturally through the inclination within them (*al-ajsāmu allatī tataḥarraku bi-al-ṭab'i bi-al-mayli alladhī fīhā*) that their source of motion is from the inclination existing in them (*anna mabda'a ḥarakatihā innamā huwa min al-mayli al-mawjūdi fīhā*) by virtue of which they move naturally. For the thing that moves them from heaviness in potency to heaviness in actuality, making them be in a state differing from that they were in, is also the cause of their motion in actuality'.

of the universe according to the opinion of Aristotle the philosopher,[126] where natural inclination or *mayl* is defined as the mover of the elements' natural movement, and identified with the heavy and the light. Philoponus too defines the relationship of the elements to their natural places as the *rhopê* in virtue of which the bodies are heavy or light.[127]

However, this term does not appear in Aristotle's text. And while in Philoponus' commentary the term *rhopê* (inclination) designates the very nature of the elements as heavy and light, in the two texts of Alexander just mentioned, it refers to the internal principle of the movement of simple bodies. Whether or not Aristotle himself considered the natural tendency of simple bodies to move up or down, in virtue of their being heavy or light, to be a positive cause of movement and therefore a mover,[128] this is certainly the view put forward by Alexander.[129] It was then taken up and defended by Philoponus,[130] and would go on to exert influence on medieval Christian, Muslim and Jewish thought.[131]

[126] (D1), A. Badawī (1947), 254,5-8 and C. Genequand (2001), §5, 44-7 (modified): 'as for the inanimate bodies, their impulse (*ishtiyāquhā*) is towards that because of which they have their natural motion, and this impulse originating from their natural disposition is the inclination towards the thing which is appropriate to them (*al-maylu ilā al-shay'i alladhī kāna mulā'imun lahā*) and the cause of the natural activity proper to them. For this is how is the destination of every body towards the natural place proper to it (*yakūnu maṣīru kulla wāḥidin min al-ajsāmi ilā al-mawḍi'i al-ṭabī'ī alladhī yakhuṣṣuhu*), and once it has settled in it it has reached the perfection proper to itself'.

[127] In 330b30: 'The discussion is about the association between the elements and their places, which is the weight-factor (*rhopê*) according to which things are called heavy and light'. And in 330b 33: 'He speaks of fire [and earth] as "extreme" and "pure" in respect of the weight-factor (*kata tên rhopên*)' (Philoponus *in GC* 229,7-8 and 16-18; trans. in Williams (2000), 140). See H. Lang (1992), 105, according to whom the inclination of the elements is the name for their nature *qua* light or heavy which she identifies as the internal mover that moves natural bodies towards their proper places.

[128] cf. F.W. Zimmermann (1987), 121, who notes that although the conception of weight as a tendency of a body to move to its natural place is Aristotle's, as well as the use of the term *rhopê* to designate this tendency, still Aristotle did not make weight a mover, i.e. a cause or source of motion; the term *rhopê* occurs in the *Physics* only once (*Phys.* 4.8, 216a13-16).

[129] Though doubts could be raised with regard to the authenticity of the two texts by Alexander that we have mentioned (concerning the inclination of simple bodies as an internal principle of movement and its identification with the nature of these bodies *qua* heavy or light), given that these texts are only extant in the Arabic version, there will be less room for doubt regarding the attribution of this doctrine to Alexander, because we find it also clearly stated in the *Quaestio* 2.3, 49,1-3, *di' hên dunamin ouketi tauta monês tês kata tên ropên kinêseôs arkhên en hautois ekhei*, and translated in R.W. Sharples (1992), 96 as well as *Quaest.* 2.18 cited above.

[130] See S. Pines (1986b), who maintains that Philoponus adopted Alexander's theory of natural inclination in a less hesitant and more explicit way than his predecessor. He clearly identifies it as *the mover* of the inanimate bodies in their upward and downward motion. See also F.W. Zimmermann (1987), 121 ff., H. Lang (1992), 97-124 and R. Sorabji (1988), 223-4 who shows that even if Alexander considers the natural inclination as the mover of the natural inanimate bodies, he nevertheless recognises Aristotle's 'generator' as a cause. This does not exclude, but rather depends on, the theory of

Alexander's account represents an attempt to reconcile the *Physics* with *De Caelo*. In *Phys.* 8.4, 255b30-1, the bodies' internal principle of motion towards their natural places is called a 'principle of passivity'. But in *De Caelo* 4 Aristotle uses the word *rhopê*, with a certain reticence, to refer to the potential of heavy or light things for 'a certain natural motion', carefully adding that these bodies 'contain within themselves, so to speak, the germs of motion'.[132] Alexander recognises this inclination as an internal principle of the movement of inanimate bodies, but goes further by drawing an analogy between the inclination of inanimate bodies and the desire of the soul in animate bodies. The two notions derive from the more general term impetus (Gk. *hormê*, Ar. *ishtiyāq*). He thus unifies all movement in the natural realm under the concept of inclination, which may manifest itself either as impulsion or as desire.

Bc: Ya'qūb b. Isḥāq's response: hot and cold as moving forces

Ya'qūb b. Isḥāq's treatment of Alexander's commentary on *GC* 2.3, 330b30-3 is polemical:[133] he aims to refute Alexander's claim that the phrase 'the two first' refers not to the two cosmic places, up and down, but to light and heavy, just insofar as they account for the movement of elements towards their natural places. His passionate argument against this view confirms that it is genuinely Alexander's, but he never sets out explicitly the opinion he is attacking.

Ya'qūb b. Isḥāq was a doctor and a pharmacologist. His interest in *GC* was directed to its theory of mixture, in which the four elementary qualities are considered to be active and passive, and this in two ways. Firstly, each of the qualities acts upon and is acted upon by its contrary. Secondly, the qualities

intrinsic nature as the efficient cause of steam rising. Heat only makes water rise by converting it into steam, which rises by its intrinsic nature.

[131] See S. Pines (1986b), 248-51, who notes that Avicenna and his successors adopt the main point of Alexander's thesis concerning the application of the principle that everything that is moved is necessarily moved by something to the natural motion of simple bodies, in that they consider heavy or light bodies to have in themselves an internal principle of movement. On Philoponus' influence on the physics of the Arabs with regard to this question, see F.W. Zimmermann (1987), 124 ff., and for a brief review of the studies of Philoponus' influence on medieval philosophers, see H. Lang (1992), n. 62.

[132] See *Cael.* 4.1, 307b30-308a2.

[133] Of the eleven treatises of the *majmū'a* attributed to Ya'qūb b. Isḥāq, seven have to do with the theory of the elements, six of these being of polemical nature: either Ya'qūb defending his doctrine, or refuting the objections of his critics. Note the incipit of treatise number 6 which presents a list of the doctrinal points of Ya'qūb's theory of elements which are the subject of controversy and which we also find in our treatise: 1) fire and earth are contraries in respect of heat and coldness, and earth is the coldest element; 2) water is not the coldest element; 3) upward movement is by means of heat and downward movement is by means of coldness; 4) the interpretation of the expression 'the two first' that Aristotle uses in *GC* as referring to heat and coldness. See A. Dietrich (1966), 175, n. 79; 177, n. 81; 178, n. 82, 83.

divide into an active pair (hot and cold) and a passive pair (dry and moist).[134] It is the latter division Ya'qūb b. Isḥāq has in mind when he argues that the phrase 'the two first' in fact refers to the elementary qualities, and in particular to the two active qualities which are worthier of primacy (48a25: *al-ḥarāratu wa al-burūdatu aḥaqqa bi-al-awwaliyyati li-annahumā al-fā'ilān*). Only hot and cold are considered active, and heavy and light are aligned with the other tangible qualities, as effects of hot and cold.[135]

Ya'qūb b. Isḥāq must therefore discuss 'the generative efficient cause' of light and heavy, since he does not consider these two qualities to be a positive cause for the movement of the elements; are heat and cold, being the agents of rarefaction and condensation, the efficient causes of heaviness and lightness?[136] He is driven to this by his concern to preserve the unity of *GC* where light and heavy are considered neither active nor passive.[137] So Ya'qūb b. Isḥāq must hold that the causality exercised in this motion is extrinsic to lightness and heaviness:

> He had in mind the efficient cause of lightness and heaviness, not lightness and heaviness [themselves]. We must therefore investigate the relation in virtue of which lightness and heaviness are generated; for it is evident from what he said that the phrase 'the first' applies to [this relation] and is the cause.[138]

He argues from two extracts of Alexander's commentary in *GC*, first to establish that heat and cold produce lightness and heaviness (47b24-5), and second that the latter are neither active nor passive (48a1). Thus he can establish

[134] In *GC* 2.2, 329b24, Aristotle does, indeed, distinguish, among the four primary tangible qualities a pair that is necessarily active, viz. hot/cold, and a pair that is essentially passive, viz. dry/moist. However, these qualities do not display their specific powers in the *GC*, where all to an equal extent act and are acted upon by each other in order to produce an elemental transformation. It is only in *Meteor.* 4 that active 'powers' will inform and organise passive contraries in order to produce a transformation in the qualities characteristic of the homeomers; see *Meteor.* 4.10, 388a20 ff. For an analysis of the role of heat and cold as active forces, see H.H. Joachim (1904), esp. 83-6 and (1922), 205-7.

[135] See Nuruosmaniye 3589, 48b3 ff. Note that Al-Kindī makes the same division and moreover considers light and heavy as mere productions of hot and cold, in *On the Explanation that the Nature of the Celestial Sphere is Different from the Natures of the Four Elements* (ed. M.A. Abū Ridā (1950-3), vol. 2, 40-6, at 41,10 ff. and 43,6 ff.). I am very grateful to Dr Peter Adamson for this reference.

[136] See *Phys.* 8.4, 256a1 ff.; cf. *Cael.* 4.3, 310a20-5. and R. Sorabji (1988), 219-22, who explains the passage of the *Physics* as stating two causes of movement for the natural bodies apart from their intrinsic nature: 'to take the example of rising steam, it is moved partly by the man who generates it by boiling the kettle, and partly by the man who takes the lid off the kettle and so removes the obstacle' (p. 220). As Richard Sorabji draws to my attention, heat should be 'the generative efficient cause' of the light, as Ya'qūb says, just as he who boils the kettle moves the rising steam up.

[137] See *GC* 2.2, 329b21 ff.

[138] Nuruosmaniye 3589, fol. 47b21-3.

that heat and cold are moving causes of elemental movement (48a25-48b2), hence reducing light and heavy to mere effects of heat and coldness.

Bc1: Ya'qūb b. Isḥāq's first argument appears as an extract of Alexander's commentary *in GC* 2.3, 330b10 ff.:

> Then he (Alexander) said, prior to this chapter, that heat is the agent for rarefaction and lightness, while coldness is the agent for condensation and heaviness.[139]

A few lines later we read:

> Then Alexander also said, commenting on what Aristotle said in order to refute the claim of those who said that the elements are <not> generated from one another: in this chapter he mentions that heat is the agent for rarefaction and lightness, while coldness is the agent for condensation and heaviness.[140]

This may be an extract from Alexander's commentary on *GC* 2.1, 329a10-13, which discusses Anaximander's notion of the Infinite.[141] Alternatively, it may refer to the passage in which Aristotle alludes to Anaximenes (*GC* 2.3, 330b9-13), in his doxography on the question of the number of elements.[142] In neither case does Aristotle cite the author he has in mind, and this is not the place to question the authenticity of the doctrines at stake.[143] The doxographers report that Anaximenes held the universe to be formed from a unique principle, air; the other elements, he believed, were generated from air by successive rarefactions and condensations.[144] Thus Anaximenes would reduce the qualitative differences of the elements to quantitative variations of a single substance. To put it another way, he makes the differences in their natures into mere differences of density: whatever is thick and dense is heavy, and whatever is fine and rarefied is light.

[139] See Nuruosmaniye 3589, fol. 47b2-24.
[140] See Nuruosmaniye 3589, fol. 48a17-19.
[141] Anaximander and his follower Anaximenes are two Presocratic philosophers of the fifth century BC who belonged to the Milesian School. Anaximander imagined at the origin of the cosmos an undifferentiated mass in which the elements and even the first qualities were not yet distinct. He called it the *apeiron*, which means 'without boundaries'.
[142] According to Ya'qūb b. Isḥāq's phrasing ['Then he [Alexander] said *before* this chapter' (*thumma yaqūlu qabla hādha al-faṣli*)] the reference is to a chapter prior to chapter 3 of book 2, and so it is the first hypothesis that is correct. The second becomes valid at the price of textual emendation as follows: 'then he [Alexander] says earlier <in> this chapter (*thumma yaqūlu qabla <fī> hādhā al-faṣli*)'.
[143] For other citations concerning the principle of Anaximenes in Aristotle, see *Metaph.* 1.3, 984a5 ff.; 1.4, 985b9 ff. and *Phys.* 1.4, 187a12. See also *GC* 2.1, 329b11 ff. where he mentions Anaximander's *apeiron*.
[144] See *Phys.* 1.4, 187a12. See also D. O'Brien (1981), 364-82.

Fire, then, would be nothing but rarefied air, and water would be condensed air, which when further condensed would yield earth. Cold corresponds to the condensation of air, and heat to its rarefaction.[145] In bringing hot and cold, light and heavy into line with rare and dense, the Presocratics explained them as mere products of differences in degrees of density.[146] But Aristotle, who rejects the existence of atoms and void in matter, instead sees condensation and rarefaction as simply the product of heat and cold, which are the only active powers *dêmiourgounta*. Note how emphatic his terminology is, in contrast to the general usage of *GC*, which calls the two qualities *poiêtika*.[147] The argument is intended to show that heat and coldness are efficient causes of lightness and heaviness through rarefaction and condensation; steam for example is rarefied as compared with the original water, and this may be related to its being light.[148]

The association between the rare and light on the one hand, and the dense and heavy on the other, in the extract attributed to Alexander seems at first curious, given that Aristotle does not here mention the light and heavy, nor say anything else that seems to justify introducing them at this point (i.e. at 330b7 ff., if this is in fact the passage in question). It is thus natural to wonder whether it might be better ascribed to Ya'qūb b. Isḥāq rather than Alexander.[149] But in fact throughout his commentary, Alexander constantly associates these two pairs of qualities as being both different in nature from, and non-reducible to, the effects of heat and cold. Philoponus tells us that Alexander explained the absence of the rare and dense among the pairs of tangible qualities enumerated by Aristotle in *GC* 2.2, 329b19-21 by aligning them with the heavy and light:[150]

> And we ask why he omits mention of the opposition between rare and dense. The interpreter Alexander says that he reduces this to heavy and light ; for the rare is light, just as the dense is heavy. But it is possible to reduce them to the same thing as the fine and the coarse; for fineness as a quality, if it is not thought of in terms of magnitude, seems to be the same

[145] This is what Plutarch reports in his *De Prim. Frig.* 947F.
[146] See O'Brien (1981), 372, and Theophrastus, *De Sensibus* 59 (DK 68A135): '<All> they say, for example, [is] that what is rare and fine is hot, and that what is dense and thick is cold: that at least is the fashion in which Anaxagoras distinguishes air and aether. Heavy and light they also account for by more or less the same factors and further by movements up and down' (trans. O'Brien (1981), 371).
[147] See e.g. *GC* 2.2, 329b26. For the use of *dêmiourgounta*, cf. *Meteor.* 4, 384b26; 388a27; 389a28 (references in H.H. Joachim (1922), 214).
[148] My thanks to Richard Sorabji for his comments on this point.
[149] Did Ya'qūb b. Isḥāq know the theories of the Presocratics? A. Dietrich (1966), 177 and n. 1, draws attention to a reference to Anaximander in the treatise no 5 of the *majmū'a*.
[150] See Philoponus *in GC*, 214,22-5, who mentions this quotation at the beginning of ch. 2 in 329b7, when he demonstrates that the tangible contrarieties are the only ones common to all bodies and that the task is to determine which ones among these are the most universal.

as rareness.[151] For we call a body that is easy to penetrate fine, and this seems to be the same as rare. Thus the coarse too <is the same as> the dense. (trans. C.J.F. Williams)

It is here worth noting that *Quaestio* 2.12, on the contraction (*sustellesthai*) of bodies, similarly aligns the two pairs of qualities. This text uses *pakhu* for 'dense', instead of the usual *puknon*, and *lepton* for 'rarefied' (usually *manon*).[152] Apart from this the *Quaestio* deals with variations in the volume of a given matter within a given space, in order to refute the argument that solid bodies contract into one another and so must be capable of interpenetration.[153]

Bc2: The second extract of Alexander's commentary mentioned by Ya'qūb b. Isḥāq addresses this topic even more explicitly:

> Then he (Alexander) said, again in a chapter previous to this one, when talking about roughness and smoothness: or it is more appropriate and adequate to say that these two qualities are neither active nor passive, just as heaviness and lightness are not. It is therefore manifest that all the other tangible differences which he names contrarieties, can be reduced to these four primary ones that were previously described, namely heat, coldness, moisture and dryness.[154]

This extract parallels *Morphology* §24,10-13 (the second part of Alexander's reply), and so is yet another sign of the authenticity of our commentary. Now, light, heavy, rough and smooth are here clearly defined as incapable of action and passion, and thus as irreducible to the effects of hot and cold, being different in nature from the latter.

The Arabic tradition provides a third textual witness to this interpretation. This is Ibn Rushd's *Middle Commentary* on *GC*, which combines the two extracts mentioned above:

[151] See *Cael.* 3.5, 303b22-5; Philoponus *in GC*, 223,9-17, who mentions the theory of Andronicus which orders under the same category of quality light and heavy, rare and dense and thin and thick. See also H.H. Joachim (1922), 204, who explains the absence of the pair rare/dense by the fact that Aristotle denies their reality in the popular sense, viz. insofar as this involves the assumption of some sort of intervals within matter, and prefers to reduce them to a sort of thin and thick.

[152] See *Quaest.* 2.12, 57, trans. R.W. Sharples (1992), 110-12 and R.B. Todd (1972a).

[153] According to R.B. Todd (1972a), 57,16-22 Bruns is based on *Phys.* 4.9, 217a10-b20, where Aristotle explains that *puknôsis* and *manôsis* cannot be reduced to the presence of void inside the body; see R.B. Todd (1972a), 298 ff. and R.W. Sharples (1992), 111 n. 365.

[154] Nuruosmaniye 3589, fols 47b24-48a3.

MS Paris B.N. Hebr. 1009, fol. 28b,1b-21b (al-'Alawī (ed.), *Talkhīṣ al-kawn*, p. 95,7-17).[155]

Wa al-Iskandaru yaqūlu: innahu innamā sakata 'an al-takāthufi wa al-takhalkhuli, immā li-annahumā taḥta al-thaqīli wa al-khafīfi, wa immā li-annahumā taḥta al-ṣulbi wa al-layyini. Wa sakata 'an al-khushūnati wa al-malāsati li-anna al-khushūnata taḥta al-yubsi wa al-malāsata taḥta al-ruṭūbati. [...] *Wa yushbihu ann yuẓanna innamā sakata 'ani al-takāthufi wa al-takhalkhuli min qibali annahumā kayfiyyatāni ghayru fā'ilatayni wa annahumā tābi'atāni ayḍan li-al-ḥararati wa al-burūdati.*

Wa sakata 'ani al-khushūnati <wa al-malāsati>, li-anna al-khushūnata tuqālu bi-al-jumlati 'alā yubūsatin mufriṭatin fī saṭḥi al-shay'i al-khashini, wa al-malāsata 'alā ruṭūbatin mā fī saṭḥihi. [...] *Wa yushbihu an yakūna hādha huwa alladhī 'anāhu al-Iskandaru.*

Alexander says that he (Aristotle) kept silent regarding rareness and density either because they are subsumed under the heavy and the light, or because they are subsumed under the hard and the soft. And he passes over roughness and smoothness in silence because roughness is subsumed under dryness and smoothness under moisture. [...] It seems that Aristotle kept silent regarding rareness and density because these are two qualities that are not active and that, moreover, depend on heat and coldness.

He kept silent regarding roughness and smoothness because roughness generally designates excessive dryness on the surface of the rough thing, whereas smoothness designates a certain moisture in the surface. [...] It seems that this is what Alexander meant.

Ibn Rushd's citation brings together the two pairs of tangible qualities that Alexander associates with the light and heavy: rough and smooth, rare and dense.[156] However, like Philoponus, Ibn Rushd fails to mention the association of the rough and the smooth with the heavy and the light. He retains only the first possibility, which subsumes these two qualities under the dry and the moist. On the other hand, he adds that the hard and soft are alternatives to the heavy

[155] See also the translation by S. Kurland (1958), 74,23-39.

[156] Ibn Rushd here conflates two passages from Alexander's commentary which are cited by Philoponus in two different places in his commentary, and which probably were not adjacent in the original (see Philoponus *in GC* 214,22-30; 223,8-17 and **Ad** above). The genre of the Middle Commentary (*talkhīṣ*) itself allows him this liberty, whereby he does not just reproduce the text being commented on, but gives a continuous exposition, and at the same time makes free use of previous commentaries, changing the order of argumentation when this is required by his own reasoning. Note that this conflation involves a leveling out of the problematic: Aristotle left out the pair rare/dense in the list of seven pairs of tangible contrarieties which he has enumerated and which include the pair rough/smooth, for which, in turn, he left out the description of the way they are subsumed by the moist/dry. For Ibn Rushd's method in his Middle Commentaries, see M. Bouyges (1983), xi, S. Kurland (1958), xv-xvi, and C.E. Butterworth (1978), 117-26, at 118 ff.

and the light as the principles of the rare and dense.[157] Though Ibn Rushd associates the rare and the dense with the light and heavy, as being likewise inactive, and though he recognises the dependence of rarity and density on heat and cold, Ibn Rushd does not draw the conclusion that the light and heavy are therefore effects of heat and cold.

Because Ya'qūb b. Isḥāq does not consider the difference in nature between these two pairs, though he mentions this in a passage that preserves a fragment of Olympiodorus' commentary on *GC* (of which the original Greek and the Arabic versions are both lost),[158] Ya'qūb encounters several difficulties. The first concerns the hot and cold as efficient causes of movement for the simple bodies that they qualify.[159] Suppose that we explain fire's upward motion because it is hot in the 'absolute' sense (*al-ḥārr al-basīṭ*)[160] – that is, qualified only by heat – so that heat characterises the nature of fire which, being essentially hot, will move upward.[161] This explanation fails, because according to *GC* earth, for instance, is essentially characterised by dryness, coldness qualifiying water.[162] So however much cold might be the principle of downward motion, we cannot use a similar account in explaining why earth moves down,[163] because earth cannot be claimed to be cold in an absolute sense.[164]

[157] See *Phys.*, 4.9, 217b11 ff. 'the dense is heavy, the rare light'.

[158] See below, Appendix. Arabic biobibliographers mention that Olympiodorus' commentary on *GC* was translated by Asṭāth (Usṭāth). See G. Flügel (1872), 251.

[159] See Nuruosmaniye 3589, fol. 48a25-b2 and below, Appendix.

[160] For the translation of *haplôs* as *basīṭ*, see G. Endress (1973), 114.

[161] cf. *Meteor.* 1.4, 342a6 and also Philoponus *in GC* 2.3, 330a30, who accounts for the lightness of air by its heat.

[162] See *GC* 2.3, 331a4 ff.

[163] cf. *Meteor.* 1.3, 340b20; 341a5 ff. and 4.6, 382b30. See also Ibn Sīnā, in his commentary on *GC* 2.3, 331a4 ff. (ed. M. Qāsim and I. Madkour (1969), 155,9-11) who, while recognising that earth is essentially dry, adds: 'But earth is also cold by nature. How could this be otherwise if weight is not compatible with heat?' (*lākinna al-arḍa fī ṭabī'atihā al-bardu ayḍan* [...] *wa kayfa lā wa al-thiqlu lā yuwāfiqu al-ḥarārata*?) and 157,17 where heat determines the movement of air towards the place of fire. Abū al-Barakāt al-Baghdādī also reproduces the association 'lightness-heat-rarity' and 'weight-cold-density' and even seems to endow heat and coldness with some kind of efficient causality in the upward and downward motion of the elements, by making lightness a product of heat and weight a product of cold: 'Theoretical reflection makes you observe that this lightness belongs to fire only through its heat and its rarity, and that heaviness belongs to earth only through its coldness and its density. So that when [what is] dense is heated it rises and floats by means of its heat, and when [what is] rare cools it sinks [to the bottom] and becomes heavy by means of its coldness'. And he adds several lines below: 'The hottest and rarest is fire and its upward region (*ḥayyizuhu*) and the coolest and densier is earth and its downward region'. See Abū al-Barakāt al-Baghdādī (1938), 127,8-10 and 18-19.

[164] The proof that Ya'qūb b. Isḥāq, when he says 'the simple cold', refers in fact to earth, is given in the incipit of the sixth treatise of the *majmū'a* (fols 30b-32a), where he refutes the criticisms by some physicians of his doctrine of the elements, particularly his statement that 'earth is the coldest of the elements and that upward motion is by means of heat and downward motion is by means of cold'; see A. Dietrich (1966), 178.

His zeal to refute Alexander interpretation leads Ya'qūb b. Isḥāq to another erroneous interpretation with regard to *GC* 2.2, 329b24-6 '*thermon de kai psukhron kai hurgon kai xêron ta men tôi poiêtika einai ta de tôi pathêtika legetai* (hot and cold, dry and moist are so called because *those* are active and *these* are passive)' (cf. Nuruosmaniye 3589, fol. 48b3-5). Here he was let down by his Arabic translation, which apparently rendered *ta men* as *al-ithnayn al-awwalayn minhum* ('the first two among them')[165] which refers simply to syntactic position, and not to any ontological priority. But Ya'qūb b. Isḥāq instead reads the phrase as referring to a priority in dignity, and hence takes this to be a confirmation of his thesis that the hot and cold are, for Aristotle, ontologically 'primary'.

Ya'qūb b. Isḥāq refuses to look beyond the immediate context of *GC*, where qualities are considered to be active only with regard to their role in the mixture and combination of elements. He thus encounters difficulties when he tries to use these qualities to explain the natural movement of the primary bodies, because he does not take into account the fact that these movements are properly studied in physics,[166] where heavy and light are considered as intrinsic explanatory principles.

The problem faced by both Alexander and Ya'qūb b. Isḥāq is, then, to establish the coherence between Aristotle's chemical theory and his physics. The difference between the two contexts resides ultimately in, on the one hand, the choice of the qualities that will explain the essential transformations of the elements, and on the other the determination of their roles in the constitution of the elements. The third book of *Cael.* is presented as an inquiry into the elements and their generation. There is no need to discuss here the limitations of this inquiry as we actually find it in Book 3.[167] But it is worth noting that Book 3 ends by determining 'the most essential differences' between the elementary bodies, as being 'differences in properties and functions and powers'.[168] What

[165] As do indeed many translations of *GC*. See E.S. Forster (1955), 271,9-10, 'the first pair get their name because they are active' and J. Tricot (1934), 101,18, 'le premier couple est actif'; C. Mugler, on the contrary, renders *ta men* ... *ta de* by 'les uns ... les autres', see C. Mugler (1966), 48,8-10. It is to be noted, on the other hand, that Ibn Sīnā, op. cit., 154, proves to be fairly literal when he says (l. 4) '*ithnatāni minhā fā'ilatāni* (two of them are active)' and further down (l. 13) '*fa-li-hādhā mā tusammā tānika fā'ilatayni wa hātāni munfa'ilatayni* (it is for this reason that those are called active and these passive)' which is the exact equivalent of *ta men*... *ta de*.

[166] See *Cael.* 4.1, 307b30-2.

[167] Book 3 of *De Caelo* establishes that the coming-to-be of the elements takes place only by mutual transformation, and this after rejecting three alternative theories of how they come to be. However, in *De Caelo* the mechanism of this coming-to-be is never explained, and it is not until the second book of *GC* that Aristotle resumes the line of his inquiry in order to lead it to its end, although from a different vantage point. See P. Moraux (1965), xx-xxi, and on the relations between *Cael.* and *GC* see F. Solmsen (1958), 295-8, and an excellent presentation by H. Hugonnard-Roche (1985), 17, who takes the tradition into account.

[168] See *Cael.* 3.8, 307b20. P. Moraux notes that loose terminology seems to have troubled Alexander (*ap.* Simplicium *in Cael.* 671,25 ff.)

Aristotle means here is established at the very beginning of the book, where he refers to the movement of bodies, on the one hand, and on the other to 'their alterations and their transformations into one another'.[169] When Aristotle turns to discuss the heavy and the light in *Cael.* 4, he is thus entering into a discussion of the fundamental properties of the elements. These are the intrinsic qualities of the bodies they qualify. Given that, in *Cael.* and in Aristotle's physics as a whole, 'it is the natural movements of simple bodies that are the most characteristic properties of bodies', lightness and heaviness have a fundamental role to play in the classification of the elements[170] and the account of their cosmological distribution according to which they realise their nature. But the context of *GC* 2.2-5 is quite different. Here Aristotle is concerned with the generation of the elements from one another, and with the four primary qualities that are shown in 2.2 to be the only ones capable of explaining this generation. By acting upon one another, they facilitate not only the reciprocal transformation of the elements, but also the generation of more complex bodies made up of elements. For the element remains 'the first constituent' of a thing, its 'constitutive and immanent principle', 'specifically indivisible into other species'.[171]

Since what Aristotle means by *stoikheion* is the simplest and most primitive constituent of a thing,[172] it is the primary contraries that deserve this denomination. Even though the elements are the most simple substances, and indissoluble into simpler constituents, they are not for all that absolutely simple. For each of the elements can be decomposed, at least theoretically, into a pair of elementary qualities. The prospect that it is the four contraries that are the ultimate 'elements' of things makes it more urgent to inquire into their nature, and into their relationship with the four simplest and more primary bodies.

C: Elements in the proper sense, and the primary perceptible bodies

At *GC* 2.3, 330b22-30, Aristotle distinguishes between the primary perceptible bodies that appear to us to be the simplest bodies in the sublunary world (*ta kaloumena stoikheia*),[173] which are however 'not simple but mixed', and the

[169] See *Cael.* 3.1, 298a32 ff.
[170] See *Cael.* 4.4, 312a8-5, 312b19, where Moraux sees an attempt to deduce the elements from weight and lightness. By positing an intermediate between the unqualified heavy and the unqualified light, which is both heavy and light and which is also double, Aristotle can deduce four specific differentiae and consequently four elements. Nonetheless, recalls Moraux, this demonstration is not an *a priori* deduction: the four elements are supposed to be known and Aristotle only observes, after examining their characteristic motions, that it is impossible to admit fewer than four specific differentiae among the simple bodies. See P. Moraux (1965), xxv-xxvi.
[171] See *Metaph.* 5.3, 1014a26 ff.
[172] See *Metaph.* 5.3, 1014a31-5; *GC* 2.1, 329a5; 2.8, 334b31 ff.; *PA*, 646a12-17; *Cael.* 3.3, 302a15-19.
[173] The expression *ta kaloumena stoikheia* appears already in *GC* 1.6, 322b1 f., and re-appears several times in the course of the treatise: see *GC* 2.1, 328b31; 329a16, 26,

elements properly speaking, which are the simple forms of these bodies. Fire, air, water, and earth are of course the primary perceptible bodies, but they are not mere instantiations of the pairs of elementary qualities that constitute them, which elements strictly speaking should be. Only a substance that is, for example, purely hot and dry, would be an 'element' in the proper sense. The fire that we perceive is similar to such a substance, but not identical to it. Aristotle refers to the pure element as the *puroeidês*, and this is characterised simply (*haplôs*) by the pair hot-dry. Thus the word 'fire' is used properly of the fire that we perceive; it is purely fire, impure relative to what is nothing more than hot and dry. It is mixed (*mikton*), because of its surplus heat, whereas the pure hot and dry, which is simple, is qualified by the hot and the dry in equal measure.[174]

This distinction raises two problems: first, it puts into question the nature of the elements. In denying that the four elements are identical to the primary bodies that we experience, Aristotle raises the question of what these proper elements really are. We must ask not only how these pure elements relate to those we experience, but also whether they are merely ideal abstractions or rather separately existent.[175] If the latter, then where do they exist? A second

where Aristotle defines the true elements as those which are prior to the first perceptible bodies, and from which these latter stem: the prime matter and the primary contrarieties. See H.H. Joachim (1922), 137, who recalls that Aristotle prefers to reserve the term *stoikheia* 'to the absolutely underivative and unanalysable immanent *arkhai*', viz. first matter, privation and *habitus*. See also 2.3, 330b2, *kata logon tois haplois phainomenois sômasi* and *Meteor*. 1.3, 339b6 (*ta legomena stoikheia*) and Alexander's commentary ad loc. (7,35-8,2) who distinguishes sublunary so-called elements from the true elements by which the former are produced. R. Sokolowski (1970), 270, has analysed the use of the term *stoikheion* in *GC* in all occurrences. He distinguishes three kinds of use: 1) Aristotle uses it simply, without any qualification, when speaking of theories of other philosophers; 2) otherwise he uses the expression *kaloumenon stoikheion* to refer to the primary bodies which he, consequently, does not consider to be the true elements; 3) finally, *stoikheion* refers to elemental qualities, particularly in *GC* 2.

[174] See *GC* 2.3, 330b21 ff. and W.J. Verdenius and J.H. Waszink (1946), 58-9.

[175] Modern commentators often consider the elements strictly speaking as 'ideal' substances (the expression is used by H. King (1956), 379). According to this view, the elements in their pure state could not exist in a concrete form in Aristotle's universe: these are ideal abstractions and the elemental transformations described in *GC* 2 are theoretical elaborations. In fact, most modern scholars have examined the question from the viewpoint of the chemical theory of elements and particularly in the light of the idea that every compound body must have a mixture of four elements as its material basis (cf. *GC* 2.8). Therefore the elements never exist in a pure state. Moreover, all the bodies that we perceive are real mixtures whereas the elements themselves cannot be perceived. In the same way, elemental qualities are considered from a dynamic point of view only in the case of mixture, whereas in the analysis of the four elements they are considered from a merely formal point of view. See R. Sokolowski (1970), 272-3 n. 18, citing G. Seeck (1964), 38-42 and 47-50; H. King (1956), 377 ff.; J. Puig Montada (1996), 1-34; and E. Lewis (1996), 40 who thinks that elemental transformations as they are described in *GC* 2 could never have taken place, because the elements do not exist in a pure state in the Aristotelian universe. Real water transforms into vapour, but this is not a transformation

problem is that Aristotle has said the primary bodies are *mikta*; with what, then, are they mixed?

Ca: Material fire

The obvious answer is that the primary bodies are mixed with one another, which is why they are not 'pure', as proper elements must be, but rather constantly altered due to mutual contact.[176] The elements would then be mixed because they are contaminated by one another. This is a preliminary answer considered by Philoponus:[177] 'Those who look at his words too hurriedly will think that what he is saying is that the elements are not simple or pure but mixed and always rendered spurious by each other, as many have held' (trans. C.J.F. Williams). On this, most straightforward reading, the mixed fire of our world is qualified by an excess of heat, as opposed to a fire that is reduced to its simple nature (*ta hapla toiauta*), i.e. the pair of qualities, hot and dry.

There is however no trace of this interpretation in the fragments reproduced by Jābir. To explain why this terrestrial fire, i.e. mixed fire, has 'an excess of heat' (*GC* 2.3, 330b25-6) Alexander says:

> By 'fire' he means the fire that is like form. As for the fire which is the matter and in which way [it is], he said that 'fire is nothing but the excess of heat', for the reason that air is hot, because what is essentially (*'alā al-qaṣd al-awwal*)[178] and properly hot is fire, for 'fire is the boiling of heat and dryness'.[179]

of the elemental water, just as the earth on which we walk is not the same as the element earth.

[176] Several lines below, at 330b34, Aristotle says that fire and earth are extreme bodies, and are very pure (*kai akra men kai eilikrinestata*) whereas water and air are intermediate and more mixed (*mesa de kai memigmena mallon*). One might ask why water and air are more mixed than other simple bodies if all four constantly transform into one another. The answer would be found in the nature of 'the twofold exhalation', described in *Meteorology* 1.3 and 4, which plays a central role in the mutual transformation of the primary bodies. The hot-moist exhalation comes from the evaporation of the water from the surface of the earth, to which it is related and whose characteristics it retains; and the hot-dry exhalation results from the action of the sun on the earth itself. It is the hot-moist exhalation that is a kind of aqueous vapour midway between water and air that involves a constant mixture of the two elements; it is always air in transition to being condensed into rain or water in transition to being evaporated into air. See H.H. Joachim (1922), 139.

[177] See Philoponus, *in GC*, 227,26-30.

[178] For this expression, which occurs fairly frequently in the Arabic versions of some of Alexander's treatises, see n. 52 to the translation.

[179] *Morphology* §29: *Fa-innamā ya'nī al-nāra bi-qawlihi anna al-nāra allatī ka-l-ṣūrati. Wa ammā allatī hiya al-māddatu wa 'alā ayyi jihatin, innamā yaqūlu anna al-nāra innamā hiya li-ghalabati al-ḥarārati, min qibali anna al-hawā'a huwa ḥārrun wa dhālika anna alladhī huwa ḥārrun 'alā al-qaṣdi al-awwali khāṣṣatan huwa nārun, wa dhālika anna al-nāra huwa ghalayānu al-ḥarārati wa al-yubūsati.*

And a few lines later:

> For, he only names 'fire' that which is properly called fire. He also names it 'domestic [fire]', because such is its condition. As for <the fire> which is the element, it is not like this, for it is neither like boiling nor like excess. This is the reason why it is very generative and fruitful (*muwallida wa muthmira*).[180]

In the midst of an apparently faithful exposition of the text, we have here a novel distinction between a 'fire that is like form' and a 'fire that is matter', which is not present in Aristotle. The distinction between mixed, terrestrial fire, which has an excess of heat and is called by Alexander 'domestic fire' (a metaphor found in Philoponus, who uses the term *to diakonikon*, translated literally into Arabic as *allatī li-l-khidma*),[181] and 'pure' fire that is reduced to its simple nature (*ta hapla toiauta*) and is essentially qualified as hot and dry. The latter is thus not fire as actuality but fire as potency, which explains why it is 'generative and fruitful'.[182] This distinction is of course properly Aristotelian.

We find this view also in *Quaestio* 2.17,[183] where Alexander asks why terrestrial fire is hotter than fire as an element, which he identifies with celestial fire (*ouk epei mallon thermon tou hôs stoikheiou puros, ho kai hupekkauma legetai*).[184] He attributes the excessive heat to the nature of the combustible: the heat of fire depends on the matter that is burning. For instance, incandescent iron is hotter than a burning flame because its heat stems from the consistency of the material of which it is made up. The nature of terrestrial fire thus depends upon that of the material with which it is mixed in order to burn. It assimilates this material and changes it into its own nature, and it is this process that will alter its composition by preventing hot and dry from being in equilibrium. Note that the combustible material in question has nothing to do with the 'matter' discussed in the passage just mentioned. Rather this material is the 'proximate'

[180] *Morphology* §35: *Wa dhālika annahu innamā yusammī nāran hādhihi allatī 'alayhā khāṣṣatan yaj'alu isma al-nāri. Wa yusammīhā 'allatī li-al-khidmati', wa dhālika anna bi-hādhihi ḥālahā. Wa ammā tilka <allatī> hiya al-usṭuqus laysat hākadhā, idh kānat tilka laysa ka-l-ghalayāni wa lā ayḍan ka-l-ghalabati, wa li-hādhā al-sababi hiya muwallidatun jiddan wa muthmiratun.*

[181] See Philoponus *in GC* 228,28, *pur entautha phêsi to diakonikon.*

[182] Since fire is essentially characterised by heat, and since the heat which constitutes it is tempered because of its constant mixture with other elements, it is generative, and acts as a principle of cohesion in the formation of the homeomers or first bodies composed out of the elements. In fact, heat and coldness have a generative power when they master the matter (cf. *Meteor.* 4.1, 379b1), i.e. when they are in balanced proportions and act as controlling powers in bringing together homogeneous substances, in the case of heat, and heterogeneous, in the case of coldness. See also *GC* 2.1, 329b24-6; Philoponus *in GC* 228,30-229,4 and below, **Cb**, for the *Middle Commentary* of Ibn Rushd which paraphrases the same passage identifying the elemental and the heavenly fire.

[183] cf. *Quaest.* 2.17, 61-2, and R.W. Sharples (1994), 14.

[184] cf. *Quaest.* 2.17, 61,32-3, and R.W. Sharples (1994), 14.

matter that is burned, and that may eventually lose its form once it is completely consumed in the fire, which will perish by the same token. This process does not affect the essential 'form-prime matter' compound that constitutes fire itself.[185] Only while it is being burned can this proximate matter affect the elemental fire's heat.

One can thus understand the analogy with ice, given at *GC* 2.3, 330b25 f. The analogy aims to demonstrate that the difference in nature between terrestrial fire and true, elemental fire is reducible to variations in degrees of intensity. Ice, as the extreme opposite of fire, is here considered to be a frozen 'cold-moist' (i.e. elemental water), which is produced when the element water takes on an excess of cold. With the destruction of the equilibrium between cold and moisture, which characterises the nature of water, water is replaced by ice. In the same way, an excess of heat entails the destruction of the form 'hot-dry'. Thus, just as ice is not water, terrestrial fire is not elemental fire.[186] The analogy breaks down, however, if we consider the relationship between the primary bodies and their corresponding elements. The analogue of terrestrial fire ought of course to be terrestrial water, not ice. But Aristotle is not attempting to give a definition of this relationship between terrestrial and elemental fire. He wants only to show that material fire, i.e. actual fire, is nothing other than the degenerative process of the element into excess. The analogy should therefore be read as follows: fire is to 'hot air' or *hupekkauma*[187] as ice is to water. If fire is analogous to ice, and

[185] See *Mixt.* 9, 222,35 ff., and R.B. Todd (1976), 132-3.

[186] See *Morphology* §33. Alexander will cite this analogy again in his commentary *in Meteor.* 1.3, 340b20, 14,25-8.

[187] Aristotle will distinguish, in *Meteor.* 1.3, 340b23 (cf. *Meteor.* 1.4, 341b) the real fire which is an excess of heat from the elements that occupies the region above the air and below the heavenly sphere, and which 'we are accustomed to call fire though it is not really fire' (trans. Lee). This substance which occupies the highest part of the sublunary realm and which is called 'fire' is the substance which is 'fire potentially', but not in actuality. We are talking rather about a kind of inflammable material which is only a mixture of heat and dryness. In the case of fire, the distinction between *hupekkauma* and air is very tenuous, because they both originate in the twofold exhalation of the sublunary region (see *Meteor.* 1.3, 339b3 ff. and on the ambiguous nature of the double exhalation, H.H. Joachim (1922), 139), and is shown by a certain terminological confusion. The equivocity has been pointed out by Alexander (*in Meteor.* 1.3, 341a9, 17,18-20) who explains the lack of terminological consistency by an effective contamination of the two elements during their reciprocal transformation. Thus when in *Cael.* 2.7, 289a20, Aristotle says that the heat and light emitted by heavenly bodies as a result of 'the friction of air by the motion of those bodies', whereas it is the fire or *hupekkauma* that must be found immediately below the heavenly sphere, Alexander apud Simplicium, *in Cael.* (439,14) explains that in this case 'air' refers to the *hupekkauma,* while noting that Aristotle elsewhere calls this *hupekkauma* elemental fire (reference from R.W. Sharples (1990a), 98-9). Sharples concludes from this that if this interpretation is in agreement with *Quaestio* 2.17, it corresponds neither to the data of *Meteor.* 1.3, 340b23, nor to Alexander's commentary ad loc. It is worth noting that in *Quaestio* 2.17, Alexander identifies the *hupekkauma* with the elemental fire, distinguishing it very clearly from the real fire described as an effervescence of fire. In our excerpts one can see the emphasis

ice is an excess, then fire must also be an excess. Elemental fire, conversely, being by nature pure and unmixed with any combustible matter, is insusceptible to any variations in intensity.

This theory may be found already in Theophrastus, who in the opening sections of *De igne* raises a doubt about the elemental nature of the terrestrial fire, given its need for combustible material. Whereas the other elements exist by themselves, fire must always come to be in some other, combustible material. For Theophrastus, an element cannot depend on a substratum (cf. §§3-6), because it will be neither elementary nor prior to the substrate or to the combustible. The only solution is that there are different types of fire: one, pure and unmixed, located in the first celestial sphere and characterised by pure heat; the other, terrestrial fire, mixed and always undergoing generation.[188]

However this proximate matter is not the only matter at stake in *Quaestio* 2.17. Alexander also says that the fire around us (*par' hêmin*) is itself matter: *hulê to toiouto pur*.[189] This is apparently original to Alexander. It is not found in Theophrastus. Alexander gives us to understand that the difference between terrestrial and celestial fire is one of matter and form. This is of course precisely the distinction found in our text, and has no direct source in Aristotle. Again, this is strong evidence for the authenticity of the commentary.

Philoponus' commentary lends further support to this conclusion. He mentions another interpretation, which he takes more seriously than the one he has already discussed (*eipousi proteron tên alêthê tou rhêtou dianoian*): this is to distinguish between pure forms, which are uniquely constituted from a pair of opposites, and the primary bodies, which are mixed and composed (*mixta kai suntheta*) from form and matter. For example 'for the form of fire which is regarded as constituted by the pairing of the qualities – I mean hot and dry – this is simple, just as matter is simple, but fire is already something composed out of both'.[190] Fire resembles the pair of qualities that give it form, but these qualities are not identical to fire (*homoiai, phêsi, tois stoikheiois, ou mên hai autai*), they are only its form.[191] Here Philoponus' explanation of the view is rather confused; he has clearly had difficulty reconciling the thesis of his predecessor with Aristotle.

Yet if we return to the text of *GC* 2.3, we see that Aristotle calls 'our' fire simply 'fire' (*pur*), as opposed to what is 'similar to fire' (*tôi puri homoion*

on the proximity of nature between the two substances, whose differences are reduced, in a way, to a difference of intensity; see *Morphology* §29.

188 See V.C.B. Coutant (1971), 5,11 ff. and trans. 4,13 ff., 'A fire in solid, earthy material is hottest because it does not flow off so readily but is sealed in by the density and because it has a fuel which is more solid, being harder and more compact. For this reason such substances are very hot when subjected to fire, as for example, iron, bronze, stone and earthen ware, substances which presumably are by nature very cold. They retain and hold the heat within them to a considerable extent, so that they burn flesh severely, as is to be expected'.

189 *Quaest.* 2.17, 61,33 and 62,11.

190 Philoponus *in GC* 330b25, 228,4-6, trans. C.J.F. Williams.

191 ibid., 228,21-5.

puroeidês). This recalls a passage in the *Timaeus* (49D-50A),[192] where Plato distinguishes on the one hand the fire called *pur*, the intelligible form, which may be called 'this' or 'that', and on the other hand sensible fire, which being a moving image of the intelligible form is only similar (*homoion*) to fire, and which is nothing but a 'such' (*toiouto*), because of its instability. Aristotle has inverted the relationship: for him the word *pur* designates sensible fire, while pure fire is called *puroeidês*.[193] Aristotle uses Platonic language, but reverses the terminology, so as better to undercut the theory of forms. Alexander resists this move and reintegrates Aristotle's theory of elements with the Platonic distinction between material fire and a fire that is like form, here sowing the seeds of the later Neoplatonic synthesis.

Finally let us return to the passage we started with: 'By "fire" he means the fire that is like form (*al-ṣūra*)' and note the echo of *Timaeus* 51B, where Plato asks whether there could be 'something like fire that is absolutely itself', answering at 52A that what appears in the Receptacle is a copy of the intelligible Form, which shares its name and resembles it. Fire here thus takes its name and meaning from its participation in the Form of fire, of which it is merely the reflection. So much for the sources of Alexander's interpretation; let us now turn to its reception in a later commentary, that of Ibn Rushd.

Cb – The genetic and cosmological theory of the elements

Our passage is reproduced in Ibn Rushd's *Middle Commentary on GC*:[194]

> Alexander said that this [i.e. the fact that nothing is generated out of fire or ice] only applies to fire that is here. As for the fire that is at the limit of the circumference, that is not in an excess of heat or boiling. For this reason, more than any other element, fire is the cause of generation.[195] This is a questionable matter that requires further investigation.

Ibn Rushd does undertake such an investigation in his *Middle Commentary on De Meteorologica*,[196] where he treats this problem in the context of a general,

[192] I am very grateful to Dr Denis O'Brien for this observation and argument.
[193] See W.J. Verdenius and J.H. Waszink (1946), 59, who point out the confusion that might arise from Aristotle's use of the term *puroeidês* precisely because of the Platonic use which designates a lower degree of being, whereas with Aristotle the pair hot/dry is called *puroeidês* because it refers to a reality superior to that of the physical world.
[194] See J. al-'Alawī (1994), 97,22-98,2 and S. Kurland (1958), 76,38-77,2.
[195] Note a departure from Alexander's text, where fire is described as highly generative, whereas for Averroes it is, among all the elements, the one that is most a cause of coming-to-be. Note also the localisation of the elemental fire at the periphery of the universe and thus its identification with the *hupekkauma*, whereas there is no reference to such an identification in our commentary. On the other hand, in *Quaestio* 2.17, as in his commentary on *Meteor.*, Alexander explicitly assimilates the elemental fire to the hot and dry substance located above the sublunary region. See 61,32-3 with R.W. Sharples (1994), 14, and Alex. *in Meteor.* 14,24-30.
[196] Ed. J. al-'Alawī (1994), 27-32.

systematic attempt[197] to reconcile the cosmological model of *Cael.* with the genetic theory of the elements found in *GC* and *Meteor*. In *Cael.* Aristotle characterises fire by its natural movement upwards, and its coming to rest in a place where it it is actualised in its first simplicity.[198] In the genetic theory, by contrast, elementary fire is described as a fiery substance that is not actual, but potential fire, and is essentially hot and dry. These two qualities allow it on the one hand to be transformed into the other elements, and on the other to combine with the other elements to form homeomerous bodies. But if, as Ibn Rushd claims, Alexander thinks that burning fire (i.e. 'actual fire') and elementary fire only share the name 'fire' equivocally, then they are two completely seperated entities and nothing about the nature and behaviour of one of these types of fire could be inferred from that of the other.

H. Hugonnard Roche has shown that, in his *Epitome of De Caelo*, Ibn Rushd juxtaposes these two theories without successfully reconciling them.[199] He raises the issue of whether celestial and terrestrial fire are called 'fire' univocally or, as Alexander thought, equivocally. He follows Alexander in his commentary on *Meteor*. The fire he characterises as 'natural' is hot and dry exhalation, in contrast to 'real' or 'non-natural' fire, which is described as an excess according to the analogy with ice in *GC* 2.3, 330b25 put forward by Alexander. He seems here compelled to accept the view that he ascribes to Alexander, namely that real and natural fire only share a name homonymously, given that (as Hugonnard Roche has pointed out) comparing the two requires appealing to the notion of the non-natural.[200]

The situation is completely different in the *Middle Commentary on Meteor*. Here, proceeding from the same premisses, Ibn Rushd reaches a synthetic

[197] As with all the commentators of Aristotle, Ibn Rushd attempted to present Aristotle's thought as a system, which explains references made in one commentary to the other, setting in relation different texts of the Stagirite. See H. Hugonnard Roche (1985), 7. For the method of Ibn Rushd in his Middle Commentaries see the references in n. 156 above, and M. Aouad (1996), who describes the specific character of the Middle Commentary as a genre in relation to other forms of exegesis as being a direct explanation of the profound sense of the commented text taken as a whole. So, the systematisation of Aristotle's thought that one finds here would be a result of a broader view than the one at work in the Long Commentaries which are constrained by their line-by-line pattern. Here the ultimate goal is to present a clearer and more precise text with a more pronounced doctrinal character. The author cites D. Gutas who notes that the terms *talkhīṣ* and *lakhkhaṣa* convey, in the classical language, the idea of determining a meaning, analysing its constitutive elements; see D. Gutas (1993), 55-6.

[198] See *Cael.* 4.3, 311a4 ff.

[199] cf. H. Hugonnard Roche (1985), 'L'Epitomé', 25-9.

[200] cf. ibid., 27, where the author presents another passage from the *Epitome* in which Ibn Rushd contrasts the rectilinear upward movement of fire with its circular motion in its natural place, qualifying the latter motion also as non-natural. There is indeed an opposition between the two kinds of movement, which moreover fall under two contradictory theories: the circular motion of fire following the sphere of fixed stars in *Meteor.*, and the rectilinear upward movement of fire and its rest in its natural place, as expounded in *Cael.*

account that denies a strong distinction between pure and actual elements. He puts the problem just as he had in his *Epitome of Cael.*, as he is still working with Alexander's commentary on *Meteor.*,[201] which included the analogy between burning terrestrial fire and ice taken from *GC*. The cross-reference from the *Middle Commentary on GC* to the one on *Meteor.* can thus be explained as stemming from the same concern for systematisation, since Ibn Rushd pursues the synthetic project of a general treatment of fire, in which both the sterile, terrestrial fire and the 'generative and fruitful' fire of *GC* would, in disagreement with Alexander,[202] be called 'fire' univocally. Note that Alexander does not pose the issue quite so sharply in terms of equivocity, being content to cite Aristotle's remark regarding celestial fire that 'we are accustomed to call it fire, though it is not really fire'.[203] Ibn Rushd tries, that is, to establish that they are two varieties of the same element. It will thus be possible to establish a relationship between them on the ground that they share the same nature.

The relevant portions of the *Middle Commentary* of Ibn Rushd[204] read as follows:

> We must investigate two things. One is what Alexander says regarding the fire that is in the concavity of the sphere of the moon: that it does not burn, and that it is given the name 'fire' only homonymously (*bi-ḍarbin min ishtirāki al-ismi*). [...]
>
> Alexander says that the hot, dry body that is adjacent to the celestial sphere is not actually fire, nor does it burn; it is only potentially fire. He claims that this is Aristotle's doctrine, and in support of this he cites what [Aristotle] says in the book *On Generation and Corruption*, namely that fire is the boiling of the hot that is dry, just as ice, which is its contrary, is the freezing of the cold that is moist. If ice is not the body that is the watery element, then it must be that the fire that is its opposite [sc. the opposite of the watery element] is not the fire that is the boiling of the hot and dry, but rather a hot, dry body that is not at the extreme [of heat and dryness]. Again, if ice is analogous to fire, and ice is an extension of (*khurūj*) the watery element toward excess, it must be that actual fire is an extension of the fiery (*nārī*) element excess. In support of this one may say that, if there were actual fire there, it would ignite the air and the other elements because of what follows necessarily from the size of that place and fire's power of transformation.
>
> Alexander says, how can one believe that this fire is synonymous (*muwāṭi'atun bi-al-ismi*) with that [fire], when that [fire] is generative, and this one destructive?

[201] See Alexander *in Meteor.* 14,24-30.

[202] In fact all the arguments that he attributes to Alexander stem ultimately from theories formulated by Aristotle in the *GC* and *Meteor.* But it seems that Ibn Rushd found it more convenient to attribute them to Alexander than to attack Aristotle directly.

[203] See above, p. 50 and n. 200.

[204] J. al-'Alawī (1994), 27,9-29,2.

Ibn Rushd thus raises two *aporiai* that show the difficulties that arise for Aristotle's theory of elements in light of the distinction between the simple elements and the primary bodies that correspond to them. These latter are of the same nature, yet not identical to them, because they are mixtures, terrestrial fire being elementary fire mixed with matter,[205] just as ice is water congealed together with terrestrial impurities. But then – and here is the first *aporia* – how can it be that the primary bodies are composed of qualities that are more intense than the same qualities existing on their own, in the pure elements?

> If it is the simple watery element that is at the extreme of coldness and moisture and not sensible water, then the body contrary to it must be the body that is at the extreme of heat and dryness. But if the watery element is not at the extreme, and ice is colder than it, then the body contrary to it must be the body that is in the same state.
> We are, then, in a dilemma: either we admit that the simple elements are at the extreme of the qualities that constitute them, and that what exists from them and is imagined to have more intense qualities than they do (the reason for this would be that these [elements] do not exist in their primary simplicity, but are always mixed with one another, as in the case of water and earth); or, we admit that there may be something from the elements that has a more intense quality than they do. For ice is not simple water, but is composed from water and earthy parts. And it is the same in the case of the fire that is opposed to it, I mean luminous, burning fire: it must be composed.
> The principles require that it is impossible that there be anything in what is composed that is more intense in quality than the simples, because the composition is produced only through mixture, and mixture necessarily requires tempering the primary powers, I mean the powers of the simples.[206] [...] There must not exist here a hot, dry body hotter than the

[205] See H. Hugonnard Roche (1985), 25,30-26,6, who reproduces the distinction drawn by Ibn Rushd in his *Epitome* of the *De Caelo*, between the visible fire on earth and superior invisible fire, opposing his own interpretation to that of Alexander. Here is a French translation by the author of the yet unedited Arabic: 'Mais il en va autrement si nous posons qu'ils sont dits feu par simple communauté (*ishtirāk*) de nom, comme le pense Alexandre qui assure que c'est l'opinion d'Aristote. Il soutient que le feu qui est en haut n'est pas brûlant comme le feu qui est sur terre, et qu'il n'y a d'ignité dans le premier qu'en tant qu'il est chaud et sec seulement, et que l'air est de deux sortes, l'une chaude et humide et l'autre chaude et sèche à laquelle Aristote applique le nom de feu. Et il infère cela de l'explication d'Aristote dans le *De gen. corr.*, selon laquelle le feu vrai est l'opposé de la glace'.

[206] The theory of mixture essentially implies the conception of degrees of intensity in the elemental qualities, whose contraries will be mutually tempered by means of their reciprocal acting and being acted upon. The intensities of contrary ingredient qualities must thus be balanced so as to be able to combine and allow the emergence of one intermediary quality produced by the attenuation of the qualities of the ingredients. See H.H. Joachim (1904).

hot, dry element, and this is necessary, as you can observe. It is amazing how this escaped Alexander, unless he only meant that fire does not burn in its place due to mixture. And mixture is probably necessary for it, as has been made evident. When Aristotle defines fire and ice in the book *On Generation* [*and Corruption*], he only defines the simples, and he gives as examples of this composed things that are closest to them in similarity, I mean, closest to them in their primary qualities.[207]

Thus the mixed nature of the primary bodies echoes the transformation of the pure elements and the interaction of their qualities. If fire does not burn in its natural place, i.e. just below the moon, it is only because of the mutual transformation of elements that causes their mixture, and thus the weakening of their qualities.[208] Ibn Rushd finally succeeds in unifying the Aristotelian cosmological accounts by appealing to a single fundamental principle: the reciprocal action of the primary contraries that constitute the elements. They explain not only mutual transformation but also the formation of homeomerous bodies. Thus they are the basis for all sublunary bodies. Similarly, the rectilinear movement of the elements can be explained by the contact between them, through which each element affects those adjacent to it. Thus a drop of water may tend towards the sphere of air as if towards its natural place, because of its qualitative relationship to air, through which it is transformed into air and thus comes to its natural place, from which it will immediately depart for an even more proper place, as it ceases to be water.[209]

This leads Ibn Rushd to the solution of his second *aporia*: does fire, unlike water, air and earth, exist as a separate, pure element in its own place?[210]

[207] See J. al-'Alawī (1994), 29,14-30,18.

[208] The first alternative, which is also the solution advocated by Averroes, stipulates that the elements are in a constant mixture, on the basis of the example of water and earth. It might have been suggested by the Aristotelian theory of the formation of compound bodies in the sublunary world which are all composed of all simple bodies. Now, the bodies that are on the earth must contain earth, because in the region in which they are there is more earth than of anything else. 'Furthermore the earth cannot remain coherent without moisture, and this is what holds it together; for if the moisture were entirely removed from it, it would fall apart' (*GC* 2.8, 335a1-3, Forster trans.). Thus the fundamental components which necessarily go together in each compound in the central region of the universe are earth and water. The presence of two others is only a result of logical deduction, 'because they are contraries of earth and water' (*GC* 2.8, 335a3-9), and the constituents of a compound must be contrary (cf. *GC* 2.2, 329b10-11, Forster trans.). On the other hand, in the context of the *Meteor.* the example of mixture of water and earth could also refer to the double nature of the exhalation produced from the earth when it is heated by the sun; it is constituted by vapour from water that exists in and on the earth, and of smoke because of its properly earthy origin (See *Meteor.* 1.4, 341b6-10).

[209] See *Phys.* 4.5, 212b29-213a10; *Cael.* 4.3, 310b1-15 and V. Goldschmidt (1956), 108-9.

[210] See J. al-'Alawī (1994), 30,19-31,1; the question that seems to imply a different behaviour of fire, could have been suggested by *GC* 2.8, 335a16, where Aristotle

> If the elements existed in their primary qualities without being mixed with one another, then there would be no generation or corruption, but they would consist of parts and a whole, and would be separable from one another. But since the heavenly bodies have stirred them up equally through their own motions, and because they are equal in their powers, an equilibrium is produced between them with respect to mixture, action and passion. [...]
>
> What Alexander says, that the fire there is a cause for generation, is true, because it is mixed and impure. It is not because its substance, insofar as it is simple, is the cause of generation, as one might understand from the way his statement appears.[211]

The transformation of the elements is necessitated by the movement of the sun along the ecliptic, which guarantees through its duality a continuing cycle of generation and corruption.[212] This transformation is thus a process that unifies all sublunary phenomena with a single efficient cause. This is something to which *GC* alludes only in passing, but it is discussed extensively in *Meteor.*, where the various phenomena described in the first three books are in the last analysis explained in terms of the exhalations produced by the action of the sun.[213]

Ibn Rushd thus appeals to the mechanics of elementary transformation, described theoretically in *GC* and given a more concrete analysis in *Meteor.*, to reconcile two central theories of Aristotle's natural philosophy: on the one hand the cosmological doctrine of elements, which emphasises the rectilinear movements of the elements towards their natural places, and on the other hand the chemical theory of *GC*, which deals with the interaction of the primary qualities. In both theories, the elements are seen as endowed with qualities through which they may affect one another. Ibn Rushd's two *aporiai* thus stem from a basic problem of internal coherence in Aristotle's system: if we admit that elementary fire is generative, we must deny that it exists only purely and simply, by itself in its natural place.[214]

specifies that 'while all [sc. the simple bodies] come-to-be out of one another, fire is the only one which is fed' (trans. Forster).

[211] See J. al-'Alawī (1994), 31,11-32,9. The question has been raised by Aristotle at the end of the *GC* (2.10, 337a11-15), viz.: why simple bodies do not remain at rest in their natural places, separate from each other? 'The reason is their reciprocal change of position; for if each remained in its own place and was not transformed by its neighbour, they would have long ago been parted. [...] Owing to their transformation, none of them can remain in any fixed position' (trans. Forster).

[212] See *GC*, 2.10, 336a31-336b15.

[213] See Alexander *in Meteor.* 19,34-21,5, where intending to give an account of the phenomenon of combustion, Alexander explains very clearly how Aristotle has construed the sublunary part of the universe from the twofold exhalation.

[214] Let us note finally that in the conclusion of the excerpt just cited, Ibn Rushd disagrees with Alexander's position in *Quaestio* 2.17, which is devoted entirely to showing that if the elemental fire is less hot than the fire that burns on earth this is not due to its mixture

I remarked above that the distinction between 'fire that is like form' and 'material fire' echoes Plato's distinction between intelligible Forms and their sensible images. In the next section I will investigate the incorporation of this idea into Aristotle's theory as it appears in the commentary of Alexander preserved in Jābir. Particularly problematic here is the status and nature of prime matter: how to reconcile 'material fire' with the Aristotelian prime matter, given that in the *Timaeus*, sensible fire is only an image, which exists only by participating in its exemplar. Though this image exists in a subject, the infamous Platonic 'Receptacle' (*hupodokhê*), it does not relate to this subject as an Aristotelian elemental form relates to its matter. The Platonic *hupodokhê* is distinct from the exemplar as well as from the image, and is thus separate. But for Aristotle, form is inseparable from matter, so that the two cannot exist independently. Thus Alexander's commentary faces the challenge of reconciling Aristotle and Plato on this point as well.

II: Prime matter and elemental hylomorphism

It is traditional to hold that for Aristotle, the subject that persists through all natural generation is 'prime matter', an unknowable[215] and inseparable substrate that is supposed to be necessary for at least one kind of substantial generation: the transmutation of simple bodies or elements into one another, as is described especially in *GC* and in *Cael.* The extracts in Jābir include only Alexander's

with its contrary. Alexander there contrasts the terrestrial fire which 'needs nourishment and is preserved for as long as it has it, and it is the opposite that nourishes a thing' (trans. R.W. Sharples (1994), 14) and which moreover depends on matter, to 'the other sort of fire which does not depend on nourishment but is unalloyed and pure, unmixed with its opposite' and 'exists in its own right as does each of the other elements' (ibid.). Alexander will maintain against the Stoics (cf. *Mixt.* 9, 222,35 ff.; R.B. Todd (1976), 133) that fire is not mixed with iron, because it is generally absurd to say that matter is mixed with form. Now, everything that is burnt or heated by the fire is its matter, even if this matter is destructible. Alexander appears to be particularly anxious to state a radical distinction between the terrestrial fire and the *hupekkauma* which alone is characterised as elemental. His description of elemental fire is dictated by this worry and is only explained by the opposition to fire on earth, which explains his insistence on the absolute nature of the element, which is characterised by purity and autonomy to an eminent degree. Thus, the nature of burning fire, incapable of existing without fuel, is incompatible with the status of first substance and of element. For this reason Theophrastus already attempted to question the elemental nature of fire (see Coutant, *Theophrastus De Igne*, §4, reference from R.W. Sharples (1994), 114 n. 59). Alexander has preserved its status only at the price of a radical distinction between the two kinds of fire, a distinction not of degree but of nature. One might also raise questions about Averroes' attempt to see the burning fire here on earth and the element fire as sharing a common nature. For even presupposing that the elements undergo mixture in their places, he concludes his demonstration by stating the irreducibility of fire and ice to their respective elements: they are only the compounds that bear the greatest resemblance to these elements in terms of their constitutive qualities.

[215] See *Phys.* 1.7, 191a8, where nature as a substratum is knowable only 'by analogy'.

commentary on *GC* 2.5, where Aristotle argues against those who held that one of the elements serves as the matter of the others. For Aristotle, all of the primary bodies are equally primary, in virtue of their reciprocal transformation, being generated from one another and not from some other, prior body.[216] But this reciprocal transformation does require a shared matter, which allows the contraries to act upon one another. Thus, 'if there is nothing — nothing perceptible at any rate — prior to the four elements', the matter will simply be intermediate between two contraries, 'imperceptible and inseparable'.[217]

Alexander's commentary directs us to Aristotle's description of prime matter as expounded in *GC* 2.1.[218] In the overview of 2.5, which precedes the exegesis of the individual *lemmata*, Alexander had already summarised Aristotle's position on the impossibility of a body prior to the four elements, in the terms of his exegesis of 2.1: 'matter is something else, other than a sensible body insofar as it is not a body. Nevertheless, it is not something separated from bodies and it cannot subsist in isolation'.[219] Likewise, in his comment on 332a35-b5, he insists again upon 'the imperceptible nature' of matter as a third principle posited as that which receives the contraries according to which elemental transformation can take place. Matter is inseparable, 'due to the fact that it [sc. the matter] is always accompanied by one of these differences, that it does not exist in actuality without being accompanied by these, and that it is not a body separated from these [differences]'.[220]

At *GC* 2.1, 329a23 ff., after a discussion and critique of the theories of his predecessors,[221] Aristotle gives his own theory: there is a matter for the first perceptible bodies, which is not separable but always accompanied by contraries, whose union constitutes the primary bodies. Aristotle understands elemental generation in terms of the general theory of change developed in *Physics* 1.6-9, which stipulates that all change, including substantial change, requires three terms: two contraries and a substrate that underlies the change and persists throughout.[222] So too prime matter, without ever existing separately, serves as the substrate of first contraries, which make the matter perceptible. Since it is from the interaction of these qualities that primary bodies are generated, prime matter is neither separate from the elements nor prior to them. The elements are the ultimate perceptible bodies, and no further physical

[216] See *GC* 2.5, 332a26. If, for example, fire were considered as hot air, in that case the transformation of air into fire would have no longer been generation, but mere alteration.
[217] cf. *GC* 2.5, 332a26 and 35 (Forster trans.).
[218] See *GC* 2.1, 329a24-6, *hêmeis de phamen men einai tina hulên tôn sômatôn tôn aisthêtôn, alla tautên ou khôristên all' aei met'enantiôseôs, ex hês ginetai ta kaloumena stoikheia*. The interpretation of this passage, of capital importance for the concept of prime matter, is still a matter of controversy among scholars. The problem is whether the pronoun *hês* refers to the contrarieties or to matter. See especially H.R. King (1956), 381; F. Solmsen (1958); H.M. Robinson (1974).
[219] *Morphology* §69.
[220] *Morphology* §91.
[221] See *GC* 2.1, 328b32-329a24 and *Cael.* 3.6, 305a14-32.
[222] See in particular *Phys.* 1.7, 190a31-b9.

analysis of them is possible.[223] This, at least, is how the tradition understood Aristotle.

A: Alexander and the tradition

Alexander's exegesis seems to be in keeping with the general pattern of this interpretation, which is at any rate held to have arisen within the commentary tradition. Several scholars[224] have questioned the view of prime matter just sketched as not being genuinely Aristotelian, arguing that it was first put forward by the Neoplatonic commentators in an attempt to assimilate Aristotle's material substrate to Plato's passive and intangible Receptacle. In so doing, it is argued, the Neoplatonists distorted Aristotle's conception of matter, sacrificing its 'stuffiness' for the benefit of a 'rationalisation and spiritualisation' of Aristotle.[225] This is not the place to go into the full details of this debate, but some discussion of the question is necessary given the relevance of the Jābir extracts for Alexander's position on prime matter. In particular, the extracts give us new insight into Alexander's view on the relationship between the primary tangible qualities and the elements; for the status and role of the primary contraries turns to a large extent on what view is taken with regard to the possibility of an underlying material substrate. To admit that the elements are themselves compounds of form and matter means an immaterial understanding of the contraries, in which they are granted the status of form, rather than an understanding of the contraries as independent corporeal powers that exercise real and autonomous forces. On the basis of Alexander's commentary on *GC*, I intend to reconstruct a less abstract, or rather more consistent, conception of prime matter, which has as a corollary the greater efficacy he ascribes to the primary contraries or 'powers'.

Because it is in *GC* that Aristotle deals with the nature and formation of the four sublunary elements (indeed this is the main topic of our commentary), this is the crucial text for the question of a substrate more fundamental even than these elements – which would thus be the foundation for a system in which each

[223] See *GC*, 2.5, 332a26.

[224] See H.R. King (1956), who was the first to question the presence of the 'doctrine' of prime matter in Aristotle's physics, followed by W. Charlton (1992), 129-45. Both rightly base their argumentation on the fact that the elements are the ultimate matter of all perceptible reality, so they are the most simple substances in Aristotle's physics. F. Solmsen (1958) and A.R. Lacey (1965) gave strong arguments against King's criticism, and more recently H.M. Robinson (1974) reacted to Charlton's arguments. The controversy between the advocates and critics of prime matter, while less heated than it previously was, still persists in the recent publications on Aristotle's physics; see particularly M.L. Gill (1989), with comprehensive bibliography on the problem, and, closer to the present text, E. Lewis (1996), 1-58, to which I shall return several times.

[225] See H.R. King (1956), 388-9, and R. Sokolowski (1970), 275 n. 23, from whom I borrow this terminology.

member of the ontological hierarchy can serve as matter for its superior.[226] Since for Aristotle, the elements are the simplest (though this need not mean they are themselves unanalysable) and primary sublunary bodies, the elements can on his view only be generated from one another.[227] Matter with absolutely no determination, inseparable, a pure potentiality that cannot exist in actuality but only within an element, seems to be a necessary prerequisite for the transformation of the elements into one another. This is, at least, how Alexander understood Aristotle's position: 'what we call fire, air, water and earth are generated from one another, and each is in the others potentially. In what follows, [Aristotle] also adds the cause of the transformation of these bodies into one another, namely that they come from a common, underlying matter'.[228]

Aa: Prime matter in *On Generation and Corruption*

GC 1.3 deals with the generation and corruption of substances, but without ever mentioning explicitly the notion of prime matter. Aristotle merely establishes a framework in which prime matter appears to be necessary as the material cause for the perpetual cycle of elemental generation and corruption, which is treated within the more general theory of change as a passage from potentiality to actuality.[229] Once Aristotle has claimed that the elements are generated from each other, and not from a prior body, the question arises of how to understand this within the theory of change in *Phys.* 1.7-8, including the need for something that persists through any change, which is itself a substance.[230] But if the elements are the ultimate substances in the sublunary world,[231] then a substrate that underlies them cannot itself be substance.

As a matter of fact, Aristotle establishes in *GC* 1.3, in response to the well-known *aporia* that nothing can change without coming-to-be, but absolute generation is impossible, that generation is indeed from something that is, but something that is in itself non-substantial: 'In one way things come-to-be out of that which has no unqualified being, in another way they always come-to-be out of what is; for there must be a pre-existence of that which potentially is, but actually is not, in being'.[232] It is being in potentiality, which is non-being in actuality, that pre-exists any generation. Thus air is generated from water, insofar as water in actuality is air in potentiality, or has a privation of air: air comes from 'what is' (water) and 'what is not' (the privation of air). Privation is of course distinct from matter; matter is distinguished by its ability to receive

226 See *Metaph.* 9.7, 1049a18 ff. and *GA* 1.1, 715a9 ff. The degree of reality of a being is measured by the place it occupies in the hierarchy of beings, where each composite substance is matter and potentiality for that which is superior to it, up until the pure actuality. See Joachim (1922), 101.
227 See *Cael.* 3.6, 305a14-32.
228 See Alexander *in Meteor.* 7,23-6.
229 See *GC* 1.3, 317b34-318a27.
230 See *Phys.* 1.7, 190a31 ff.
231 See *Metaph.* 11.10, 1066b36 f.; *Cael.* 3.6, 305a22-4 and *GC* 2.5, 332a26.
232 cf. *GC* 1.3, 317b15-17 (trans. Forster).

either form or privation of form.[233] This description of the underlying substratum required by generation applies likewise to proximate matter, since the water presupposed for the generation of air is a concrete and informed substance that is water in actuality and air in potentiality. Up to this point, prime matter does not seem to be absolutely necessary. It becomes essential when the generation of one thing is simultaneously the destruction of another: when a certain quantity of water is generated, the same quantity of air must perish.[234] But then what underlies the transformation, since it can be neither air nor water? A material cause is required, 'in virtue of which generation always occurs'.[235]

It is thus in the context of the transformation of the elements into one another, as described in *GC* 2.4-5, that the notion of a matter more fundamental then the elements will appear in our commentary—where, as in Aristotle text, it will never be designated by the label 'prime matter'. Alexander does speak of a 'third principle' required for all change,[236] 'which does not necessarily imply that it be a third body, "for the matter is intermediate", and it is a substrate (*mawḍūʿ*) for these [sc. the contrarieties] in respect of which change takes place, in so far as it is not sensible by nature'.[237] Thus the very imperceptibility of prime matter, which makes the modern reader so suspicious of the whole idea, is for Alexander absolutely required, because of the tangibility of the primary qualities it receives. Admitting an inseparable matter as the third principle means *de facto* accepting that the contraries can play the role of the two additional principles, form and privation. On the one hand we have an unknowable and inseparable prime matter; on the other tangible forms. This suggests that we ought to locate the change in which one element is generated and another destroyed in the realm of form, as being the disappearance of one form and the appearance of another in the prime matter that underlies the change. Described in these terms, elemental 'generation' becomes a transformation of perceptible qualities within an imperceptible substrate; but this, properly speaking, is alteration.[238]

Ab: Generation and alteration

Alexander's awareness of the difficulty of distinguishing between 'alteration', i.e. qualitative change, and 'generation' regarding the generation of elements is clear from his comments on the beginning of *GC* 2.4 where, in a demonstration whose obscurity has frequently been noted,[239] Aristotle appeals to alteration as

[233] See *Metaph.* 8 1, 1042b1-3.
[234] See *GC* 1.3, 318a23 ff.
[235] ibid., 317b34-5; 318a9 and 23-7.
[236] cf. *Phys.* 1.7, 190a13 ff.
[237] cf. *GC* 2.5, 332a35 and *Morphology* §91, which continues: 'Furthermore, the change of elements into one another takes place in respect of sensible differences only, for change takes place in respect of a tangible difference'.
[238] I follow the terms in which the problem is stated in G. Morrow (1969).
[239] See *GC* 2.4, 331a8-10 and H.H. Joachim (1922), 220. The demonstration starts from the postulate that perception attests to the fact of coming-to-be. The alteration is related

proof that the elements are generated. Alexander expands on the difference between alteration and generation, but does not make clear the basis of the distinction in this context:[240]

> This is manifest owing to the fact that he calls the reciprocal change of the primary bodies in respect of form, 'alteration'. This is evident from what he said: 'because alteration is only in respect of tangible affection'. Because what is generated in respect of [tangible affection] is generated through alteration, for alteration is, strictly speaking, only alteration and is not, in respect of [tangible affection], generation. [...] Not only do we observe that [bodies] change only in respect of tangible differences, but we say so because through these differences, [bodies] change in a manner that is known through sensation. These are their forms affected by a nature (*munṭabi'a*), and we observe that these forms belong to them for the sake of their change into one another, so that simple bodies may be generated into one another, otherwise there would be no alteration. Moreover, we observe that simple bodies are generated. For alteration is their change into one another.

The distinction between generation (*genesis*) and mere alteration (*alloiôsis*) is all the more difficult to make out in this passage because Aristotle simply assumes the familiarity of the distinction, and makes use of it to establish the reality of generation. Generation of the first bodies from one another takes place through the reciprocal change of their tangible qualities, in so far as they are informed by these qualities. But alteration is precisely the change of bodies according to their tangible affections. It is an indeniable matter of fact that this occurs, since we perceive directly 'that a [body], which is at times <hot, is at times> cold and vice versa'.[241] Now, alteration presupposes the generation of one body from another. Thus the observable fact of alteration is supposed to prove the reality of generation.

It is at the beginning of *GC* 1 that Aristotle gives two criteria for distinguishing generation from mere alteration. The first concerns the nature of the thing that undergoes the transformation: when a thing changes in its essence or definition, this change is a generation. If it changes only in its accidental qualities, the change is an alteration.[242] The second criterion has to do with the nature of the substrate: 'alteration is when the sensible subject, while remaining the same, changes in its qualities, which may be either contrary or intermediate. [...] But when the whole changes, without anything sensible remaining the same [...] [for example] when air comes from water, or air is entirely changed into

to perception (cf. 314b13-15), because alteration is the change of a tangible body in respect of its perceptible properties (319b8-10). The observable fact of alteration therefore implies a change in the properties of tangible bodies.

[240] *Morphology* §44, with relation to *GC* 2.4, 331a8-9.

[241] *Morphology* §44.

[242] See *GC* 1.2, 317a23-7.

water, such a change is the generation of one thing and the corruption of another'.[243]

The first criterion presupposes that the forms involved in generation participate in the thing's essence; that is, they are substantial forms. But if this is applied to the elements, there is a difficulty: if we assume that the elements are in fact substances,[244] then the essence of fire, for example, will be heat and dryness. For these two qualities belong to fire *kath' hauto*, and constitute the *logos* that defines it. But then the generation of simple bodies is nothing other than change in perceptible qualities; but this corresponds precisely to the definition of alteration.[245]

Only the second criterion will allow us to distinguish alteration from generation in the case of the elements.[246] Since the substrate underlying

[243] See *GC* 1.4, 319b10-18, *alloiôsis men estin, hotan hupomenontos tou hupokeimenou, aisthêtou ontos, metaballêi en tois heautou pathesin, ê enantiois ousin ê metaxu, hoion to soma hugiainei kai palin kamnei hupomenon ge tauto, kai ho khalkos strongulos, hote de gônioeidês ho autos ge ôn. hotan d'holon metaballêi mê hupomenontos aisthêtou tinos ôs hupokeimenou tou autou, all' hoion ek es gonês haima pasês ê ex hudatos aêr ê ex aeros pantos hudôr, genesis êdê to toiouton, tou de phthora.* There is no unity among the translators on this passage. Tricot, followed by Forster, renders *holon* in 319b14 as 'la chose prise comme un tout', considering that it refers not to a whole thing, but to a *sunolon*, because the first matter always persists *qua* substrate. By contrast, the literal translation that I adopt is also reproduced by Gill who sees here, on the contrary, evidence for the total disappearance of the subject of coming-to-be, cf. M.L. Gill (1989), 46.

[244] See G. Morrow (1969), 158, who draws attention to Aristotle's hesitations as to whether the elements should be regarded as full-fledged substances. On the one hand, water, air, fire, and earth are natural things and therefore substances (see *Phys.* 2.1, 192b8-13 and 33), as *Metaph.* 7.2, 1028b10 and *Cael.* 3.1, 298a29 confirm. On the other hand, the essentially binary nature of the elements, each of which is constituted by two tangible qualities, is difficult to reconcile with the definition of substance as essentially one and indivisible. In *Metaph.* 7.16, 1040b5 ff., Aristotle excludes the elements, taken individually, from the scope of the concept of substance, because 'none of these elements or parts is a unity: they are as a heap until they have been either concocted or made into some unity'. On the feebleness of elemental forms, see also R. Sokolowski (1970), 263-75.

[245] See *Phys.* 3.1, 200b34; 5.1, 225b8; 5.2, 226a26; 7.3, 246a2; *Cael.* 1.3, 270a27; *GC* 1.2, 317a27; 319b23; 320a14.

[246] M.L. Gill (1989), 48 ff., questions the argument concerning the nature of the substrate which is regarded as persisting in two cases of change, *qua* perceptible in the case of alteration and imperceptible in the case of generation, in accordance with *GC* 1.4, 319b10-18. On the basis of a reconstruction of *GC* 1.4 and particularly 319b15 she attempts to prove, against the standard interpretation, that what is different in each case is not the nature of the substrate, but its role, because in both types of transformation we are talking about a perceptible whole which persists through the change of accidental properties in alteration, but disappears and is replaced by another underlying subject in generation, because of the destruction of its essential characteristics. To avoid this one would need to show how a perceptible substrate could endure through substantial generation, and yet still distinguish generation from alteration. Gill then goes on to consider that in 319b21-4, where Aristotle describes a situation in which a perceptible

elemental transformation is not perceptible, nothing perceptible survives such a transformation; such a transformation must therefore be a generation.[247] Alexander's commentary on *Metaph.* 1.3, 983b6 ff. refers to this argument when he links the Milesians' inability to explain how generation and corruption are possible, with their embrace of a single material principle in actuality. Because they ignored prime matter, they were unable to distinguish simple generation from alteration:

> The consequence, for those who make matter a kind of body in actuality and not, as Aristotle says, potentially, is that nothing whatever is either generated or destroyed in an unqualified sense, but that generation so called is alteration, as he showed in his treatise *On Generation.* For <they say> that matter exists in actuality and is forever permanently the same, since they assume that the principle is incorruptible and unchangeable in its substantial nature, and that it alters the modifications of the substances coming-to-be out of it; for alteration is change with respect to a modification.[248]

Alexander reproduces the two criteria that allow us to distinguish between alteration and generation: (1) alteration implies an actual material substrate that persists through change, whereas generation requires a potential substrate; and (2) alteration is a change of affections, whereas generation is a change in the thing's essence.

In our extracts, Alexander, following Aristotle's text, focuses on the nature, rather than the function, of the qualities involved in alteration, which is here defined as a change 'with respect to tangible qualities'. He does not discuss the nature of the substrate of such a change. This is despite the fact that Aristotle has never distinguished alteration in terms of the *nature* of the qualities involved; nor does he say that perceptible qualities are proper to alteration, even though it is a fact of experience.[249]

property (coldness or transparence) persists in a substantial generation such as a transformation of air into water, the prime matter is rendered perceptible by the accidental qualities which characterise it, such as the transparence or the cold. In her view, the problem consists in establishing a structural parallel between substantial generation, which requires a subsistent *pathos* and the replacement of the substrate, and alteration, which involves a permanent substrate and the *pathê* that are replaced. In any case, this reasoning does not seem to take into account the difference between underlying and persisting: does the *pathos* that persists in the case of substantial generation assume the role of the substrate of this generation?

[247] cf. *GC* 1.4, 319b15.

[248] See Alexander, *in Metaph,* 1.3, 23,24-24,6, translation from W.E. Dooley (1989), 46.

[249] cf. *GC* 1.1, 314b13-15. Note Alexander *in Meteor*. 378b28, 181,22-3, trans. E. Lewis (1996), 67, which presents striking affinities with our paragraph.

Philoponus takes up this point in his own commentary,[250] and denounces the 'absurdity' of Alexander's remarks regarding the distinction between generation and alteration.

> If, he says, generation for the simple bodies is not from one another, there would be no such thing as alteration, because generation for them is by change of their tangible qualities, in so far as it is by these that they are specified; but if these tangible affections are said to be unchangeable by those who deny the generation of elements from one another, they deny also alteration given that alteration is understood in terms of the tangible affections. But we ought to think of alteration, not, as Alexander does, of generation; for the sense of the remark will not be found appropriate if it is taken as saying that if generation is not from one another there will be no generation. Alteration, then, must be understood as change, in the general sense, in respect of quality, whether the quality is accidental or substantial.[251]

Philoponus considers the tangibility of affections as a starting point, since Aristotle's purpose here is to demonstrate that the primary bodies are generated into one another by means of tangible affections. He takes 'alteration' in a broad sense as a matter of perception, in which the tangible qualities involved in the change may be either accidental or essential. Philoponus rejects Alexander's interpretation on the basis that Aristotle's reasoning presupposes the distinction between generation and alteration. The passage is incomprehensible unless we take this for granted, and worse still, Alexander's reading would make generation and alteration coincide in the case of the elements, insofar as the elements are essentially defined by their tangible qualities. It must be said though that Philoponus' critique here is in bad faith; he clearly has not tried to understand Alexander's interpretive aims in the passage, and has perhaps deliberately ignored them. Alexander is concerned precisely with the difficulty of bringing to bear on this passage Aristotle's distinction between generation without qualification and that other kind of qualified generation which is alteration – between a change of substance and a change of qualities, in the case of a substance that is actually constituted from its tangible qualities. There is too the further difficulty that, as Philoponus himself is aware, alteration cannot be reduced to tangible qualities. Alteration derives its perceptibility from its substrate but can concern any kind of affection.

B: Elemental change and prime matter

In *GC* 2.4, Aristotle describes the four kinds of elementary transformation. This is the chapter of Alexander's commentary that is best represented in the

[250] Philoponus *in GC* 2.4, 331a8, 231,28-232,6.
[251] Trans. C.J.F. Williams (2000), 142-3.

Morphology.[252] At issue is the demonstration that none of the primary bodies is prior to the others, since all are generated into and from one another. This is related directly to *Cael.* 3.6,[253] where Aristotle refutes previous theories of the elements, without yet presenting his own theory, which he will complete in *GC* 2.

In his introduction to the chapter, Alexander recites Aristotle's general principle from *Phys.* 1 that all change occurs between two contraries.[254] Thus the opposing qualities that characterise the elements are not just accidental affections, but their constitutive differences.[255] Contrary to one another, they account for their transformation one from another. Though the continuity of this transformative process would seem to require a substrate, there is no mention of prime matter in *GC* 2.4. Instead the contraries are here given the leading explanatory role; so much so that it is tempting to reify them, and eliminate the need for prime matter completely.

Ba: Elemental change and time

The first kind of elementary change involves 'adjacent' elements, i.e. those that share one of the two qualities that constitute them. Such a change is quick and easy, because only one quality needs to be replaced by its opposite. For example, air is generated from fire when dryness gives way to moisture.[256] The second kind, the slowest and most difficult, occurs between two non-adjacent elements that share no qualities. Here both qualities must change into their opposites.[257] The third involves a generation of one element from two others, in which each of the original elements changes one of its qualities but keeps the

[252] As pointed out above, p. 13, the chapter is reproduced by Jābir almost in its entirety, except for a short paragraph 331b21-4. He seems more interested in Aristotle's text than in Alexander's exegesis, as the length of some lemmata interspersed by only two lines of commentary indicates (see e.g. *Morphology* §51). Consequently, the fact that the chapter is reproduced almost in its entirety does not imply that Alexander's commentary has been excerpted with the same generosity.

[253] Alexander and Philoponus in turn interpret Aristotle's allusion at 331a7 to 'before' (*proteron*), as a reference to *Cael.* 3.6, where Aristotle announces that he will deal with the generation of the elements but in fact devotes the rest of his exposition to a study of the theories of his predecessors on the same topic. Alexander also refers to *GC* 1.1, 314b15-26, as indicates *Morphology* §44. On the relations between the third book of *De Caelo* and the second book of *GC* see P. Moraux (1965), xx-xxi, and F. Solmsen (1960), 295-8.

[254] See *Phys.* 1.7, 190b29 ff. and *GC* 2.4, 331a14-16.

[255] See *Morphology* §48: 'not just anything can change into anything no matter what it is. But, all the elements in relation to each other, are contraries. Therefore, all the elements are generated out of one another and change into one another. He has explained that the elements are contraries <from> the fact that the differences through which they exist, are contraries, and it is through these differences that the elements change and are generated'.

[256] See *GC* 2.4, 331a23-b4 and *Morphology* §§50-2.

[257] See *GC* 2.4, 331b4-11 and *Morphology* §§53-4.

other one. This is quicker than the second type, since only one quality per element need change; thus earth may be generated from water and fire together, when these two change their moisture and heat into dryness and cold, respectively. The remaining qualities then constitute the form of earth.[258]

The time factor involved in these transformations, especially in the case of non-adjacent elements, has in my view been overemphasised by those who use it as evidence for a 'stepwise' change of elements. On this 'stepwise' interpretation, the element would change first with respect to only one of its contraries, while the other contrary serves as a principle of continuity for the change, so that there is no need to posit prime matter.[259] For example, in the case of the second type, in which the element must change in respect of two qualities, if both qualities perish together nothing would persist. Thus Gill remarks: 'a transformation involving elements that share no common features might seem, in particular, to require prime matter to serve as the continuant'. But she rejects such an interpretation, arguing that 'if prime matter is a silent partner in the business of elemental change, as many commentators would like to think, they need to explain why a change of fire into water takes longer than a change of fire into air'.[260]

The explanation is to be found in the natural disposition of the elements, that is to say, the structure of the sublunary world. Aristotle orders the four elements in concentric circles, in which consecutive elements always share one quality and differ in one quality. This disposition is structurally static, even though its parts are in constant motion, and is thus able to account for the movement of simple bodies towards their natural places, which in turn explains how they are able to change into one another. Conversely the qualities of the bodies

[258] See *GC* 2.4, 331b12-26 and *Morphology* §§55-8; Aristotle will specify that this third mode is not valid in the case of the adjacent elements, because from it either one pair of contrary qualities will result, or one pair of identical qualities, both cases being inadequate for the constitution of an element. See *GC* 2.4, 331b27-34 and *Morphology* §§62-5.

[259] See M.L. Gill (1989), 74-5, who describes the slow change as a change caused by one element that acts first in respect of one of the characteristics, and then in respect of another one. Water can be generated directly out of fire by a direct action of water on the original fire, first by acting in respect of its moisture, thus overcoming the dryness of fire to produce transitory air, and then, in respect of its coldness, yielding water as a final product. The transformation of fire into water therefore is not a mere replacement of entities, but presents a continuity that pertains to all change. See also E. Lewis (1996), 39-42: 'I will now briefly discuss Aristotle's theory of elemental transformations, demonstrating that it is in harmony with the view that the elements are composed out of the contraries as matter, and that it is the contraries that persist as substrate in cases of elemental transformations. I claim that only by allowing the contraries to remain and underlie various stages of elemental transformations can one make sense of the actual mechanics of these transformations, which Aristotle discusses in *GC* 2' (40), 'if the elements are composed out of the contraries as matter, then the temporal properties of elemental transformations are easily explained. If the material substrate of the elements is some sort of prime matter, elemental transformations remain mysterious' (42).

[260] cf. M.L. Gill (1989), 73,18 f. and 74,12 f.

determine their relative positions. When a quantity of water (cold, moist) is generated from a quantity of fire (hot, dry), this implies first a change of fire into air (from dry to moist), and then a change of this 'intermediary' air into water (hot to cold). This is the only way we can understand why this kind of change is slower than the other two: elements can only change into those adjacent to them, and no element can simultaneously lose both of its constitutive qualities. For the natural order of the elements determines a natural order for changes in which 'one is like matter, the other form', each element being actuality for what is 'below it' and potentiality for what is 'above it'.[261] Similarly the third kind of elemental change is quick, and more like the first kind than the second, because the changes involved are between adjacent elements, even though they do not change into one another, each one changing into the element adjacent to it. There is no *continuity* of the elements because of their contraries, but there is *contiguity*[262] which allows for contact between them, a contact which is realised as an interaction of action and passion amongst their respective qualities.[263]

Hence the time involved in the transformation of two non-adjacent elements into one another does not allow us to dispense with prime matter. Gill claims that continuity would be preserved because 'the change occurs in two stages', so 'a different factor can be left at each stage', preserving continuity. For instance if fire has to be changed in water, first the dryness of fire will be overpowered 'to yield an interim air, and then the heat can be overpowered finally to yield water'.[264] But what is described here is two quick changes and hence the need for prime matter to underlie the change remains the same. The distinction Gill tries to draw between two quick changes and one slow one is overemphasised, as her constant appeal to an 'interim' element during the change shows. The surviving contrary cannot play the role of matter since the form of an element,

[261] See *Phys.* 4.5, 213a1-5.

[262] For the difference between contiguity and continuity see *Phys.* 5.3, 227a6-10. Both involve a contact between the bodies, but whereas continuity presupposes the unity of things that come into contact, contiguity occurs when two things are in contact at their limits, yet remain distinct.

[263] See *GC* 1.6, 322b21 ff. However the conditions of contact between physical bodies involve specific factors not included in the general definition of contact in the *Physics* that applied to mathematical and geometrical objects as well. Now, contact strictly speaking applies only to things that 'have a position' and these must be in a place. A body that is in a place must be heavy or light, and by virtue of that it is active or passive. This deduction is not incompatible with *GC* 2.2, 329a20-2, where Aristotle denies that lightness or weight can be a source of acting or being acted upon. The elements are essentially passive and active, because they are in a place, and as such, they are necessarily heavy or light. But the fact that they are active and passive in respect of each other is not a consequence of their lightness or weight. See on this H.H. Joachim (1922), 146. Let us note that the contact that is presupposed by the elemental transformations is never invoked in *GC* 2.4. On the other hand, it is mentioned explicitly in *GC* 2.2, 329b8-10, where the requirements of these transformations are stated: 'the contrarieties that constitute the forms and principles of bodies are those that are by contact'.

[264] cf. M.L. Gill (1989), 74,31 ff.

even if interim, needs two constitutive qualities. The dry alone does not determine any kind of element; it is only when coupled with the hot or the cold that it constitutes fire or earth respectively. So if we are to accept this interpretation, on which the contraries provide continuity, then we must accept that the contraries can function both as form and matter,[265] insofar as they are responsible for the tangible nature of the elements, which makes the change possible.

Moreover, things that can make one another change must necessarily be contraries within the same genus,[266] or even contrary forms in the same matter. Thus action and passion, which are facilitated by the contact between simple bodies, and which in turn, facilitate elementary change, must involve opposite determinations of the *same* substrate. This substrate provides the *generic unity* necessary for the exercise of actuality and potentiality. Furthermore, the substrate must have a material nature: an incorporeal form is absolutely impassive, and thus cannot receive contraries.[267]

Alexander emphasises the issue of generic unity several times, notably when he describes the function of primary contraries that 'originate (*al-muḥditha*) the species (*al-anwāʿ*)', or again, 'the differences out of which the species of the primary body (*anwāʿ al-jism al-awwal*) originate'.[268] The analogy between genus and matter does have its origin in Aristotle, but Alexander takes the analogy much further. So too in his commentary on *Metaphysics* 5.28, where Aristotle mentions 'the genus as matter' (1024b8), Alexander explains:

> He means that *genos* as matter is the common [constituant] predicated of several things differing specifically. And he makes clear the aspect in which this *genos*, [the genus], is matter by saying, 'for that to which the differentia or quality belongs is the underlying subject, which we call matter'. [1024b9-10] For because the differentiae belong to [the genus] as

[265] See M.L. Gill (1989), 77, on whose view contraries are intrinsic characteristics required by the elemental changes where in every transformation one of the contraries will remain, thus guaranteeing a continuity beween the perishing of an element and the coming-to-be of another one. The contrary which survives a transformation can thus be considered as a substrate and 'will play the role' of matter, in the same way as the replaced contrary will 'play the role' of form. See also E. Lewis (1996), 23. He emphasises, furthermore, an important difference in this respect between his own theory and Gill's, on whose view the contraries that play the role of material substrate throughout the elemental transformations are only material to the extent that they persist through such changes. According to Lewis, the contraries play this role because they are the matter of the elements (42 n. 65).

[266] See *GC* 1.7, 323b31 ff.

[267] See ibid., 324b7 f. and 324b19 ff. See also Alexander, *Mixt.* 13, 229,8 ff, 'only enmattered bodies can be acted on. Hence only where active bodies share in the same matter are they reciprocally acted on. Of bodies that do share in the same matter it is only those that have some mutual contrariety that can interact. [...] Interaction, then, occurs among bodies with the same underlying matter and a mutual contrariety' (trans. R.B. Todd (1976), 149).

[268] See *Morphology* §89.

> to a substrate, and because the genus is converted into species by the differentiae, as matter too [is determined] by the form, the genus would be matter. [...] Since the substrate of qualities is called 'matter', the genus too is matter of the qualities that are differentiae.[269]

Once the equivalence between differences and qualities has been established, Alexander feels able to describe the differences as inhering in their underlying substrate, even though the relation between difference and genus is not a relation of inherence or immanence; the differences are not *in* the genus.[270] The forms of the elements are thus seen as species in an identical matter, considered as an ultimate genus. It is from this viewpoint that we must understand Alexander's preference for calling the primary qualities 'differences', while Aristotle usually calls them 'contraries'.[271] Does he, then, think of them as simple logical divisions? If so it would be easy to conclude that the four elements are species produced from the informing of prime matter by the four contraries or 'differences'.[272] But Alexander does not draw this conclusion. When he explains how Aristotle himself relates prime matter to a first genus, he says:

> For the primary matter would be in some way a genus of the things under it, for the proximate matter of a statue is the bronze, but its ultimate matter is water, if water were the matter both of bronze and of all things that can be melted. Or 'the primary matter' could be an even more remote [matter], which would be in turn a genus both of the matter of water and of that of bronze'.[273]

[269] W.E. Dooley (1993), 117-19.
[270] See W.E. Dooley (1993), n. 545.
[271] In *GC* 2.1-5 Aristotle frequently uses the term 'contrarieties' which occurs more than fifteen times as opposed to five occurrences of 'difference'. In our commentary, it is the latter term that is privileged, as witnessed by Alexander's ample use of it; for the occurrences of the term in our text, see lexicon, *s.v. f-ṣ-l*.
[272] See *Morphology* §89, 'If the contrarieties that originate (*al-muḥditha*) the species (*al-anwā'*) are more than one, it is impossible that elements be two' and 'the differences out of which the species of the primary body (*anwā' al-jism al-awwal*) originate'. See also H. King (1956), 384, who, considering the four elements as the ultimate matter of the sublunary world, describes them as being generically prime matter. Taken 'as one', they are the underlying matter common to all compound bodies. But taken specifically, this prime matter is differentiated into four elements, each being different by nature, but each sharing a common contrariety with another and each capable of being generated out of others. If, however, in our commentary, the elements are described as species of the same genus, what is at issue is precisely the prime matter which underlies and is common to *them*.
[273] See *Metaph*. 5.24, 1023a26-8 and Alexander *in Metaph*., 421,31-6, and Dooley (1993), 108.

Bb: Tangible contraries and elemental forms

Though Alexander calls the tangible qualities 'differences', he describes them more fully in our extracts as 'the differences through which the form of the body is affected by a nature (*yanṭabi'u*)', or again, as 'the sensible contrarieties by which bodies are given a form and affected by a nature (*tanṭabi'u ṣūratu al-jismi*)'.[274] The Arabic version uses the VIth verbal form (*inṭaba'a*) to describe the formative action of the qualities. *Ṭaba'a*, the root verb, means 'to imprint', 'to stamp' or 'to impress with a stamp or a seal', 'to give form or character', and thus implies the action of a craftsman, whose effect is the impression. It may also mean shaping or modelling a malleable substance. *Inṭaba'a*, then, suggests aptitude for receiving a character or nature understood as the imprint of a craftsman, or even a creator.[275] One might well suppose that this term was added by a translator and has no basis in the Greek, especially given that it is in our extracts always accompanied by a near-synonym, *taṣawwara* (to become informed)[276] – this sort of double translation is a common feature of early Graeco-Arabic translations. But a Greek basis is suggested by a parallel usage in the extant Greek of Alexander's commentary on *Meteor.*, whose fourth book begins with a summary of the theory of elements, as presented in *GC*. A term frequently used for the endowment of the elements with form is the passive *eidopoieisthai*; Alexander mentions several times the 'four causes that inform (*eidopoieitai*) the elements'.[277] And *eidopoieô* means to endue with form, to give

[274] See *Morphology* §42: *al-fuṣūlu allatī bihā tanṭabi'u ṣūratu al-jismi*; and §69, *al-mutaḍāddātu al-maḥsūsatu allatī yataṣawwaru al-ajsāmu wa bihā yanṭabi'u*. See also §44, *fa-hādhihi ṣuwaruhā munṭabi'atun* ('these are their forms affected by a nature'); §56, and §61, *al-faṣlāni* [...] *alladhāni bi-himā yanṭabi'u ṣūratu al-mā'i* ('both differences in respect of which the form of the water is affected by a nature'); and further *Morphology* §89 and §109, *in kānat al-mutaḍāddāt allatī bihā yanṭabi'u ṣuwaru kulli wāḥidin min al-ajsāmi* ('if the contrarieties, in respect of which the forms of each of the bodies are affected by a nature').

[275] See W. Lane (1893), 1823-4, who states that the substantive *ṭab'* is more general than *khatm* (seal) and more particular than *naqsh* (engrave, carve). Note also that *ṭab'* signifies nature understood as a proper and innate character, or disposition referring to an act of creation. So while the Greek *phusis* signifies the coming-to-be of things as well as nature, the Arabic *ṭabī'a* which translates *phusis* signifies originally *imprint*, *impression*, or a *shaped form*. According to R. Walzer (1976), 387-8, the choice of *ṭabī'a* to render *phusis* stems from looking at nature as subordinate to divine will, and carrying the imprint of God.

[276] See *Morphology* §69, 'since the perceptible contrarieties by which bodies are given a form and affected by a nature'; see also §56, 'they both (sc. dryness and coldness) <constitute> the form of the earth' and §61.

[277] See Alexander *in Meteor.* 4, 179,14 ff. and Lewis (1996), 65: 'Aristotle is reminding us of the matters set out in the second book of the *Generation and corruption*. There he has shown that there are four causes according to which the first bodies, the elements *are given form* (*eidopoieisthai*): these causes are heat, coldness, dryness and moisture. They were shown to be the first tangible contrarieties, and by the first tangible contrarieties the elements *are given form*. [...] For this reason the elements number four, because the things by which they *are given form* are also four'. See also 181,14 ff. and Lewis (1996), 67, 'Having shown that [two] of the four [powers] by which the first bodies *are given*

something shape, figure, endow with a character, etc.[278] It thus seems at least plausible that the Arabic *inṭaba'a* translates *eidopoieisthai*; Lewis has already pointed to its frequency in other works of Alexander.[279] The term is incidentally original with Alexander; it does not appear in Aristotle.

Thus the qualities that characterise the elements also account for their perceptible nature. Alexander underlines the role that the qualities play in elementary change by stressing their twofold function. By the mere fact of informing the elementary bodies they affect them with a nature, because they are essentially tangible.[280] They do not merely explain the opposition of the elements, but also the perceptible nature of the elements, thus combining the two chief requirements of elementary change (i.e. contrariety and tangibility).[281] Alexander recalls this leading role in introducing the fourth chapter: 'These are their forms affected by a nature (*munṭabi'a*), and we observe that these forms belong to them for the sake of their change into one another, so that simple bodies may be generated into one another'.[282]

form are active, namely the hot and the cold, and that [two] are passive, namely the moist and the dry'.

[278] See H.G. Liddell, R. Scott, H.S. Jones (1968), 482, s.v. *eidopoieô* that gives also 'characterise' or 'receive a character'.

[279] See Lewis (1996), n. 6 of the translation.

[280] With Alexander, the emphasis is on the sensible nature of the first contrarieties. We find numerous additions of attributes qualifying the primary contraries as tangible (*malmūsa*) or sensible (*maḥsūsa*) in Alexander's exegesis. (e.g. *Morphology* §24, *Fa-ẓāhirun anna jamī'a al-ajnāsi wa **al-fuṣūli al-malmūsati** al-bāqiyati wa huwa yusammīhā al-mutaḍāddāt*; §69, *yubayyinu annahu lammā kānat **al-mutaḍāddātu al-maḥsūsatu**, allatī yataṣawwaru al-ajsāmu wa bihā yanṭabi'u* §91, *Wa al-usṭuqussāti innamā yakūnu lahā al-taghayyuru ba'ḍuhā ilā ba'ḍin **bi-fuṣūlin maḥsūsatin**, idh kāna dhālika **bi-faṣlin malmūsin***). These additions seem to belong properly to the exegesis, since they make no systematic appearance in the *lemmata*. We find similar additions in other works by Alexander, such as *De Anima* where there is an analogous case: enumerating elemental qualities, Alexander mentions, citing *GC*, other tangible contrarieties (*haptai enantiôseis*) that can be reduced to the four primary ones. Reference from F.W. Zimmermann (1994a), 43, who picks up the same kind of addition in D27d and D7, two Arabic versions of the *Quaestio* 2.11, which mention, refering to *GC* 2.2, *al-ṣuwar al-mutaḍādda al-malmūsa*, where the Greek has only *tôn aitiôn enantiôseôn*. Having discussed several conjectures as to the origin of these additions, the author concludes that there is no sufficient evidence to decide whether or not we are dealing with an error of translation. Cf. 58,27-59,1. But the frequency of these additions in Alexander's commentary *in GC* weakens the hypothesis of a translator's error. Moreover it is worth noting that Philoponus' commentary *in GC* 330a12 displays the same addition; see 221,14 (*tas haptas antitheseis*).

[281] See *Morphology* §48.

[282] See *Morphology* §44; see also §48. Cf. *Mixt.* 13, 229,26 ff., and translation in R.B. Todd (1976), 151: 'The bodies described here have the same matter and a mutual contrariety in form, as it is a proprium of matter that it can remain identical in receiving both of a pair of opposites, since all bodies that come to be and pass away belong to the same matter as one another, while they are differentiated by forms and accidental qualities'.

The primary tangible contraries are thus linked both to the elements, which they make perceptible, and to prime matter, which is not separable.[283] So there is little point in asking whether the elements come from the contraries rather than prime matter, since the relationships here obtain necessarily: if the elements come from one, they come also from the other.[284] Thus the problem of a 'prior' prime matter that is necessarily imperceptible need not be posed in the same way, insofar as the elements are the ultimate perceptible sublunar bodies;[285] it is impossible to go down further vertically. Only a 'horizontal' analysis of the components of the four elements is possible, but one must remember that the elements only exist through their composition. The elements come neither from a prior prime matter nor from the contraries. They are *constituted* by prime matter and a pair of contraries but are *generated* from one another. When, at *GC* 2.1, 329a26, Aristotle refers to a more precise definition of these concepts given 'elsewhere' (*diôristai de peri autôn en heterois akrithesteron*) the tradition sees this as an allusion to *Phys.* 1.6-9. There, Aristotle speaks not of prime matter but of the need for 'a substrate for the contraries' in change generally.[286] The contraries are understood there as form and privation.[287] The same analysis applies to elemental change. But the elements are not contrary to one another,

[283] See *Morphology* §§83 and 91.

[284] See on this *GC* 2.1, 329a24-6, which recapitulates Aristotle's theory of prime matter: *hêmeis de phamen men einai tina hulên tôn sômatôn tôn aisthêtôn alla tautên ou khôristên all' aei met' enantiôseôs, ex hês ginetai ta kaloumena stoikheia.* (As for us, we say that there is a matter of which the perceptible bodies consist, but that it is not separable but always accompanied by contrariety, and it is from this that the so-called elements come into being [trans. Forster modified]). See also the discussion of H. King (1956), 381, who thinks, against the Oxford translation, that the relative pronoun *hês* (gen., sing., fem.) refers not to *tina hulên tôn sômatôn tôn aisthêtôn* (a matter of the perceptible bodies) understood as the prime matter, but to *enantiôseôs* (contrariety). This, according to him, undercuts the interpretation of the advocates of prime matter: Aristotle's underlying matter appears to be linked with the contrarieties, which thus render it perceptible. And because it is in virtue of diverse associations of these perceptible contrarieties that the elements are generated from each other, 'the elements come to be from the contrarieties', and Aristotle's matter is neither separate nor prior to the elements. However, King's translation and interpretation cannot conceal the fact that Aristotle mentions two different entities: (1) a matter of perceptible bodies; (2) the contrarieties, if only to emphasise that they are inseparable. So one may accept that the elements come from the pair of contraries, without necessarily denying the existence of prime matter. It is not its reality, but its role that is in question.

[285] See *Cael.* 3.6, 305a23. At *in Metaph.* 5,28, Alexander considers the elements earth and water not only as irreducible to one another, but also as unanalysable into a *perceptible* substrate that is common to both, 'It is therefore things whose substrate allow nothing of this kind that are called "other in genus", as stone and bronze, for their substrates are, respectively earth and water, which are not resolved either into each other or into some other perceptible substrate that is the same [for both]'. Trans. W.E. Dooley (1989), 118.

[286] See *Phys.* 1.6, 189a22-6; 1.7, 189b30-190a21 and 190b33.

[287] See *Phys.* 1.7, 191a3-5; 12-14 and 1.9.

and in any case Aristotle says that substances cannot oppose each other.[288] Thus elemental change can only be a change in contrary tangible qualities, those standing in turn for form and privation. Aristotle does not hesitate to call a change from earth to fire a generation from non-being, because the cold that qualifies earth, for instance, is a privation of heat.[289] The commentators' view that Aristotle's reference here is to the canonical discussion of change in the *Phys.* seems not implausible, insofar as it manifests how Aristotle understands prime matter in *GC*: as a substrate for primary contraries that are understood as the two poles of elemental change.[290]

Considering the first contraries as the matter of the elements,[291] as do some recent discussions of this issue, seems to be grounded on an *a priori* definition of matter, which seems rather misleading at least in the context of *GC*. According to such a definition 'something is *truly* matter when it is an ingredient of that of which it is the matter, while something is truly form when it is an arrangement or structure of "true" matter'.[292] On this view, showing that the contraries are the *ingredients* of the elements is tantamount to identifying them with the matter of the elements. Hence 'all four contraries are conceived of as the matter of the elements'.[293] Of course there is an Aristotelian basis for this description. In *Phys.* 1, Aristotle says, 'I call matter the first subject of each thing, out of which the thing comes to be non-accidentally, and which is immanent to it'.[294] Matter here is seen as a constitutive element of a thing, its ingredient, unlike privation, which can only be the origin of a thing and never a constituent.[295]

288 See *Phys.* 1.6, 189a32-3.

289 See *GC* 1.3, 318b10 ff. and 2.5, 332a22-5 and *Morphology* §§75-6.

290 See H. King (1956), 382, who maintains that *GC* 2.1, 329a27 does not make a reference to *Phys.* 1.6-9, precisely because Aristotle there treats matter only as a substrate of contraries, and all the examples of substrate that he lists concern also proximate matter. He suggests rather earlier passages in *GC* or *Cael.* 2, where Aristotle describes in detail the nature of the elements.

291 See E. Lewis (1996), 15 ff.

292 A definition proposed by M.L. Gill who examines the role of matter in the coming-to-be and constitution of composite substances in Aristotle, and adopted by E. Lewis (1996), 18: 'Yet it is unclear what being an ingredient amounts to. This gets to the crux of the problem. I contend that on any account of "being an ingredient" that one might plausibly derive from the Aristotelian corpus, the contraries count as ingredients of the elements'.

293 See E. Lewis (1996), 23, '*GC* is concerned primarily with the composition of the elements and with the contraries' role as the material substrate through elemental transformations. It therefore emphasises the role all four contraries play as the matter of the elements'.

294 See *Phys.* 1.9, 192a31-2, and 2.3, 194b23-6; *GA.* 1.18, 724a23-6; *Metaph.* 5.4, 1014b17-18 and M.L. Gill (1989), 63 f.

295 See J. Moreau (1962), 91-2, who grounds Aristotle's theory of change in the distinction between the two meanings of *ex hou*, one referring only to the origin *out of* which a thing comes to be, but of which it is not made, i.e. privation that is essentially non-being, and another involving an ingredient, i.e. that which remains in a thing.

If we operate with this definition, the question becomes whether the *ingredients* of a thing are exhausted by its *constituents*. For there is no doubt that the contraries are in fact the constituents of the elements. Alexander recalls this in his commentary on *GC* 2.5, 332a27-9 in order to stress the fact that the elements are generated from each other and not from something prior to them: 'He also showed this (sc. that elements are generated out of one another) in the book *On Generation and Corruption* in the passage where he showed that [elements] come from contrarieties. For he said that fire, water, air, and earth are compound, and that they are compounded from heat, coldness, moisture and dryness'.[296] He emphasises the immanence of the contraries, which is mentioned several times in *GC*.[297] Those who seek to avoid attributing the theory of prime matter to Aristotle consider such passages as confirming that the contraries are ingredients, in the sense in which things are said to 'come from (*ek*)' their matter in *On the Generation of Animals*.[298] If the contraries are the ingredients of the elements and if, moreover, they are 'immanent' to them, then they should be their matter.[299] This analysis is grounded on a passage in *On the Parts of Animals*,[300] which explicitly recognises the contraries as matter, though the passage concerns composed bodies and not elements. Analogous passages in *Meteor.*,[301] which say that passive potencies have the status of matter, would lend further support to this interpretation.

However, the Aristotelian definition of matter in *Phys.* 1 suggests that matter has some sort of *separate* existence, that is, as matter that pre-exists the generated compound – even though it is of course immanent to the complex whole of which it is the matter, once the generation has occurred. This notion of matter, as shown by further examples given by Aristotle (brass or stone for the statue, wood for the table, etc.),[302] is a notion of *proximate* matter, in other words matter that already has some other form. But Alexander's treatment of the

[296] See *Morphology* §83.
[297] See *GC* 2.4, 331b4.
[298] See *GA* 1.18, 724a20-30, 'There are, however, numerous senses in which one thing is formed or comes into being "from" another [...] as a statue is formed from bronze, or a bedstead from wood, and all those cases where we describe things as being formed from some material; here the finished whole has been fashioned into a certain shape from something which was there to begin with' (trans. Peck) and E. Lewis (1996), 19, 'What tests does Aristotle employ for being an ingredient of some compound? It seems that things are composed out of their ingredients (regardless of whether there is a temporal act of their composition), and so an examination of passages on composition may shed light on what it is to be an ingredient. [...] One which Gill discusses is *GA* 724a20-30'.
[299] Because E. Lewis (1996), 20, adds an additional test in order to prove that one thing is a matter or an ingredient of another: 'if X is the matter of Y then X inheres in Y'.
[300] See *PA* 646a13-18; this is generally the main evidence adduced by most critics of prime matter.
[301] See *Meteor.* 4.1, 378b33-379a1 and Alexander *in Meteor.* 224,12-16.
[302] See *Phys.* 1.7, 191a7-12.

primary contraries emphasises precisely their inseparability.[303] There is no sense in which they can exist independently of prime matter or the elements.

It is crucial that the text from *On the Parts of Animals* just mentioned has to do with compound bodies, and not elements. The four contraries are described as the ultimate matter of *compound* bodies only insofar as they are the constituents of the elements from which these bodies are constituted. Likewise, in *Meteor.* 4 passive contraries are matter, but for homeomerous, not elemental, bodies. So there is no contradiction between these various texts:[304] in *Meteor.* Aristotle is analysing compounds more complex than the elements studied in *GC*. For all homeomerous bodies are composed of the four elements, insofar as the latter are characterised by the primary qualities.[305] But *GC* examines only the process of elemental combination and interaction of the constitutive qualities that leads to the generation of the homeomerous bodies. Here the homeomerous body is seen as the product of a chemical combination, a mixture of simple bodies whose constituents are the contraries. In such a combination the members of each pair of contraries react to produce an 'intermediary'.[306] In *Meteor.*, by contrast, Aristotle deals with mixture involving homeomerous bodies that have already been constituted. Only here, in the chemical combination of the four elements, are heat and cold considered to be active 'par excellence', while dry and moist are passive 'par excellence' and thus seen as matter.[307] The unification

303 See *Morphology* §§83 and 91.

304 Which seems to be the worry of E. Lewis (1996), 23.

305 See *GC* 2.8, 334b31-2; 335a9 and 22.

306 See *GC* 2.7, 334b16-19 and the discussion at H.H. Joachim (1922), 241-3.

307 Aristotle mentions this distinction already in *GC* 2.2, 329b24 and 2.3, 330b12-13. He will develop it in *Meteor.* 4, only insofar as it applies in the production of composite bodies, whereas in *GC* it is the transformation of all the elements into each other which is at issue, so that all the qualities are alike reciprocally active and passive. See Philoponus *in GC* 329b24, 216,27-217,23, trans. C.J.F. Williams (2000), 127-8: 'For if all the elements change into one another, wet and dry are bound to act upon one another; for it is he himself who says that earth changes into water, which makes it necessary that what is wet should be active with reference to what is dry, and similarly water into earth, where what is dry is manifestly active with reference to what is wet. Why, then, does he here make an absolute distinction, saying that hot and cold are capable of acting, whilst wet and dry are capable of being affected? This difficulty, then, we can solve by appealing to things that are said in Book 4 of *Meteorology*, claiming that *this is said in connection with the coming-to-be of composite bodies*. For these are found around the central place of the universe, I mean around the earth, as would be expected of things which share same portion of earth; for they could not be composed of this alone. For earth by itself is loose and easily dispersed, so it is held together by water binding and moistening it, just as the water is circumscribed by it. But when these are mixed they hold each other together, though they cannot by themselves achieve a perfect fusion, but require heat and cold to fuse them together and endow them with form (*eidopoiountos*), wet and dry presenting the role of substratum and matter, heat and cold being analogous to form. [...] *This then <is what happens> in the case of composite things. But in the case of their coming-to-be from one another they are all alike capable both of acting and of being affected*'.

of the components which characterise a mixture in the proper sense[308] occurs when the active contraries act upon the passive ones so as to 'dominate' them. But this already requires the combination of the four elements, in order to bring together the four contraries. It is thus only in homeomerous compounds that are already constituted from the four elements that we can consider the effect of heat and cold as active powers on the dry and moist as matter.[309] This is indeed the purpose of *Meteor*. 4,[310] which examines the different ways that the dry and moist can, as matter, be organised by the hot and cold.

In *GC* Aristotle works at a more basic level in the hierarchy of beings, a hierarchy in which each level (i.e. each compound substance) is matter for the one above it and form for the one below it.[311] Here (unlike in *Meteor*.) the four contraries all play the same role, a role that is essentially subordinate to the forms of the elements; for the contraries determine prime matter and give it form by qualifying it. One might object to saying that the elements have 'form', given their primitiveness and lack of function. While form involves an organisation of the matter according to an end, the contraries that constitute the elements merely qualify the matter that underlies them.[312] There is no denying that, the further we descend down the hierarchy, the harder it is to discern the function and hence the form of each thing. Yet Aristotle recognised that even simple bodies like fire and water have a formal aspect and a sort of teleology, though it may not be apparent because of the dominance of matter.[313] Their *logos* is nothing more the way the primary contraries qualify their underlying matter.[314]

Following Aristotle, Alexander recognises that the elements have a function and so a formal aspect:

> It is even less clear in the case of the simple bodies which we call the elements, such as fire, water and the rest. For it is least of all clear what the particular purpose is of each of these bodies, in which matter plays the greatest part, that is, which are nearest to matter. Those are the nearest to matter which are the first to be produced out of matter, and these are the elements. Hence in compounds, these have the definition of matter. [...]

[308] See *GC* 1.10.
[309] See *Meteor*. 4.1, 378b10 ff.
[310] See *Meteor*. 4.2, 379b10-12.
[311] See *Metaph*. 9.7, 1049a18 ff. and *GA* 1.1, 715a9 ff. where Aristotle shows that each physical entity can be a matter for another, of a higher order.
[312] On the weakness of the form of the elements, see above n. 244 and R. Sokolowski (1970), 264-75, who nonetheless recognises a formal dimension in the elements, in the sense that powers operate on the model of form in determining the form of the underlying matter (272 ff.).
[313] See *Meteor*. 4.12, 390a2-4: 'The distinction is less clear in the case of flesh and bone, and less clear again in the case of fire and water. For the final cause is least obvious where matter predominates' (trans. Lee).
[314] See R. Sokolowski (1970), 274.

And form is nothing other than the definition (*logos*) according to which matter is given form.[315]

A few remarks on this passage are in order. First, the form belonging to any matter is the product of its organisation, since the way that a thing is organised determines its function and therefore its form. Unlike *Meteor.* 4, where Aristotle studies the different ways according to which matter can be organised and especially the different ways according to which dry and moist as matter can be organised by hot and cold,[316] *GC* sees each element as constituted from an active and passive contrary, which together constitute its form.[317] The active/passive dichotomy of *Meteor.* is only hinted at and not argued for in *GC*,[318] which puts the contraries on an equal footing. For instance, as we have seen, our extracts use the reflexive form *taṣawwara* (to become informed), with or without *inṭaba'a* (to be affected by a nature), to render the passive *eidopoieisthai* (to be informed),[319] in descriptions of the action of the primary contraries. And this is applied to all four contraries, whereas in Alexander's commentary on *Meteor.* 4, the term is applied only to the bestowal of form on the passive contraries by the active contraries. Note however that the introduction to this commentary alludes to the doctrine of *GC* and uses *eidopoieisthai* for the action of the four causes.[320]

Second, for Alexander the corporeal state of the elements constitutes their form and determines their *telos*, according to which they acheive their nature. So, 'just as [flesh and liver are flesh and liver] when they produce that which is expected of them, so too [the elements are elements], when each of them retains its own nature and its particular function'.[321] The elementary forms may be humble, but they are still forms, and like all other forms are determined by the organisation of underlying matter. Without the distinction between this matter and the contraries, we cannot understand how the contraries bring about form, and without the action of the contraries, we cannot explain how matter is anything other than inert and amorphous.

At this stage it is worth asking whether these elemental forms which are nothing other than mere affections may be echoes, albeit weak ones, of the 'imprinted images of eternal beings (*tôn ontôn aei mimêmata, tupôthenta ap'*

[315] See Alexander *in Meteor.* 224,10 ff. and E. Lewis (1996), 122.
[316] See *Meteor.* 4.1, 378b27-8.
[317] See *Morphology* §56.
[318] See *GC* 2.2, 329b24-5.
[319] *eidopoieisthai* is absent from Aristotle's text. However, E. Lewis notes that *GC* 329b9 gives a description that in his view is close to this concept. Aristotle there maintains that it is not all the qualities that 'constitute the forms and principles of bodies (*eidê kai arkhas poiousin*)'. Lewis mentions other occurrences of the term in the works of Alexander (e.g. *in Metaph.* 57,7; 54,8; 59,15, etc.). In addition we may note the frequent use made of it by Philoponus in his commentary *in GC* always with the same meaning. In active form it signifies 'bestow a form'. See E. Lewis (1996), 24-5 and above 69-80 and n. 277.
[320] See Alexander *in Meteor.* 179,14-180,5, and E. Lewis (1996), 65-6.
[321] See Alexander *in Meteor.* 224,33-5 (Lewis trans.).

autôn)' in the Receptacle. This is particularly plausible since the Platonic *khôra*, i.e. the material or milieu within which these images appear, is described as a nature that receives all bodies (*tês ta panta dekhomenês sômata phuseôs*), and indeed always receives all things (*dekhetai te gar aei ta panta*).[322]

Bc: The receptivity of matter

The notion of receptivity appears only implicitly in our extracts, in an allusion to matter's disposition for receiving contraries. Matter is described as 'a substrate (*mawḍū'*) for these [sc. the contrarieties] in respect of which change takes place, in so far as it is not sensible by nature'.[323] The surrounding exegesis is purely Aristotelian, since Alexander carries on saying that matter 'is always accompanied by one of these differences, that it does not exist in actuality without being accompanied by these, and that it is not a body separated from these [differences]'. Yet the first formulation might lead us to see the contraries as somehow exterior to matter – or even to suppose that matter has a kind of pre-existence in which it possesses an aptitude for receiving the contraries, or further that matter is already qualified by the aptitude for receiving contraries and is hence separable.[324]

The use of *dektikon* to characterise prime matter appears frequently in the independent treatises ascribed to Alexander. *Quaestio* 2.11 describes matter as receptive (*hulê dektikê*)[325] of the forms that characterise it. But matter's inseparability is also emphasised: it is impossible for any form that matter receives to exist actually without matter, or for matter to be without form; they are inseparable as far as their actual existence is concerned. Actually, matter informed by the contraries is in turn receptive of them. The two Arabic versions of this *Quaestio*, D 7 and D 27d, despite their divergence in their handling of the Greek, both render the concept of receptivity and adjective *dektikon* and its derivatives using the Arabic *qābila*.[326] *Quaestio* 2.12 likewise insists on matter's

[322] Things in the phenomenal world are produced by the images of the Forms in the Receptacle. The latter receives the images of Forms and is at the same time constitutive of the bodies. This tension between the constitutive and spatial aspects of the Receptacle, which does not lead to a contradiction between the two, has been well analysed by L. Brisson (1974), 208-20 and K. Algra (1995), 72-120.

[323] See *Morphology* §91.

[324] Almost all the Greek commentators were confronted, in a more or less explicit way, with the problem of the nature of prime matter: is it actualised only by the form of the element, or does it have a prior form that explains its corporeality? Could prime matter, for example, be an indefinite extension able to receive, among other things, three-dimensionality? See on this R. Sorabji (1988), 3-43 who begins his analysis from *Metaph.* 7.3, especially 1029a16 ff.

[325] See 56,6.8.27.30 and R.W. Sharples (1992), 107-10. There are two Arabic versions of this *Quaestio*, classified under the sigla D 27 (MS Istanbul, Carullah 1279, 63a-b21) and D 7 (Badawī, *Arisṭū*, 286,4-287,29), the second being an adapted copy of the first, made probably in the al-Kindī circle; see on this F.W. Zimmermann (1994a), 16-19.

[326] See for D 27d, MS Carullah 1279, fols 63a24-63b21, at fol. 63a29, *innahu* (sc. *al-hayūlā*) *yaqwā an* ***yaqbala*** *jamī'a al-ashyā'i* and 63a35, *in kāna al-hayūlā* ***qābilan*** *li-*

receptivity of the active qualities of bodies.[327] Matter is properly that which underpins the qualities of the elements; it is receptive of the four contraries, and thus assures the reciprocal transformation of primary bodies. *Quaestio* 1.10 also calls matter the 'ultimate receptive substrate of successive contraries'.[328] And finally, at *De Mixtione* 13, 229,30 ff., in a summary of Aristotle's doctrine on the interaction of the elements, Alexander emphasises the function of prime matter, which Aristotle fails to mention in *GC* 2.4: transformation occurs between the elements through the qualities that characterise them, but it is matter that loses its qualities in favor of the qualities of the dominant body. Here the notion of receptivity is emphasised; though very close to that of potentiality, it is nonetheless distinct.

The description of matter as receptive is not properly Aristotelian.[329] It implies that matter has the autonomy of a receptacle with respect to the characteristics it receives. For one thing cannot receive another without having some sort of independent existence and disposition for this very reception.[330] Does Alexander then substitute the notion of receptivity for the more orthodox description of matter as pure potentiality, and thus compromise the idea of an immanent, unknowable and inseparable prime matter, with the exteriority of an immutable and permanent receptacle[331] in which properties appear and disappear, 'enter' and 'leave'?[332]

Alexander's talk of 'receptivity' has been seen merely as a terminological innovation, important only in its reinforcement of Alexander's classical interpretation of Aristotle on matter as *prima materia*.[333] But this is more than a figure of speech. Of course Alexander's understanding of matter is integrated into the Aristotelian tradition, but his notion of receptivity suggests he is not quite the stolid Peripatetic he is reputed to be. For we must admit that when he

jamīʿi al-ṣuwari, 63b2, *fa-law lā annahu lam takun fīhi* (sc. *al-hayūlā*) *quwwatu* ***qubūli*** *tilka al-ṣūrati, lamā istaḥāla ilayhā* and 4, *al-hayūlā mutahayyi'atun* ***li-qubūli*** *al-ṣūrati* and for D 7, MS Damascus 4871, fols 114a23-b20, 114a29, 30, 31, 35-6, 38, etc.; see also A. Badawī (1947), 286,9; 287,2, 5, 7.

327 See 57,22, trans. R.W. Sharples (1992), 110-12 and R.B. Todd (1972a), 299.

328 See 20,33, trans. R.W. Sharples (1992), 49 and n. 125, where he points out that the phrase 'the ultimate substrate which in itself lacks shape' is a combination of *Phys.* 1.9, 192a21 and 2.1, 193a11. See also *Quaestio* 1.15, 27,2, and R.W. Sharples (1992), 60, 'the matter which is the substrate of the things subject to coming-to-be and passing-away'.

329 Let us note however that in *GC* 1.4, 320a2 ff. Aristotle describes the prime matter as 'the substratum which admits of coming-to-be and passing away' and in *Metaph.* 10.4, 1055a29-30, he defines the contraries as 'the things that differ most in the same material substrate that receives them'; references cited by R.B. Todd (1972a), 299 n. 18.

330 It should be recalled that *hupodokhê* in the *Timaeus* reaches the rank of a *ti*, which can be designated by *tode* or *touto*, see *Tim.* 49E.

331 See *Tim.* 50B.

332 R.B. Todd (1972a), 299, notes that in his independent treatises, discussing in a most developed way the notion of matter, Alexander does not at all describe it as a potency; Todd refers e.g. to *De Anima*, 2,10-11,13.

333 See R.B. Todd (1972a), 299.

speaks of a matter *receiving* the first qualities or losing its prior qualities for the form of a dominant body,[334] he implies that there is an underlying matter that seems to be independent and to be prior the qualities in something other than a merely logical sense. Yet our commentary says clearly, several times, that prime matter is neither actual nor exists without the primary qualities that inform it.[335] The same idea appears as explicitly as it could in *Quaestio* 1.17, which asks precisely whether it is proper to consider prime matter as a substrate.[336] Shall we then give in and consider that *dektikon* is a mere terminological fancy?

But we cannot ignore *Quaestio* 2.7[337] and its description of prime matter as 'possessing a suitability (*epitêdeiotês*, literally, 'fitness for') and potentiality according to which it is able to admit qualities'.[338] The term *epitêdeiotês* seems to be the necessary correlate of *dektikos*; both are close, but not identical, to the idea of being in potentiality.[339] They imply that matter can exist in a sort of 'no man's land'[340] between the state of being qualified and the state of being without qualities; 'for a thing of which the being consists in being able to admit of certain things in turn, will not depart from its own proper being either in not being in some one of [these conditions] or in being in it'.[341] 'Suitability' to

334 See *Mixt.* 13, 230,5-7, and R.B. Todd (1976), 151.
335 See e.g. *Morphology* §§69, 78, and 91.
336 See 29,30-30,22, trans. R.W. Sharples (1992), 64-6, especially 64, 'But it is not possible for anything to be in primary matter as a substrate because such matter is not even a substrate in actuality in the first place, but needs form in order to be in [real] existence'. See also *Quaest.* 1.8 and 1.26.
337 See 52,20-53,30, trans. R.W. Sharples (1992), 102-4.
338 See 52,29-30, trans. R.W. Sharples (1992), 103.
339 S. Sambursky (1961), 73-4, and (1962), 104-10, distinguishes between the properly Aristotelian concept of potency which is a necessary but not a sufficient condition of change, and the later concept of *epitêdeiotês*, 'aptitude', which is a sufficient condition, in the sense that it involves the presence of the conditions required for a transition to actuality. For example, wood has the potency to burn but it will not burn unless it is dry; only in this state can it burn. Sambursky briefly reviews the use of the term in the post-Aristotelian literature and concludes that it was employed as a technical scientific term from the second century, and that it became widespread after the rise of Neoplatonism. The term is notably used by Plotinus to illustrate his doctrine of different degrees of participation according to the capacity of the receiver (*Enn.* 6.4.11.3 as well as in the context of theurgy, Proclus *Elem. Theol.* 39 and 140). Sambursky believes that in certain cases the notion of aptitude is substituted for that of potency while in other cases the former complements the latter, supplying a more specific connotation. He draws attention to Philoponus' use of it in this sense (e.g. 149,10-14). These conclusions were contested by G.E.L. Owen (in A.C. Crombie (1961), 97-8) who sees in the concept *epitêdeiotês* only a terminological variant making no significant addition to the various kinds of potency already distinguished by Aristotle. Recent scholarship (R.B. Todd (1972b), 25-35; F.A.J. de Haas (1997), 153 ff., and S. Berryman in her introduction to C.J.F. Williams (1999), 5), follows him in judging the distinction between *epitêdeiotês* and *dunamis* as being a result of overinterpretation.
340 See R.W. Sharples (1992), 103, n. 1, who explains that *methorios* is in fact the border line separating two States, and 53,3.
341 See 53,4, and R.W. Sharples (1992), 103.

receive a thing is somewhere in between that thing and its privation and cannot be identified either with the possession or privation of that thing (it cannot be a privation, for this vanishes once the new quality is received).[342] Nor is it being in potentiality: matter is independent of what it is 'fit' to receive, whereas potentiality is a possibility immanent in one thing that allows it to change into another. Matter is thus below actuality but beyond potentiality; neither a sensible thing nor a pure abstraction, it is the condition for the appearance of sensible things. Matter, being by nature unqualified, is equally distant from privation and form, for aptitude to become something can be identified neither with form nor with privation. It is distinct from privation insofar as it does not disappear with the generation of the thing. As *dunamis* matter is characterised by a tension that links it both to the related form and potentiality, and is thus 'not a determined nature or an indeterminate nature that conserves it but something that is not yet the future quality and that is not purely and simply that which is'.[343] Receptivity does not include this 'tension toward', which is closely connected to the notion of act, and which entails that potentiality cannot be thought of without its correlate.

It thus seems reasonable to hold that Alexander, even while remaining very close to the Aristotelian text, borrows several aspects that may be broadly associated with the Platonic Receptacle. This suggests that he anticipates the Neoplatonic project of reconciling Plato with Aristotle on this issue. In this context it is worth remembering that Aristotle himself compared Plato's *khôra* to his own prime matter,[344] and that the commentators were thus only following his lead. There are limited points of similarity, too, between the Receptacle and Aristotelian prime matter conceived as substrates of properties, even though they remain superficial and do not resist a thorough examination.[345] In *Metaph.* 7.3, 1029a20 ff., Aristotle describes prime matter as a substrate stripped of all properties; similarly Plato insists that the Receptacle has in itself no qualities, so that it may take on all properites (he compares it with the odourless fluid used as a base for the production of perfume).[346] In turn Alexander insists that receptivity need not be considered a quality of matter, because matter's aptitude to receive qualities is nothing more than its lacking any qualities of its own.[347] It

342 See references above, n. 339.
343 de Haas points out that Philoponus identifies the level of tri-dimensionality, which by his time was regarded as an intermediary between the elements and the prime matter, with the permanent substrate that persists through the change. In other words, he does not reject the traditional function of prime matter, but only its representation. See F.A.J. de Haas (1997), 162.
344 See *Phys.* 4.2, 209b11-13 and *GC* 2.1, 329a14-24.
345 See R. Sorabji (1988), 34, who discusses the limits of such an assimilation.
346 See *Tim.* 50C and D; 51A where Plato also uses other metaphors (the work of a goldsmith or a printmaker) that involve a neutral material which can show the determinate features of a form it receives.
347 See *Quaest.* 1.15, 27,20 ff.; R.W. Sharples (1992), 61. Along the same lines, Alexander compares, in his commentary *in Meteor.* 4, 382a8-9, the faculty of vision to the faculty of touch: the former can receive all the colours precisely because it is devoid

seems to be not so much a simple metaphysical principle as the natural foundation of being, since it receives all attributes without itself being received by anything more fundamental.[348]

Conclusion

The discovery and examination of the extracts of Alexander's commentary in Jābir's *Morphology* shed a new kind of light on Alexander's philosophy of nature. For the first time, we are in possession of significant extracts of a commentary by Alexander preserved in Arabic. Previously, it is only the Arabic transmission of the *Quaestiones* that has been studied. But these short treatises present the original thought of Alexander, in a context where he need not subordinate his own views to those of Aristotle. Moreover, as some superb recent research has shown, the Arabic versions of independent treatises ascribed to Alexander show considerable traces of manipulation: 'Proclus Arabus' and 'Philoponus Arabus' have both been found 'disguised in the clothes of Alexander'.[349] This tends to cast a veil of suspicion over the corpus of 'the Arabic Alexander'. The experienced Hellenist usually considers this Alexander to be a mere product of Neoplatonist syncretism, having nothing to do with the real, Greek Alexander, apart from sharing the same name. By contrast, the present extracts of Alexander on *GC* testify to Alexander's direct exegetical activity, and preserve a faithful Arabic translation. It is also of clear textual importance – we have alluded above in several instances to passages that preserve readings older than our oldest Greek manuscripts of *GC*. As for the philosophical interest of these extracts, it is worth saying that the interest of an avowedly orthodox Aristotelian exegesis may reside precisely in the gap between the commentary and the text that it comments upon.

of all of them, while touch is not devoid of tangible properties, since no body can exist without tangible properties (cf. 200,25 ff.).

348 In the *De Anima*, 3,28-4,4, Alexander explicitly describes the matter and substrate of simple bodies as 'a simple nature, lacking form, formless, without a form and shape'. F.A.J. de Haas (1997), 76, n. 76, from whom I borrow this reference, points out that Alexander here is closer to Plotinus than Aristotle.

349 I borrow the metaphor from A. Hasnawi, who has made this discovery in his remarkable article, A. Hasnawi (1994).

Alexander of Aphrodisias
On Aristotle On Coming-to-Be and Perishing

apud Jābir b. Ḥayyān, *Book of Morphology*

Translation

Signs and Abbreviations

The *lemmata* taken from the *De generatione et corruptione*, and quotations from it reproduced in the commentary, are in bold characters.

References to the text of Aristotle, *De generation et corruptione* are to the Bekker edition followed by H.H. Joachim (1922).

<...>	lacuna in the text
<text>	Arabic text supplied
[text]	a word or a group of words added in English to make the meaning clear

About the Text

The following text is a translation of the first part of an edition of Jābir b. Ḥayyān's *Kitāb al-Taṣrīf* (*Book of Morphology*), soon to be published in *Mélanges de l'Université Saint-Joseph*, Beirut. The edition is based on three manuscripts:

1 (P) Paris, Bibliothèque Nationale, ar. 5099, fols 128b1-147b21.[1]

This ms. of 269 folios is a composite manuscript of Iranian origin. The first part, up to fol. 64b, is much more recent: at fol. 15, in the watermark of the paper appears the beginning of a date (18...), so that this part may be dated as no earlier than the beginning of the 19th century. The second part of the ms. is earlier, dated 1023H/1614, at fol. 95b. The script, a plain *neskhī* in black ink, is of several hands, with red headings for titles and with figures and diagrams also in red. Our text is very corrupt and cut off in the middle of a sentence at fol. 147b21. Here a marginal note in Persian indicates that the lacuna was already present in the exemplar from which our manuscript was copied, since the exemplar had two blank folios between the end of the present treatise and the following one. The same method is followed in our manuscript.[2]

2 (D) Teheran, Dāneshgāh-e, Ketāb-khāna-ī Markazī 491, fols 151b20-177a21.

The manuscript is undated. However it seems recent and should not be earlier then the 19th century. *K. al-Taṣrīf* is cut off in the middle of a sentence, as in the MS Paris, B.N. ar. 5099, but the copyist did not indicate the lacuna and moved on to the following treatise as if it were the sequel of the same treatise. For this

[1] See G. Vajda (1953), 681.

[2] I am very grateful to Dr Francis Richard for his oral description of this beautiful manuscript. The (as yet unpublished) notices of G. Vajda were also helpful.

reason the catalogue gives a much higher number of folios for this treatise than it in fact includes.[3]

3 (M) Teheran, Ketābkhāne-ye Mellī-ye Malek 6206, pp. 247,17-286,17

Dated 13th/19th century. 542 pages. This manuscript reproduces the same error as the Dāneshgāh 491.[4]

These three manuscripts are collections of treatises all attributed to Jābir b. Ḥayyān. They all include nearly the same texts and M even reproduces the treatises included in P in the same order. All three were copied in the same cultural sphere and belong to the same family.

About the Translation

The following is a translation of the first half (nearly 10 fols) of *K. al-Taṣrīf* (*Book of Morphology*), which includes the fragments of Alexander's commentary *in GC*. Something should be said about the method followed in the present translation. The complete and unabridged text of the first half of the *Book of Morphology* has been translated, including Jābir's words when they occur. These passages are identified in the notes to the translation.

I have aimed to produce a translation as close as possible to the original Arabic while still being readable. I have thus tried as far as possible to translate the same Arabic word by the same English word, in order to allow the reader to feel the original roughness of a bare technical text. Sometimes, however, this was impossible for reasons of readability.

The notes to the translation are intended, firstly, to clarify technical points related to the original text, concerning especially Arabic terminology and Graeco-Arabic translation issues; and secondly to follow closely the argument of the text providing references to Aristotle and other commentators (mostly Philoponus). Philosophical issues are dealt with in the introduction.

[3] For the description of this manuscript and its content, see M.T. Dānesh-Pazūh, *Fehrest-e Ketāb-khāna-ye ehdā'ī-e āqā-ye Sayyed Muḥammad Meshkāt be Ketāb-khāna-ye dāneshgāh-e Tehrān*, vol. 4, Teheran 1953, 1012-35.

[4] For a description of this manuscript see I. Afshār and M.T. Dānesh-Pazūh (1992), 254-63.

1 The book of Morphology, work of Jābir b. Ḥayyān, may God be merciful to him

2 In the name of God, the Merciful, the Compassionate. Praise be to God, the Lord of all worlds and peace and prayers be upon Muḥammad the Seal of the Prophets

3 We have written many books before the present one about the science of Balances and we have taught within these books the aspects of their mutual reactions, but we did not indicate the way to work with these Balances. We have taught the qualities[1] of things through letters according to the principles[2] which are heat, coldness, moisture and dryness, but without referring to quantity.[3] For it is another science, that has nothing in common with the

[1] *Kayfiyyāt* designates here primary qualities, though Jābir normally prefers the more concrete word *ṭabā'i'* (Natures). See P. Kraus (1986), 165 and below n. 9.

[2] Jābir will often name the primary qualities *uṣul* ('roots' or 'principles', sing. *aṣl*: see *K. Maydān al-'aql*, P. Kraus (1935), 210,15; 211,11.13.15 and *K. al-Mizān al-ṣaghīr*, *Textes*, 431,7; 454,2) thus giving them an originary status. See P. Kraus (1986), 162, n. 3 who points out that the Arabic *aṣl* corresponds to the Greek *rhiza* rather than to *arkhê*. Jābir seems here not only to compare the four primary qualities with the letters of the alphabet, but also to cultivate the analogy with the roots of words. For the Balance of Letters which he expounds is based on a real identification between the noun and the intimate structure of the thing it designates, in so far as there is a correspondence between the Natures or qualities which constitute a thing and the letters which make up a word. On these grounds, Jābir believes he can extract the quantitative and the qualitative structure of words by analysing them. This analysis requires reducing each word to its roots (*ḥurūf uṣul*). Hence, the primary qualities correspond the the words *ḥurūf uṣul*.

[3] Jābir's task is to submit the Natures to measurement and to determine the quantity or the intensity in which they are represented in the bodies. Measuring the Natures of a body means measuring the quantities that the world soul appropriated when it entered into the matter, pervading matter according to the intensity of its desire. 'The principle of the Balance thus derives from the desire of the Soul for the elements' (*K. Maydān al-'aql*, P. Kraus (1935), 212,1-2). The science of Balances studies this desire, and thus is able to calculate the share and intensity of the Natures in bodies, as apportioned by the world soul. (Unlike Alexander, Jābir follows the Platonic tradition, that begins in the *Timaeus*, of accepting a single soul that orders the entire cosmos.) By reducing all qualitative changes of the physical world to quantitative changes, the theory of the

foregoing, that shows the quantitative [aspect] of these; thus we have left it off to another book.

4 Having shown that there can be no language without the combination of letters — actually, an isolated letter cannot be pronounced — and having also shown the simples (*al-basīṭa*)[4] and their positions,[5] it has become necessary for us to describe how to manipulate these letters which are simples or compounds — so that the benefit becomes, henceforth, great and sublime. It has also become necessary for us to show how to achieve the use of the simples (*al-basīṭa*) and the compounds,[6] in order to make comprehensible, in our present books, how they may be manipulated.

5 Since the case at hand (*mawḍi'*)[7] concerns the transmutation (*taṣrīf*) of the simples into one another and the interaction between them all, I described my book as the *Morphology* (*taṣrīf*).[8] As the grammarians name that case (*mawḍi'*), as far as the combination of letters is concerned, morphology, and the

Balance will thus make it possible to reduce all the data of human knowledge to a system of quantity and measurement; see P. Kraus (1986), 159-67.

[4] Jābir will often simply designate the primary qualities as 'simples', calling them *al-basīṭa* (simples) or *al-basā'iṭ al-uwwal* (primary simples), in opposition to the elements that are in fact composed from them (see also *K. al-mīzān al-ṣaghīr*, P. Kraus (1935), 412,11).

[5] *Mawāḍi'* pl. of *mawḍi'* ('position'), as opposed to *mawḍū'* ('subject'). The four Natures or primary qualities are divided into four groups of seven degrees of intensity each, which means 28 positions that are indicated by the 28 letters of the Arabic alphabet. Thus to each degree of intensity corresponds a letter. Hence, the quantitative structure of a thing depends on the order of the letters in the noun that designates it, because the position of the letter in the word designates a quality and determines its degree of intensity. Jābir believes in the absolute correspondence between the Letters and the Natures. On the Balance of Letters, see P. Kraus (1986), 223-70, and P. Lory (1985) and (1996).

[6] This probably refers to the elements which are composed out of the primary qualities, hot, cold, dry and moist. First, the Natures were endowed with corporeal form by the substance, then two of these corporeal isolated Natures combine again to form a composed primary body; see P. Kraus (1986), 166 and references there. See above, Introduction, p. 10.

[7] *Mawḍi'* means the grammatical 'case' of a word, so that its use here hints at the correspondence between the position of the letters in a word and the degree of intensity of the Natures. The term *mawḍi'* means not only the situation or the position of something, but each form of a word's inflexions, and thus refers directly to the Arabic *taṣrīf* (see next note).

[8] The word *taṣrīf*, which originally means *taghyīr* (change), was progressively established as an entire separate discipline among the grammatical sciences. Its subject is the formation of words and Form variations that they undergo, for instance the transmutation of letters (*qalb*) (see above, Introduction, p. 11-12). Thus, I have translated the word *taṣrīf* with 'morphology', where the word is used with a general sense, as it is here. Morphology generally designates the study of the exterior configuration of a body, and thus could be applied to its constitutive qualities. However I have translated *taṣrīf* with 'transmutation' where it has the more specific meaning of a transmutation of letters or words, Natures or elements.

philosophers name this case as far as simples are concerned, morphology, the book could not have any other title but *On Morphology*.

6 [Here is] an illustration: the *Qāf*, the *Alef* and the *Lām* are isolated letters that, when combined, become *qāla* (to say). The root of *qāla* in Arabic is *qawala* with vocalization of the *Wāw*. After a frequent use, the *Wāw* became unvowelled and the word became *qawl*; for because the *Wāw* became unvowelled and the letter preceding it vocalized by a *fatḥa* (*infitāḥ*), the *Wāw* was transmuted into *Alef* and <the word> became *qāla*.

7 Having found this in language and having previously shown that language is completely [founded] on letters, and that there is no language except through the combination of letters, therefore it became necessary to apply this to Natures.[9] It is fair to say that the morphology of Natures is like the morphology of letters, since the syllogism is necessarily made up of three [terms] that are the two Extremes and the Middle.[10] Know this.

8 In our present book, we will describe, by way of instruction, the morphology of the Natures, their states and quantities, and the aspects of their

[9] Jābir often calls the primary qualities *ṭabā'i'* (Natures), thus conferring on them a physical reality and an autonomy which the Aristotelian qualities lack. The elements are composed of the Natures and could be decomposed into them. They are more than mere accidents existing in the first bodies. See P. Kraus (1986), 165 ff., who notes that *phusis* always designates an independent reality in the philosophic Greek lexicon. P. Kraus connects the theory of Jābir concerning the elementary qualities to that of a group of Arab Hellenists who were called *aṣḥāb al-ṭabā'i'* by the theologians, and who were vigorously opposed to the Mu'tazilites. Besides deriving all the phenomena from the mixture and interaction of the Natures, they considered the latter to be bodies. Shahrastānī compares Jāḥiẓ to *aṣḥāb al-ṭabā'i'*, because he attributes Natures to bodies (trans. D. Gimaret and G. Monot (1986), vol. 1, 257). He himself often uses the term *ṭabā'i'*, especially when describing the cosmological system of the Ismā'īliyya, where 'after the spheres came to exist the simple Natures (*al-ṭabā'i' al-basīṭa*), which started moving with a rectilinear [movement]' (see D. Gimaret and G. Monot (1986), vol. 1, 557 and 209; 628). This term is also frequently used by the mutakallimūn, who give it, however, a broader meaning which encompasses each and every corporeal entity, rather than just the simple primary qualities; see R.M. Frank (1974). It is also encountered in the Aristotelian tradition. In fact, *ṭabā'i'* appears in *Al-Kitāb al-Mu'tabar* of Abū al-Barakāt al-Baghdādī, where it designates the four primary qualities, which he considers to be the primary corporeal constituents which give form to the elements (*fa-takūnu mabādi'u al-ḥudūdi minhā, li-annahā awwaliyyātun ḥissiyyatun*). Like Jābir, he refuses to consider the primary matter and the first contrarieties as logical divisions informing the elements. The ultimate constituents of the natural bodies must be corporeal (cf. Abū al-Barakāt al-Baghdādī (1939), *al-Juz' al-thānī min al-'ulūm al-ṭabī'iyya* (*K. al-Samā' wa al-'ālam*) §8, 147-53). Throughout, I translate *ṭab'*, pl. *ṭabā'i'* as 'Nature(s)', capitalised so as to avoid any possible confusion.

[10] Jābir will remind us many times throughout his treatise of the definition of the simple syllogism. There is a play here on the word *qiyās*, which means both 'reasoning by analogy' and 'syllogism'. The first meaning is relevant to the correspondence between the Letters and the Natures, because the grammarians use the term *qiyās* in this context, as he will explain at length in the second part of this work. But the second meaning suggests that his reasoning is demonstrative.

union; this way our book will be accomplished. Consider, may God leave you in good health, these gifts I am giving you, guard yourself and persevere in contemplating them, though I provided you with explanations,[11] in this book, according to your need and even more.

9 We say: as we have previously said, you should know the cause of the Natures and their morphology.

10 We know that[12] **the capacity for filling up (*al-imtilā'*) belongs to moisture, because it[13] is not confined within confines of its own but is confined by the confines of something else[14] and follows necessarily the**

[11] In the margin of the manuscript of Paris, the reviser or the author wrote *shafaytuka* (I quenched [your thirst]). The basic meaning of the verb is 'to cure'. The author thus creates a play on words: he is quenching the reader's thirst for knowledge and at the same time curing him from his ignorance, like the elixir which is supposed to 'cure' the metals. This explains the concessive clause (*ma' innī*: 'even though I provided you ...'): it refers back to the wish for the recipient's good health.

[12] The actual commentary abruptly starts at *GC* 2.2, 329b34-330a4. The chapter has already begun and the premises of the demonstration have already been set down. Aristotle is to define the primary tangible qualities which characterise the primary perceptible bodies as such. These must be informed by contrary qualities since they must be capable of combining. These qualities must be tangible, for the bodies must be reciprocally *pathêtika*. Of all tangible qualities, only the hot, the cold, the dry and the moist are primary, because they are the only ones which are reciprocally active and passive on their own, not through anything else. All of the other tangible qualities are therefore derivatives of these four primary qualities, and their definitions are derived from the definitions of the primary qualities. Cf. *GC* 2.2, 329b6-25.

[13] The demonstrative pronoun *hu* annexed to *anna* clearly refers in this case to *imtilā'* ('filling up'), while the neutral Greek *to* in 329b35 remains undetermined (most translators take it as referring to *tou hurgou*, 'the moist'). The Arabic translation is thus less ambiguous than the Greek text: the definition of the word 'moist' has already been given and is no longer in question. The passage concerns rather the word 'fine' and the reduction of the fine to moisture through their common characteristic: the fact that they are *anaplêstikon* (i.e. they fill up or penetrate whatever they contact).

[14] *Lā yanḥāzu bi-ḥayyizin khāṣṣin wa yanḥāzu bi-ḥayyizin ghayrihi* is not the exact translation of *to mê hôristhai men euoriston d'einai*, but rather that of *to aoriston oikeiô horô euoriston on* (*GC* 2.2, 329b31). It could be a copyist's mistake, by homoioteleuton for example. But when did the mistake occur? Did it already exist in the translation of Abū Bishr Mattā, or is it the fault of Jābir himself? Or that of one of the copyists of *K. al-Taṣrīf*? Another possibility is that this homoioteleuton already existed in the Greek original of the commentary of Alexander. The infrequent usage of the word *ḥāza* as a translation of the Greek *hôristhai* ('define' or 'delimit') is worth noting, and I have tried to render it with the somewhat cumbersome translation 'confine'. The 7th Form of the radical *ḥ-w-z*, *ḥayyiz* can mean 'the border' or 'limit' of something just as it can mean the 'container' or 'the place' (cf. R. Dozy (1927), 335 and W. Lane (1893), 668: 'The inner surface of a container, which is contiguous in every part to the outer surface of the thing contained'). Dozy also mentions an expression whose meaning is interesting for our context: *lā yanḥāzu* could mean 'incompressible'. Widely used by the translators in its 7th Form, *inḥāza*, *munḥāzun*, means 'separated' or 'isolated' and generally convey the meaning of the Greek word *apokrinein*. This word is often associated with *munfaridun* ('separated'), stressing its meaning. See for instance the Arabic version of

shape of that which comes into contact with it. That which is fine is capable of filling up, for it consists <of fine parts, and that which has small parts> is capable of filling up because the whole of it may come into contact with the totality of the thing. And the fine is properly as such. It is then manifest that fineness is derived from moisture and that thickness is derived from dryness. (*GC* 2.2, 329b34-330a4)

11 Aristotle presented this in his book *On Generation and Corruption*. You should understand, here, the explanation (*basṭ*)[15] and the interpretation (*taṣrīf*)

Aristotle's *Physics*, by Isḥāq b. Ḥunayn: *laysa khalā'un muḥāzun bi-nafsihi* (400,13) and *Phys.* 4.9, 217b20 *out'apokekrimenon kenon estin*. Closer to our own meaning, *inḥiyāz* renders *diôrismenon* in *Phys.* 8.4: *a'nī inḥiyāza dhālika* (sc. *al-khafīfu*) *bi-fawqi wa inḥiyaza hādha* (sc. *al-thaqīlu*) *bi-asfali* (840,16-17) and *Phys.* 8.4, 255b16-17, *to men* (sc. *to kouphon*) *tô anô to de* (sc. *to baru*) *tô katô diôrismenon*. P. Kraus notes the occurrence of this term in the writings of al-Fārābī, meaning 'natural place' (cf. *Kitāb al-jam' bayn ra'yay al-ḥakīmayn Aflāṭūn al-Ilāhī wa Arisṭūṭālīs* in F. Dieterici (1892), 29 and 30); we can also find it very often with this latter meaning in the writings of Ibn Sīnā (see A.M. Goichon (1938), 95-7, who gives it a broader sense than the *makān* or 'place' having a direct contact with the surface of the localised body, so as to consider the common place rather as 'a natural place for the localised body'). We should note that Jābir himself sometimes uses this word with this same meaning.

In his *K. al-Mu'tabar* Abū al-Barakāt al-Baghdādī gives the same definition of the dry and the moist as that of the *Book of Morphology*: '*wa yaqūlūna anna al-yābisa ma yataḥayyazu bi-nafsihi, wa al-raṭba ma yanḥāzu bi-ghayrihi*' (see Abū al-Barakāt al-Baghdādī (1939), vol. 2, *al-Fasl al-khāmis min al-samā' wa al-'ālam*, 137 and 150). Abū al-Barakāt uses *ḥayyiz* frequently throughout his long commentary, giving it the meaning of natural place. However, the definition which interests us makes another use of the word, exactly identical to that mentioned in the *Morphology*. The question arises whether this should be attributed to Abū al-Barakāt, or whether he is quoting Aristotle or another, later commentator (hence *yaqūlūn*, 'they said'). If this terminology were to be attributed to Abū al-Barakāt, it would be worth questioning whether it constitutes, in the commentary mentioned in the *Morphology*, an interpolation by Jābir, thus underlining the corporeal characteristic of the primary qualities and hence, their ability to be 'localised'. Like Jābir, Abū al-Barakāt believed in the concrete reality of the primary qualities, which he also calls *tabā'i'* ('Natures'). He considers that the latter exist as an hypostasis in the intelligible world, where they have their own *ḥayyiz* ('limit') at the border of the material world. Nevertheless, we should note that this definition appears in what seems to be the opinion of the Ancients (*yaqūlūn*), whereas Abū al-Barakāt often uses *yatashakkalu* instead of *yanḥāzu* (op. cit., 137). We know that Abū al-Barakāt had the texts of Aristotle and other commentators at hand (he is said to have been deeply influenced by Philoponus for instance), which he probably quotes literally, especially when definitions were to be cited (cf. S. Pines, (1979), 96-108). Finally it is worth noting that the verb *ḥāza* occurs once in the Arabic version of Alexander's *De Providentia* (D18, Greek original lost), by Abū Bishr Mattā, the translator of Alexander's commentary in *GC*, see H.J. Ruland (1976), 23,1: *al-ashyā' allatī yaḥūzuhā sulṭānuhu* (things that fall within the scope of his authority).

[15] Notice the opposition between *basṭ* ('explanation') and *taṣrīf* ('interpretation'), the latter conveying the meaning of interpretation which accompanies every exegesis, and so the notion of transformation, or transmutation of the word.

of the book so that what you intend to produce[16] and to analyse becomes easier for you.

12 We have showed that fineness is subsumed under moisture, just as man is subsumed under animal,[17] **'because the fine is capable of filling up, for that which is fine has small parts and that which has small parts is capable of filling up, for it may come into contact with the thing in its totality'**,[18] and it penetrates[19] and sinks [into it].[20] Now, it is the moist that comes into contact, for that which comes into contact **'is not confined within confines of its own but is only confined by some other thing'**,[21] therefore it necessarily sinks into that which comes into contact with it, and becomes encrusted[22] into it. This is the condition of the moist, and for this reason it is easy to confine. Therefore, fineness comes from the action of moisture. If that is so, the <contrary>

[16] *Takwīn* refers here to artificial generation; as alchemy leads not only to the transformation of bodies into one another but also to the production of new bodies from their constitutive elements; see P. Kraus (1986), 97-8.

[17] This example is probably an addition of Jābir's, especially given that in the second part of the treatise, he explicitly insists on the division of the natural beings into genus and species, and mentions in the very same words how man as a species is subsumed under the genus animal.

[18] cf. *GC* 2.2, 330a1-3.

[19] *Dākhala* refers to *tadākhul*, which is the term generally used to translate the *krâsis di' holou*, the perfect interpenetration of the bodies (see P. Kraus (1986), 176 and Baffioni (1986), 421-2). However, *dākhala* is also used by Abū Bishr Mattā, in his translation of Alexander's *On Providence*, in a wider sense: *yudākhilu al-nāsa al-bardu* (the cold penetrates the people) and further *al-ḥarāratu allatī tudākhilu al-nuḥāsa* (the heat that penetrates the copper), see H.J. Ruland (1976), 41,2.4 and P. Thillet (1980), 20.

[20] *Rasaba*, 'to drown', 'to sink', is very often used in texts on the philosophy of nature: it occurs many times in the Arabic version of the *De caelo* (see for instance *Cael.* 4.4, 311a23.26 and A. Badawī (1961), 375,10.12), rendering *huphistêmi* ('to sink'), and also in the Arabic version of *GA* (cf. 2.7, 747a5 and J. Burgman and H.J. Drossaart Lulofs (1971), 90,13), where it translates *khôrô* ('to give way', 'make room'). We also find it in the Compendium of the *Meteorology* attributed to Yaḥyā b. al-Biṭrīq, where *rasaba* and its derivatives occur in paraphrases which have no equivalent in the Greek text, whereas *huphistêmi*, which often appears in the Greek text of the *Meteor.*, is never translated. Ibn Sīnā uses it quite often in his commentary on *GC*. It is only in its second Form *rassaba* that it properly pertains to the alchemical terminology, signifying 'to precipitate', 'to deposit'. However, this usage does not appear at all in our commentary. In addition *rasaba* translates the Greek *hupokathizô* ('to sink under') in the translation of the *Placita Philosophorum* by Qusṭā b. Lūqa. We also find it having this meaning in the Arabic version of Nemesius of Emesa's *De Natura Hominis* by Isḥāq b. Ḥunayn, see M. Haji-Athanasiou (1982), 94,9: *rasaba al-turābu fī asfali al-mā'i.*

[21] cf. *GC* 2.2, 329b31.

[22] P. Kraus (1935), 394,16 transcribes *laḥḥa* and not *laḥaja*. I reject this amendment because the written form of the MS Paris B.N. ar. 5099, fol. 129a5, followed by the two other manuscripts, was clear at this place, and the meaning of *laḥaja*, which incidentally is not far from that of *laḥḥa*, suits our context well, for *laḥaja* also means 'to plunge' or 'to settle' (see W. Lane (1893), 2653).

quality[23] must derive from a contrary quality, so that thickness must derive from dryness.[24]

13 Moreover, viscosity derives from moisture, for viscosity is nothing but moisture that has been adulterated by a certain affection (*shābahā ta'thīrun mā*),[25] as in the case of oil. Its contrary is derived from dryness, for it is what is extremely dry, so that it petrifies through lack of moisture. (*GC* 2.2, 330a4-7)

14 The explanation of this is given in the same manner: viscosity is subsumed under moisture and its contrary under dryness. That viscosity is subsumed under moisture is evident because **'the viscous is the moist together with a certain affection'**.[26] For things that are moist and not easily divided off – though if a part is divided it slides off them – such as glue, liquid pitch and oil, are called viscous. Likewise the brittle[27] derives from dryness, for the **[brittle] is the thing which solidifies[28] through lack of moisture.**[29]

[23] The term *kayfiyya* (quality) is very rarely used in the commentary of Alexander to designate the primary qualities, which he more often calls *fuṣūl* (differences). See above, Introduction, p.68.

[24] For the whole paragraph, cf. Philoponus *in GC* 220,6 ff. The demonstration is extremely similar, and the argument is the same, with the addition of an example in Philoponus.

[25] *Shāba* means 'to blend', 'to mix with'. *Shābaha ta'thīrun mā* should be the translation of *peponthos ti estin* (*GC* 2.2, 330a5). Although *peponthos ti* ('a certain affection') is correctly translated by *ta'thīrun mā*, by introducing *shāba*, the Arabic shifts the meaning of the preposition in the direction of the blending. The Arabic stresses the idea of mixture, of addition of an extra element, and even that of adulteration, whereas the Greek insists on the idea of affection, and so on that of the passivity of the affected subject. *Ikhtilāṭ* is, in general, the term which corresponds to the Greek *mixis* ('mixture') in the vocabulary of the translators. *Shāba* definitely has a negative connotation which we perceive in the way the translators use it; see for instance the Arabic version of Alexander *in Metaph.* 12, as reproduced in the long commentary of Ibn Rushd on Aristotle's *Metaphysics*, where *shāba* occurs very often in the exegesis without appearing even once in the *lemmata* (ed. M. Bouyges (1938-52), 1565,8; 1566,1.4; 1567,8; 1576,2). It is worth noting that the extracts of Aristotle's *GC* in the Middle commentary of Ibn Rushd ad loc. use the term *khālaṭa*.

[26] cf. *GC* 2.2, 330a5.

[27] Concerning the usage of *qaḥalun* to translate *krauron* ('brittle'), cf. C. Baffioni (1986), 425, who points out that in the Greek texts on the philosophy of nature, the word *krauron* is not used much anyway. Thus, it is hardly mentioned in the text of *Meteor.* and in Book 4 (387a14), it is *psathuron* which is the contrary of *gliskhron* ('viscous'). However, it is worth noting that *qaḥalun* occurs in the Middle Commentary of Ibn Rushd on Aristotle *GC* (ed. J. al-'Alawī (1994), 93,17; 94,7) with the same meaning as that of our own commentary to designate the opposite of *lazijun*.

[28] The Arabic has two words where the Greek has only one: *pepêgenai* (*pêgnumi*) is sometimes translated by *yastaḥjiru* (to become petrified) and other times by *yan'aqidu* (to solidify). The process of the double Arabic translation of the same Greek word is frequent in our commentary, where, either it serves the purpose of specifying the meaning by giving it an extra nuance, or it focuses simply on the meaning, and it is then a pure question of rhetoric. On the double translation of Greek terms, see G. Endress

15 Furthermore the soft is derived from moisture, for the soft is that whose mass sinks into itself due to pressure (*mā ṭubi'a wa inghamara fīhi razānatuhu*)[30] but does not move, and only the moist does this. That is why it is not moisture that is subsumed under <the soft, rather the soft is subsumed under moisture. And the hard is subsumed under> dryness, for the hard is the thing which is solidified and petrified. (*GC* 2.2, 330a 8-12)

16 The soft and the hard[31] are subsumed under moisture and dryness. For the soft is that which can be impressed and whose mass shrinks, but does not move as does the moist.[32] For the moist moves, while the soft shrinks and is impressed, but does not move. So, the soft is [something] moist that has been adulterated by a certain affection, like the viscous; that is why the soft is subsumed under dryness but not the other way round. For, despite the fact that it belongs to the soft to shrink, it also belongs to it not to move, as does the viscous which is [something] moist that has been adulterated by a certain affection.[33] The moist extends then further than the soft. And the hard is subsumed under the dry, for the hard is that which is solidified and petrified and that which is solidified and petrified is dry.[34]

17 Aristotle said in the book *On Generation and Corruption*: the moist and the dry are each said in several senses. For the moist and the damp are opposed to the dry. Again the dry and the solidified are opposed to the moist. (*GC* 2.2, 330a12-14)

18 The explanation of this is that once [Aristotle] has defined the moist and the dry strictly speaking, saying that 'the moist is that which <is not> confined within confines of its own but is easily confined within foreign

---

(1973), 158, who considers this to show hesitance regarding terminology, which would be typical of a first period of translation. In our commentary, though, double translations seem to have been used systematically, which rules out this explanation. In any case double translations are also found in later translators, despite other advances in translation technique. Cf. P. Thillet (1980), 30-2, who reproduces a certain number of double translations in Abū Bishr Mattā's translations and others like Isḥāq b. Ḥunayn. It does seem that Ḥunayn's contemporaries and those who came after him used this technique less frequently. It is worth noting that whereas *in'aqada* and its derivatives are very often used in the *Middle Commentary* of Ibn Rushd on Aristotle's *GC* (ed. J. al-'Alawī (1994), 94,8.12.18; 95,1.2), *istaḥjara* and its derivatives are never found.

[29] cf. *GC* 2.2, 330a7. For the whole paragraph compare with Philoponus *in GC* 220,20-4.

[30] I have here adopted the emendation suggested by P. Kraus (1935), 395,14, the original text being as follows: *mā ṭaba'a al-ghamzu fīhi razānatahu*. However it is worth noting that we find the term *ghamzu* used in the same context in the Arabic version of *Meteor.*: *wa ba'ḍu al-ashyā'i al-ladinati yu'aththiru fīhā al-ghamzu. Wa mā aththara fīhi al-ghamzu, fa-innahu yu'ātī li-al-jablati ka-l-mūmi al-mu'aththiru fīhi al-ghamzu* (see C. Petraitis (1967), 118,12-119,2), which is a paraphrase of *Meteor.* 4.9, 386a17. *Al-ghamzu* translates in this case the Greek *thlasis* ('crushing').

[31] The Arabic has *al-ṣalāba*, literally 'hardness'. But given the nearby occurence of the pair 'soft and hard' this looks like a copyist's mistake.

[32] cf. *GC* 2.2, 330a8-9.

[33] cf. *GC* 2.2, 330a5.

[34] cf. *GC* 2.2, 330a11-12.

confines' and saying that **'the dry is that which is not easily confined within foreign confines but is easily confined within confines of its own'**,[35] he started showing, through that statement, that under these two contraries – moisture and dryness – are subsumed and arranged all the other contrarieties.

19 He said: **'since the moist and the dry are each said in several senses'**.[36] That these two are said in several senses can be explained first from the two things that are opposite to them. For when a thing has several opposites, it is one of the things that are said in several senses.[37] This is true concerning the things to which, at the moment, <numerous things> are opposed. For moist [things] and damp [things] are opposite to dry things and these two qualities are different from one another. [Aristotle] thus explains that **the moist and the dry are each said in several senses** and that all the other senses that they designate are subsumed under these first two that define them alone. <...> in so far as he thereby wants to show that the hard is subsumed under the dry, just like the soft is subsumed under the moist, when one uses this statement, namely **'that the hard is solid and petrified[38] and that the solid is dry'**.

20 Having shown[39] [that] to each of the moist and the dry can be opposed more than one thing – for to the dry he opposes sometimes the moist and sometimes the damp, and to the moist he opposes sometimes the dry and sometimes the solid – because he opposed to each one of them <more than one thing, and when the same thing has more than one thing opposed to it, it is something that is said> in several senses. Having[40] shown this, and having furthermore shown in how many senses each of [the moist and the dry] can be said, inasmuch as he took here two opposites for each of them, namely **the moist and the damp for the dry, and the dry and the solid for the moist, these [qualities] deriving from dryness and moisture <that> are said <of> them all, and belonging to those which we previously stated**, I mean those included in the definition of the [dry and the moist], he then said that **'these**

[35] cf. *GC* 2.2, 329b30-2.
[36] cf. *GC* 2.2, 330a12.
[37] cf. Philoponus *in GC* 221,21, 'in order to show this he says that "wet" and "dry" have more than one sense. And in showing that these <words> have more than one sense he uses the argument from opposites; for when the same thing has more than one thing opposed to it, it too is something that has more than one sense' (trans. C.J.F. Williams (2000)). Concerning the part of the demonstration dealing with the opposites (§§19-20), cf. Philoponus *in GC* 221,14-222,3.
[38] *Jāmid* is used here as a synonym for *mustaḥjir* and translates *to pepêgos* ('the petrified'). We already saw above in §§15 and 16 that *mutaḥajjir* or *mustaḥjir* coupled with *mun'aqid* always translate *to pepêgos*. In our extracts, *jāmid* and *mun'aqid* are equally used to translate *to pepêgos*.
[39] Lit.: when you will have shown. The Arabic uses here the second person singular. In all likelihood, this marks it as an incursion by Jābir, who is accustomed to address his reader and disciple directly when presenting his demonstrations or his experiments.
[40] Lit.: you will have (see previous note).

***stoikheia* (*ḥurūf*)[41] are reduced to these two (the dry and the moist)'**. For all the things that are opposed to the dry are subsumed under moisture and all the things opposed to the moist are subsumed under dryness, so that the moist and the damp are then subsumed under moisture and the dry and the solid under dryness. The dry that is taken as an opposite is something else, different from the dry in general, this is what we have made clear if God Almighty wills it.

21 You should know that **such is the condition of the solid and of the moist. For the moist strictly speaking is that which contains moisture of its own in its depth, <while the soaked is that which contains foreign moisture in its depth>. And the solid is that which is deprived <of such moisture>; so that, of these two, the solid derives from dryness and the latter (the soaked) from moisture.** (*GC* 2.2, 330a20-4)

22 Since we have presented the explanation of what Aristotle said on this topic and finished with it, we say that **the moist strictly speaking is that which contains moisture of its own in its depth**, for we call that which is soaked moist. However, it is manifest that the soaked is other than the moist, for we say that **the soaked is that which is reached by foreign moisture in its depth,**

[41] *Ḥarf* can sometimes designate 'a mode' or 'a way', cf. W. Lane (1893), 550. The choice of this word might not be innocent in the context of the *Book of Morphology*, and could reflect a Jābirian incursion, but it looks more likely to be a literal translation of *to stoikheion* ('element'). It is worth mentioning that *to stoikheion* at first meant what is arranged in series, and then went on to designate the letters of the alphabet, as, however, constituting elements of the syllable and the word. The comparison between the principles of physics and the letters of the alphabet seems to have been first introduced by the atomists, and Plato uses the term with this meaning, though always recalling its metaphorical character. See Alexander *in Metaph.* 1014a26, 354,30-355,1, trans. W.E. Dooley (1989), 24, where he examines the comparison between the elements and the syllables regarding the definition of the element as specifically indivisible. He concludes that the syllable is not an element of a word because the simple bodies are not divisible into parts of different kinds, whereas the syllable is divisible into letters of different kinds. That is, a particle of water is water, whereas a part of a syllable is not a syllable, the latter being a group of individual letters. The letter is thus the equivalent of an element, though it is not quantitatively divisible, unlike the element. It is Aristotle who first used the word *stoikheion* to designate the physical elements (for the occurrences of this term in *GC* as referring to the four primary bodies, fire, air, water and earth, see the index of the edition by H.H. Joachim (1922), 278-96) by completely isolating the term from its concrete origin (see C.H. Kahn (1960), 120). However, what Aristotle properly calls *stoikheion*, is the simplest, most primitive immanent constituent of a thing (see *Metaph.* 5.3, 1014a31-5; *GC* 2.1, 329a5; 2.8, 334b31 ff.; *PA* 646a12-17; *Cael.* 3.3, 302a15-19) i.e. matter, form, privation (see especially H.H. Joachim (1922), 137). More systematically, this definition is also more fundamental than that which designates the elements as parts of the universe (see *Cael.* 3.1, 298a29-32). Earth, water, air and fire are in fact made up of the primary contrarieties which further deserve the appellation *stoikheion*, being simpler and more primitive than the elements which derive from their combinations. Concerning the history of the word *stoikheion*, cf. H. Diels (1899), 58 ff. and more recently, W. Burkert (1959), 167-97. Dr Stephen Menn kindly provided me with this last reference.

while the moist is that which contains its own moisture in its depth.[42] It is then manifest that the solid is contrary to the [soaked] for this is what is deprived of such moisture. From this [sort of moisture] it became evident that the moist which is in this state is the opposite <...> – in the sense in which we took the moist and in the sense in which we took the dry – but in order to demonstrate through the [soaked], the damp and the moist, proving true that each of the present kinds is <such> as he has defined it, for the soaked is different from the damp: **'the damp is that which has foreign moisture on its surface, while the soaked is that which has foreign moisture in its depth'.**[43] Furthermore, the soaked is different from the moist because **'the moist contains moisture of its own in its depth while the soaked contains foreign moisture in its depth'.**[44] They have in common the fact that their moisture <is internal>. The soaked is, <as> we already said, [subsumed] under the moist. You should know that, by aiming at its content, you will reach your benefit, if God, Almighty wills it.[45]

23 Aristotle said: manifestly then all the other *stoikheia* (*al-aḥruf*)[46] can be reduced to the four kinds. (*GC* 2.2, 330a24-5)

24 You should know that the matter is as **Alexander said**: one must enquire why roughness and smoothness are subsumed under dryness and moisture. In answer to that, we say that roughness derives from dryness, for what is rough is solid while the smooth derives from moist, for the smooth is something fluid and liquid. Or, it would be better and more appropriate [to say] that neither of these qualities are active or passive, just like heaviness and lightness are not that either. Manifestly, then, all the other remaining genera and tangible differences that [Aristotle] names contrarieties are reduced to the first four that we have previously described, namely: heat, coldness, dryness and moisture.[47]

25 'That all the other remaining [contrarieties] are reduced to these' is manifest. But **'that these cannot further be reduced to a smaller number'**,[48] is the same as saying that A is not said in any way of either B, H or D and the same applies to each one of them. Aristotle has dealt with this subject exhaustively in *On Generation and Corruption* and he excelled in it. He wanted

[42] cf. *GC* 2.2, 330a21-2.
[43] cf. *GC* 2.2, 330a16.
[44] cf. *GC* 2.2, 330a21-2. For the whole paragraph (§22) cf. Philoponus *in GC* 222,33–223,22 who attributes this argument to Alexander of Aphrodisias: 'He brings in "sodden" according to Alexander, in order to clarify "moist" and "wet" in terms of what differentiates them from it, to lend credence to the view that each of them is such as he has defined it; for as I said, what is sodden differs from what is moist in having alien wetness in its depths whilst the latter has it on its surface, and from what is wet in the specific sense by having alien <wetness>, whilst the latter has its own wetness in its depth'.
[45] This injunction to the reader is typical of the style of Jābir. We find similar examples in all of the treatises of the Corpus.
[46] See above, n. 41.
[47] Concerning §24, see above, Introduction p.19 ff.
[48] cf. *GC* 2.2, 330a24-5.

[to say] thereby, [as] I already said, that it is impossible that these four simples (*hādhihi al-arba'a al-basā'iṭ*) be three or two and become fewer, or increase in number up to five or six or even more. This is a true statement that does not contain any defect. We did not bring it up here because I have dealt with it in previous books.[49]

26 Then Aristotle resumed saying: **likewise with the solid and the moist.** (*GC* 2.2, 330a20)

27 For the moist is what is soaked, as we have previously shown.[50] Thus, he said last what we have said first. You must know <this> and relate one part of reasoning with the other. You should know that only the excellent philosopher can explain my present book, because it is the most difficult and the richest in science, and we related <it> to difficult and long sciences. Its benefit lies in this.[51]

28 Furthermore, he said that fire is an excess of heat. (*GC* 2.3, 330b25-6)

29 By 'fire' he means the fire that is like form. As for the fire which is the matter and in which way [it is], he said that **'fire is nothing but the excess of heat'**, for the reason that air is hot, because what is essentially (*'alā al-qaṣd al-awwal*)[52] and properly hot is fire,[53] for **'fire is the boiling of heat and dryness'**.[54]

[49] §25 is all the work of Jābir, as is shown by his calling the primary qualities *basā'iṭ*, and by alluding to the letters which generally configure the terms of the syllogism. We are in the presence of four terms absolutely independent from each other, which cannot be linked in any relation of subordination.

[50] This paragraph should logically and chronologically follow §22 in order to have its full meaning. Jābir probably purposefully displaced it, according to the principle of the dispersion of science (*tabdīd al-'ilm*), as seems to be indicated in the rest of his words. This trick of composition pertains to an esoteric principle aiming at obscuring the meaning or, at least, making it difficult to understand, in order to discourage charlatans. In its most common form, it consists in disseminating the teaching in many different books, which explains why the treatises of Jābir have the appearance of a patchwork, where many themes with no real link are placed side by side. However, for the first time, we find in the *Book of Morphology* this principle applied within a single treatise, certain parts of which seem to have been deliberately interchanged, with the reader having to bring the puzzle together. Thus the exegesis of Alexander has been 'severed' in some places and redistributed in an incoherent manner. In the present passage, this is clearly signalled by the author of the treatise. §§36-45 below also suffered the same consequences. P. Kraus described and analysed the application of this principle in the Jābirian corpus, and furthermore traced its history to Antiquity and the Middle Ages, see P. Kraus (1943), xxvii-xxxiii.

[51] Here ends the commentary of chapter 2 on the second book of *GC*. Chapter 3 begins as abruptly as chapter 2, half of it being also severed, which suggests that Jābir has selected only certain sections from the commentary of Alexander in light of own interests.

[52] *'Alā al-qaṣd al-awwal*, which literally means 'according to the first intention', found only once in our extracts, is a somewhat frequent expression in some of Alexander's treatises which unfortunately exist only in Arabic. For example, see the Arabic version of Alexander's *De Providentia* (D 18), edited and translated in German by H.J. Ruland (1976), 59,2.7; 63,7.11; 65,5; 67,7. See also the edition and French translation of P.

Thillet (1980); the *Treatise of Alexander of Aphrodisias: on the principle of the Universe according to the opinion of Aristotle the philosopher* ([D 1] edited in A. Badawī (1947), 253-77 at 256,15; translated in A. Badawī (1987), 121-39); and especially the *Treatise of Alexander of Aphrodisias answering Galen's attack on Aristotle's view that every mobile cannot move except by a mover* ([D 28] edited and translated by N. Rescher and M.E. Marmura (1965), 76,17; 82,17; 86,6.7; 105,9-11.14; 107,4 etc.). There, it especially has an adverbial meaning signifying 'firstly', or 'mainly'. S. Pines notes that the expression *'alā al-qaṣd al-awwal* occurs three times in the Arabic version of Aristotle, *Topics* where it translates the Greek *prôton* (cf. S. Pines (1986d) and *Top.* 5.8, 138b13-15; Badawī (1948), vol. 2, 621,4-7). The author indicates that in the Latin version of Ibn Rushd, Great Commentary on Aristotle, *De Anima*, attributed to Michael Scot, where Aristotle's text is cited *in extenso*, the expression *prima intentione* translates in one passage the Greek *prôtôs* ('firstly'), while in another *kuriôs* ('properly'): see *Averrois Cordubensis Commentarium Magnum in Aristotelis De anima libros*, ed. F. Stuart Crawford (1953), 38 and 138 and *DA* 1.2, 405a5 ff. and 412b9. However, *'alā al-qaṣd al-awwal* renders in numerous cases *proêgoumenôs* ('primarily'), thus opposing *kata sumbebêkos* ('accidentally'). P. Merlan (1963), 71 n. 2, was the first to put forward this hypothesis; for the meaning of the verb *proêgeomai* and the adverb *proêgoumenôs*, see R.W. Sharples (1975), 37-64, at 49, quoted by Thillet, and including references concerning the occurrence of the opposition between *proêgoumenôs* and *kata sumbebêkos* in the works of the commentators. *Proêgoumenôs*, is, in fact, very frequently used in the *Quaestiones* of Alexander of Aphrodisias concerning providence (cf. *Quaest.* 2.21, 65,22.31; 66,5; 68,14, also 3.4, 87,9-10 (Alexander distinguishes here between *ta proêgoumena* and *ta deutera*, 'the primary' and 'the secondary'), 12-13.17; 3.7, 92,11, and 3.14, 109,1.28.33). Hence, whatever happens *'alā al-qaṣd al-awwal* is precisely what is required by divine providence, i.e. the movement of the spheres, whereas what is *'alā al-qaṣd al-thānī* ('according to second intention') without being purely accidental, is a derivative effect, a consequence of the main action, i.e. the cycle of generation and corruption which is generated by the movement of the spheres. In the *Treatise of Alexander of Aphrodisias answering Galen's attack on Aristotle's view that every mobile cannot move except by a mover*, *'alā al-qaṣd al-awwal* is synonymous with *bi-dhātihi* ('essentially') to which it is constantly associated, and is opposed to *bi-ṭarīq al-'arḍ*, things changing by accident (*kata sumbebêkos*) versus things changing by themselves (*kath' auta*) (see N. Rescher and M.E. Marmura (1965), 76,17; 82,17; 86,6.7; 104,14; 105,8-9.11; 106,12; 107,4.6-7.11; 108,18-19; 109,6 etc. See also *Phys.* 8.4, 254b7 ff.). It is worth noting that *proêgoumenôs* can also be used in the same meaning as *prôtôs*, and thus translated by the Arabic *awwalan* (K. Gyekye (1971), 32-3, points out that the expression *'alā al-qaṣd al-awwal* is used in the Arabic translation of Porphyry's *Isagoge*, where it translates literally the Greek *proêgoumenôs*, (ed. A. Busse (1887), 17,9) which Boethius translated by *principaliter*. In noting that in other paragraphs of the *Isagoge*, the Greek word is translated by *awwalan*, Gyekye recalls that the Greek *proêgeomai* means 'to move forward and indicate the way, to precede'). In our extracts, the expression *'alā al-qaṣd al-awwal* rather translates *kuriôs*, especially given that it is associated with the adverb *khāṣṣatan* (*wa dhālika anna alladhī huwa ḥārrun 'alā al-qaṣdi al-awwali khāṣṣatan huwa nārun*). It thus has the meaning, in our context, of 'properly' or by essence, as opposed to *kata sumbebêkos* ('accidentally').

[53] cf. Alexander *in Metaph.* 20,14-15, trans. W.E. Dooley (1989), 42.

[54] cf. *GC* 2.3, 330b29. This paragraph cannot be understood except in light of the first part of the chapter which was omitted by Jābir, where Aristotle establishes a distinction between the perceptible primary bodies, fire, air, earth, and water, the 'so-called

30 Furthermore, he said that ice and snow[55] come from excess and prolongation[56] of cold. (*GC* 2.3, 330b25)

31 By analogy, **'freezing and boiling will be excesses',**[57] just as he himself said that: **'fire is an excess of heat, just as ice is an excess of cold'.**[58]

He spoke further, by way of explaining what Plato had said <in order to> explain what Socrates had said, these words having been transmitted orally in former times. Know this.[59]

elements' (*ta kaloumena stoikheia*) which appear as such (look like real elements), but which are in fact 'not simple but mixed', and the real elements which are the simple forms of the primary elements (330b21-5). The elementary fire is not real fire, but it resembles it as having the 'form of fire' (*puroeidês*), because it is reduced to the couple of qualities which constitutes it, i.e. heat and dryness, whereas the perceptible fire which burns is already something composed out of matter and form. For an analysis of this paragraph, see above, Introduction, p. 45 ff., and *Quaestio* 2.17 which identifies the elementary fire with the *hupekkauma*.

[55] Straightaway, we think of an addition of Jābir's or even of that of a zealous copyist. It is however worth noting that we can find the same usage in Abū al-Barakāt al-Baghdādī, *K. al-Mu'tabar*. In the latter's commentary on Aristotle's *Physics* (*al-juz' al-thānī min al-'ulūm al-ṭabī'iyya, al-faṣl al-thāmin*), he opposes snow and not freezing (*al-jumūd*) to terrestrial fire, for example, see 151,5, *ka-al-ḥarārati fī al-nāri wa al-burūdati fī al-thalji wa humā ḍiddān fī al-ḥarri wa al-bardi al-ṭabī'iyyayni* (like heat in fire and coldness in snow, these [sc. fire and snow] being contraries in respect of natural heat and cold). Abū al-Barakāt considered snow to be a fifth element: *wa qad qīla anna hādhihi al-'anāṣira al-arba'a hiya al-arḍu wa al-mā'u wa al-hawā'u wa al-nāru. Fa-al-arḍu akthafuhā, wa yalīhā al-mā'u. Wa al-nāru alṭafuhā wa yalīha al-hawā'u. Wa narā khāmisan huwa al-thalju, fa-innahu fī al-kathāfati bayna al-arḍi wa al-mā'i* (It was said that these four elements are earth, water, air and fire. Earth is the densest and water follows it. Fire is the rarest and air follows it. However, we observe a fifth [element], namely snow, which is between earth and water in terms of density) (148,14-16). Having said that, the addition of *al-thalju* (snow) in our lemma could simply be the result of a double translation (see above, n. 28).

[56] The Arabic grammatical form is incorrect, because the coordination of two genitives determined by a particle (*ḥarf jarr*) entails the repetition of the particle. Hence, we can suggest that *imtidād* (prolongation) is an addition. But if so, that leaves open whether it was added by the translator or by Jābir himself.

[57] cf. *GC* 2.3, 330b27.

[58] cf. *GC* 2.3, 330b25-6.

[59] The meaning of this sentence is obscure, and its function in this context is not clear either. Plato is mentioned in the first part of the third chapter of *GC*, Aristotle having touched very briefly on a Platonic theory, whose uncertain character caught the attention of the commentators. Cf. Philoponus, in *GC*, 226,16-30, who quotes Alexander on this subject. However, it is tempting to believe it is an addition by Jābir himself. It was a common practice for the alchemists in general, and for Jābir in particular, to cite the authority of the Ancients, thus placing themselves in an uninterrupted tradition of transmission of knowledge. Jābir considers Socrates as 'the father and the master of all philosophers' and sees him as the model of alchemists. Moreover, it is worth noting that the Arabic tradition ascribed to Plato alchemical works (Ibn al-Nadīm mentions his name in the list of the alchemists); see P. Kraus (1986), 48 ff.; R. Walzer, 'Aflaṭūn' in H.A.R. Gibb (1960-), vol. 1, 234-6, at 235; G.C. Anawati (1997), 113.

32 They said that **boiling and freezing are excesses, the one being an excess of heat and the other an excess of cold. If, therefore, ice is the freezing of what is moist and cold, so fire will be the boiling of the hot which is dry.** (*GC* 2.3,330b26-9)

33 The explanation of this is that fire is the boiling of the hot which is dry.[60] The same is true about ice, because ice is the opposite of fire, since the difference between the two of them is extreme, for ice comes from an excess of coldness and fire from an excess of heat. So if ice is the contrary of fire, it will be the freezing of <something> cold that is moist, while fire will be the boiling of [something] hot that is dry; because freezing and boiling are the excess of things and their attainment the excess and the extreme limit. They are present in [the things], in their contrarieties into one another: hot to cold and moist to dry.

34 Then he said: **that is why nothing is generated either out of ice or out of fire.** (*GC* 2.3, 330b29-30)

35 For the proof for that was established on the ground of those two [fire and ice] being excesses: fire being the excess of heat and ice the excess of coldness. He said that **'nothing is generated out of these two'**, because nothing is generated out of that whose state of heat is such, nor is anything generated out of that which is cold like this. For, he only names 'fire' that which is properly called fire. He also names it 'domestic [fire]',[61] because such is its condition. As for <the fire> which is the element, it is not like this, for it is neither like boiling nor like excess. This is the reason why it is very generative and fruitful (*muwallida wa muthmira*).[62]

36 He said:[63] **simple bodies being four in number, every two[64] of them belong to each of the first two.**[65] (*GC* 2.3, 330b30-2)

[60] I suggest excluding 'fire is the boiling of the hot which is dry', as a repetition by homoioteleuton with the preceding lemma in §32, to yield: 'The explanation of this is that the same is true about ice…'

[61] cf. Philoponus, in *GC*, 228,28, *pur entautha phêsi to diakonikon* of which *allatī li-l-khidma* is the exact translation.

[62] cf. Ibn Rushd's Short Commentary on *GC*, ed. J. al-'Alawī (1994), *Talkhīs al-kawn wa al-fasād*, 97,22-98,2, *wa al-Iskandaru yaqūlu: inna hādha innamā yūjadu li-al-nāri allatī hāhunā, wa amma al-nāru allatī fī nihāyati al-muḥīṭi fa-laysat tilka fī ghāyati al-ḥarārati wa al-ghalayāni, wa li-dhālika kānat al-nāru akthara al-ustuqussāti sababan li-al-tawlīdi*, trans. S. Kurland (1958), 76,38-77,2.

[63] The part of the text which concerns §§35-44 does not figure in this particular order in any of the three manuscripts of the *Book of Morphology*. I have restored, in what follows, what I believe to have been the original order of the exegesis of Alexander. This order is disturbed in the text as it has come down to us. Quite possibly the arguments were switched intentionally, making it difficult to understand the text; see above, n. 50.

[64] The partitive *ithnayni ithnayni* should translate the Greek *hekatera* (H.H. Joachim (1922), 42, 218). However, this reading is not shared by all the editions of *GC*, some of them preferring *hekateron*; see above, Introduction, p. 26. Cf. Philoponus *in GC* 229,12-14 who bears out this reading: *hekatera gar toin duoin, toutesti tôn duadôn tôn duo hekatera hekaterou tôn topôn, hê men tou anô hê de tou katô; hekatera gar eipen oudeterôs, hoionei ta hekatera tôn duo* (for 'each of the two pairs', i.e. of the two pairs

37 For the relation they have with places is divided, and in accordance with this they are heavy or light, the [natural] places being two, namely the upper [place] which is adjacent to the extreme body and the lower, which is adjacent to the one in the middle. Among the elements, two correspond (*munāsiba*) to the upper place, namely fire and air, and the last two correspond to the lower, namely water and earth. Therefore, the first two are light and the latter two heavy.

38 By saying **'belong to each of those first two'** he means that the upper elements, just like the lower elements, are connected with two extreme places, those to the upper [place] and these to the lower. For the two extreme places and the first two are one and the same thing: namely the upper and the lower.[66]

39 Furthermore he said that **fire and air rise up towards the end and the boundary whereas earth and water are carried along towards the centre.** (*GC* 2.3, 330b32-3)

40 He means that fire and air belong to the light body and are subsumed under it. It is this body that is carried along towards the boundary, so that it is named the end and the uttermost limit, and it surrounds the world (*al-'ālam*).[67] The world and water belong to the body that becomes (*yaṣīru*) the centre,[68] which means that they belong to the heavy body. It is therefore possible, that by saying **'of those first two'**, he did not mean the extreme places, but he meant

one each, belongs to each of the places, the one to the upper, the other to the lower; for he says 'each' in the neuter <plural>, as if he had said 'one or other of the two pairs'; trans. W.E. Dooley (1989)).

[65] Regarding the reading *prôtôn*, translated here by *al-ithnayni al-awwalayni* (the first two), instead of *topon* ('place'), which all of the modern editions of *GC* have adopted, it is worth noting that it corresponds to the oldest of manuscripts which we have of *GC* (E = MS Parisiensis Regius 1853 [tenth century] and J = MS Vindobonensis, phil. Graec. 100 [first part of the tenth century]). See above, Introduction, p. 26.

[66] Concerning this paragraph, cf. *Cael.* 4.4, 312a3 ff. §37 constitutes the first solution proposed by Alexander. This is the simplest solution, which is to hold that the expression 'the first two' refers to the two extreme places.

[67] The occurrence of the term *'ālam* ('world') in this context is very curious indeed, since it could suggest that fire surrounds the entire cosmos, rather than just the sublunar world. However, we should note that *'ālam* is used in Islamic philosophic texts with the meaning 'sphere of existence', likely referring, in this context, to the terrestrial sphere. See P. Kraus (1986), 149, who surveys its usage by Arabic translators, often to render *pân, holotês*. Nevertheless, even in this case, *'ālam* is not used alone, but always coupled with a qualifier. For Avicenna's use of this term, see M.A. Goichon (1949), 248. It is worth noting that in the cosmology of the *Book of Morphology* the universe is represented in concentric circles, which Jābir calls worlds. In any case the following sentence makes it clear that here, 'world' means the sphere of earth, because '*'ālam wa-mā*'' must mean 'earth and water'.

[68] For the identification of the centre of the earth with that of the universe, cf. *Cael.* 4.4, 296b9-21.

the heavy and the light in so far as he assimilates them (*yushabbihuhā*) as two kinds.[69]

41 Then he said: **however, since [the elements] are four, each one consists without qualification of one thing: earth of dryness rather than cold, water of cold rather than moisture, air of moisture rather than heat and fire of heat rather than dryness.** (*GC* 2.3, 331a3-6)

42 Though <this> is manifest, it has nonetheless a wondrous sense. Since the differences through which the form of the body is affected by a nature (*yanṭabi'u*)[70] are four, namely heat, coldness, moisture and dryness – this is the reason why the primary bodies are only four – some of these differences occur in reality, because of the large quantity [in which they happen to be] in all the elements.

Someone might raise a difficulty about water and air: for what reason does water gets its form properly from coldness and air properly from moisture?[71] We say: it is necessary that it be so, I mean that each of the [elements] gets its form according to that by which it dominates what shares with it one and the same power (*quwwa*).[72] Air and fire have heat in common, by which fire dominates air, because the dry is linked to the fact that fire is hotter than air. Air and water have moisture in common, by which air dominates water, for air is easier to configure and enclose than water, which is the proper [characteristic] of the moist;[73] this is the reason why air is <more> moist than it is hot. Moreover, the water whose moisture is dominated by the moisture of air, dominates earth by its coldness. That is the reason why coldness is more

[69] The second solution proposed by Alexander. See P. Moraux (1979), 99: 'Il est bien dans la manière d'Alexandre de proposer successivement deux ou plusieurs interprétations différentes d'un passage, d'une phrase ou d'une tournure particulièrement difficiles, en les introduisant par *ê … ê*'. He states (102) that Alexander does not hesitate to give several successive different, yet equally plausible, interpretations of the same passage.

[70] Concerning the expression *tanṭabi'u ṣūratu al-jismi*, and its closeness with the Greek *eidopoieisthai* ('to bestow form') frequently used by Alexander, especially in his commentary in *Meteor*. 4, see above, Introduction, 67-70 and n. 277.

[71] Philoponus raises the same problem concerning the qualification of water by coldness rather than by moisture, while experience teaches us that it is water, more than air, which moisturises things. He relates this characteristic to Aristotle's definition of the moist as something which is not easily defined by its own limits, and this definition obviously suits air more than water, *in GC* 230,22 ff.

[72] Notice the change in terminology. Since it is a matter of power relations between the constitutive qualities of elements, Alexander calls the qualities *dunameis* ('potencies') here, and not contrarieties or differences.

[73] We find an argument of the same kind in the *Quaestio* 1.6 (14,1-15,22, trans. R.W. Sharples (1992), 37-40), which also questions the qualification of water by coldness rather than by moisture; the difficulty raised there is similar but not identical to the one raised here: 'for water is denser, and for that reason it fills things up, while the fluidity of air is fine' (14,21-2, trans. Sharples).

prevalent in water. Therefore, it is necessary that the form of what dominates by coldness occurs in this way. That is manifest in what he said.

43 Then they all said: **since we have said previously**[74] **that simple bodies are generated out of one another – not only do we observe this with our own eyes, but we sense that they must be generated, <for otherwise> there would have been no alteration,**[75] **for alteration exists only in respect of tangible affection – we should then explain in which way they change into one another, and explain the possibility of the claim made about these things: whether they can be generated or not.** (*GC* 2.4, 331a6-12)

44 For having shown out of which thing each of these bodies consist strictly speaking, he <started showing how each> inclines towards being connected with the other, or the manner of their change and their generation out of one another, since their generation is only out of one another. Aristotle has explained this in the book *On the Heavens*, and saying **'since we have said previously'**,[76] he reminds us of the demonstration he has presented there. He said: **'this is manifest to sensation, for otherwise there would have been no alteration'**.[77] This is manifest owing to the fact that he calls the reciprocal change of the primary bodies in respect of form, 'alteration'. This is evident from what he said: **'because alteration is only in respect of tangible affection'**.[78] For what is generated in respect of [tangible affection] is generated through alteration, because alteration is, strictly speaking, only alteration and is not, in respect of [tangible affection], generation.

He also said that **'he has defined in what has been previously said, that generation of simple bodies is into one another'**,[79] for he said that in the treatise *On Generation and Corruption*, in the passage where he replied to Empedocles.[80] Moreover, he has made clear this idea in the treatise *On the Heavens*,[81] as we said. This is evident through sensation, because if [simple bodies] did not change into one another, there would have been no alteration, while we observe that [a body], which is at times <hot, is at times> cold and vice versa. The same applies to the rest of the <bodies>.

As for the formulation it is as follows, for he says that: **'the generation of simple bodies is into one another'**, **'nevertheless we observe through sensation that <simple bodies> are generated'** is inserted in the middle and followed by the words: **'moreover, we also observe through sensation that**

[74] See *Cael.* 3.6, 304b23 ff. and *GC* 2.1, 329a35 ff. See H.H. Joachim (1922), 220 who believes that Aristotle refers here only to the *Cael.* The rest of our commentary however shows that Alexander also turns to the *GC*.

[75] For the distinction between alteration and generation, see Introduction, p. 59 ff.

[76] cf. *GC* 2.4, 331a6.

[77] cf. *GC* 2.3, 331a8-9.

[78] cf. *GC* 2.3, 331a9-10.

[79] cf. *GC* 2.3, 331a7-8.

[80] cf. *GC* 2.1, 329a35 ff. And, for the distinction between generation and alteration, 1.1, 314b15-26.

[81] *Cael.* 3.6, 304b23.

[simple bodies] are generated, and that it is evident that bodies change and alter in respect of a tangible difference'.[82]

Not only do we observe that [bodies] change only in respect of tangible differences, but we say so because through these differences, [bodies] change in a manner that is known through sensation. These are their forms affected by a nature (*munṭabi'a*), and we observe that these forms belong to them for the sake of their change into one another, so that simple bodies may be generated into one another, otherwise there would be no alteration. Moreover, we observe that simple bodies are generated. For alteration is their change into one another.

45 All of what he said, – the discourse having been put in this order of priority and posteriority – has been said.[83]

46 The statement: **'for alteration is in respect of tangible affection',**[84] follows both of the [other] statements on the same [topic]. We make use of [this statement] in saying: **'we observe through sensation too that [simple bodies] are generated'.** This implies that he explains how [simple bodies] are generated out of one another, and whether all of them change into one another and with respect to one another or whether some of them do not change, as Plato thought, although he had at first admitted that all [simple bodies] are generated out of their change into one another.[85] Like for example the alphabet (*al-mu'jam*) which, according to the grammarians, does not change, except the *wāw*, the *yā'* and the weak letters (*dhawāt al-'ilal*).[86]

47 Aristotle said in his book *On Generation*: **that all of them change evidently into one another, is manifest. For generation takes place into**

[82] P. Moraux (1979), 136, notes that Alexander is willing to emend the text he is commenting on when he is displeased with its structure.

[83] This sentence indicates the end of the passage which was intentionally deconstructed, and whose parts were interchanged. It signals the reader who tries to reconstruct the text that he has been successful. See above, n. 50.

[84] The Arabic text has *bi-tadbīr*, instead of *bi-ta'thīr*, which is probably due to a copyist's mistake.

[85] cf. *Timaeus*, 49C-D, where Plato describes the transformation of all the elements into each other in a circle. This is then revised at 54B-D, where Timaeus explains that 'it appeared as though all the four kinds could pass through one another into one another; but this appearance is delusive' (54B, trans. F.M. Cornford), because earth cannot be transformed into any of the other three elements, since the square surface of the cube with which it is associated is composed of a different type of triangle, the isosceles triangle with angles of 45, 45, and 90 degrees. The remaining three elements can be transformed into each other, because their surfaces are made of equilateral triangles, and these are all formed from identical scalene right triangles with angles of 30, 60, and 90 degrees. Cf. L. Brisson (1992), 248, n. 347, and F.M. Cornford (1937), 215 f. Thanks to Dr Stephen Menn for providing me with the mathematical data of this note.

[86] It is evident that this sentence is an addition of the author of the *Book of Morphology*. The three letters of the Arabic alphabet called *ḥurūf al-'illa* or *al-ḥurūf al-mu'talla* (the 'weak' letters) are the three long vowels *alif, wāw* and *yā'*. The three of them are *sākina* (unvowelled). When vocalised they change into another letter, as for instance a *hamza*. For the details of the grammatical point made here, cf. H. Fleish, 'Ḥurūf al-Hijā'', in H.A.R. Gibb (1960-), vol. 3, 617-20.

[one] contrary and out of [the other] contrary, and all the elements have a contrariety to one another, because their differences are contrary [to one another]. For in some of them both differences are contrary, such as in fire <and water>: for fire is hot and dry and water is cold and moist. In others only one of the two differences is contrary to the other, such as in air and water: for air is hot and moist and water is cold and moist. It is then manifest that all are by nature generated <out of> all. (*GC* 2.4, 331a12-21)

48 The demonstration is as follows: he said that **'contraries are generated out of one another'**, for contraries change into one another, as I have explained in the foregoing of the book *On Generation*, for not just anything can change into anything no matter what it is. But, all the elements in relation to each other, are contraries. Therefore, all the elements are generated out of one another and change into one another. He has explained that the elements are contraries <from> the fact that the differences through which they exist, are contraries, and it is through these differences that the elements change and are generated.[87]

49 Then he said: **it is not difficult to see how this happens for each of the elements [taken individually].** (*GC* 2.4, 331a21)

50 He moved on to the second [part] of the enquiry and started explaining the manner of their generation out of one another.[88] We say that the elements have differences which are their counterpart in relation to each other (*fuṣūl hiya ghāyātuhā baʿḍuhā ʿinda baʿḍ*),[89] because the elements have [some] differences which are held in common and shared with one another, and some that are contrary. In explaining [this], he said that **'it is manifest how the elements change into one another, from those among them that <change> easily and [whose changing] is not hard or difficult'**. This is how [Aristotle] establishes the easy way of changing.

51 Then he said: **for all may be generated out of all, but there will be a difference between them owing to the fact that some are generated more quickly and some more slowly, some more easily and some with greater difficulty. For the change will be quicker for those which have something in common with one another, and slower for those that don't, because the change of one thing [sc. one quality] is easier than the change of many. For example: air will be generated out of fire by the change of one thing, for fire is hot and dry and air is hot and moist, so that when moisture dominates dryness, air is generated. Again, air will become water when**

[87] cf. Philoponus *in GC* 232,24-31, whose exegesis is completely identical to that of Alexander.

[88] cf. Philoponus *in GC* 233,2-5.

[89] *Fuṣūlun hiya ghāyatuhā baʿḍuhā ʿinda baʿḍin* paraphrases the Greek *sumbola* which Aristotle uses for the first time in *GC*, 2.4, 331a24. The sense of the term *sumbola* in this passage comes from its meaning as the 'halves of a bone or coin, which two persons broke between them, each keeping one piece' (Liddell-Scott). See H.H. Joachim (1922), 220-1. Aristotle uses this term to designate the common quality of the two consecutive elements: thus, the heat in fire and air. Normally the word *ghāya* means 'limit' or 'end', with a sense close to the Greek *telos* (see W. Lane (1893), 2312).

coldness dominates heat, for air is hot and moist and water is cold and moist, so that water will be generated when the heat changes. In the same way, earth will be generated out of water and fire out of earth, for both [members] of each pair have something in common,[90] **for water is cold and moist and earth is cold and dry, so that when moisture is dominated, earth is generated. Again, since earth is cold and dry and fire is hot and dry, then if coldness were to perish, fire will be generated out of earth. It is then evident that generation of simple bodies is cyclical; and this way of changing is very easy, because the elements which are consecutive have something in common.**[91] (*GC* 2.4, 331a22-331b4)

52 As for the first way <in which> the elements change, it is the one by which the elements change one after the other, [each] keeping for itself only one of the differences belonging to it. As for the second way of changing, where they are consecutive, it is evident, and I have made it evident with this statement.[92]

53 Then he said: **that water be generated out of fire, and earth out of air, and again that air and fire be generated out of water and earth, is possible though difficult and hard, because the change takes place through more than one thing [sc. quality]. For when fire is generated out of water, both moisture and coldness must necessarily perish. And again, when air is generated out of earth, then necessarily coldness and dryness must perish too. Therefore, when air and fire are generated out of earth and water, then necessarily both [differences] must perish, so that this generation takes longer.** (*GC* 2.4, 331b4-11)

54 Consider the subtleties that you now have at your disposal, contemplate them with the eye of pure intellect, take foolishness away from me and <...>.[93] This is the second of the two ways of the elements changing into one another.[94]

55 As for the third way of the elements changing into one another, he shows what it is about in the next statement. [Here] is the beginning of this statement: **‘if any one of the two [differences] belonging to each of the two [elements]**

[90] The Arabic *wa dhālika anna kilayhimā lahumā ‘inda kilayhimā mushāraka* is the literal translation of the Greek: *ekhei gar amphô pros amphô sumbola* (331a24). My translation somewhat distorts the Arabic to avoid awkwardness, because *mushāraka* is used here in an absolute way as a *maṣdar* (verbal noun) and would thus be more accurately translated as ‘community’ or ‘participation’.

[91] 331b4, *dia to sumbola enuparkhein tois ephexês*. For ‘cyclical’ as opposed to ‘rectilinear’ elemental transformation, see H.H. Joachim (1922), 227-9, who states that to be ‘cyclical’, the transformation of the elements cannot stop at one element, and none of the elements can be a principle for the rest. Otherwise the transformation would be ‘rectilinear’, since it would have to start from one of the elements and proceed in a straight line upwards or downwards.

[92] Jābir must have summarised Alexander’s exegesis very briefly here, being concerned only to establish a transition between the two modes of elementary transformation described by Aristotle.

[93] The Arabic ends the sentence with ‘*wa isra‘ ilā al-hawā*’’ which is hardly intelligible.

[94] This paragraph is entirely due to Jābir.

were to perish'.[95] Since he had defined the change of the elements close and adjacent to each other – and had explained about them that they have something in common, and said that **'[this change] is very easy'** – <now, regarding the elements that are> far from and contraries to one another, in so far as they perish in respect of both their differences into the contrary, he said this is difficult and hard because the change takes place not out of a single thing. Thus, this change [the third way] is more difficult and harder than the first one which is when the elements have [something] in common in relation to one another, and it is easier than the second, because the change takes place for two elements into one only.

As for the first two changes, they are those of two elements <...> one, to which does not belong the change that belongs to the elements that are consecutive, <...> or in respect of two differences in those that are consecutive.[96]

56 As for the change he is explaining now, it is that of the generation of two elements <into> one, in so far as each of the two differs from the other in respect of only one difference and keeps the other difference that belongs to it. This way, earth will be generated out of water and fire, I mean out of both at the same time, when they change, fire with respect to heat and water with respect to moisture. For in addition to these two, remain coldness and dryness: from fire dryness and from water coldness, and they both <constitute> the form of the earth. And if these two [fire and water] would change in respect of their two other differences, so that the heat of fire and the cold of water be resolved (*inḥallat*), air would be generated out of these two. Likewise, out of air and earth will be generated water and fire, in so far as each of the two [air and fire] changes in respect of each of its differences. This is the third way of changing, which I made clear in this statement.[97]

57 Aristotle said: **if one of the two [differences] of each of the two [elements] were to perish, their change will be easier but not reciprocal; but out of water and fire, air and earth will be generated, and out of air and earth, fire and water will be generated. For when the coldness of water and the dryness of fire perish, air is generated because the heat of fire and the moisture of water remain. When the heat of fire and the moisture of water perish, earth is generated, owing to the fact that the dryness of fire and the coldness of water remain. Therefore, out of air and earth, water and fire are generated. For when the heat of fire and the dryness of earth perish, water will be generated, for the moisture of the air and the coldness of the earth will remain.** (*GC* 2.4, 331b12-13)

58 This statement is manifest and evident, for the third way of changing has been clearly explained thereby.

[95] cf. *GC* 2.4, 331b12.
[96] This sentence is rather abstruse, the manuscript being very corrupt in this place.
[97] Concerning the entire paragraph, cf. Philoponus *in GC* 233,21-234,2.

59 We carry on with this saying: **the generation of fire is evident**[98] **to sensation, for fire is most properly flame <and flame> is smoke, and smoke is [composed] of air and earth.** (*GC* 2.4, 331b24-6)

60 We say that this sort of generation can be properly observed as belonging to fire, for fire is believed[99] to be flame in the proper sense and the flame is generated <out of> nothing but air and earth.[100] **For flame is smoke being consumed and burning *(yanfudu wa yash'ulu)*, and smoke is from the mixture of air and earth.** For smoke is an exhalation from moisture existing in those things.[101] And when these change, earth in respect of coldness and air in respect of moisture, the flame is generated, getting the dryness of earth and the heat of air.[102]

61 Someone may inquire:[103] how can he say that the change into one [element] out of two is easier than the change <into> the contrary [element], which is the change that takes place when the thing changes in respect of both its differences together, so that what is contrary to it is generated? For just as in that [change], the two differences that perish and change are two, it is the same in this change too, where two [elements] change into one, for in this sort of generation two differences change too.

To this we answer that when water becomes fire, owing to the fact that both differences in respect of which the form of the water is affected by a nature perish together, and change into their contraries <...> whereas in the change where two change into one, both differences still perish, yet the two differences which are contrary to them are not generated, {but there is desiccation (*al-*

[98] *Ma'dan* ('metal') in the Arabic text. This could be a copyist's error, the written forms of *ma'dan* and *bayyin* being similar. However, cf. *Quaestio* 2.17, where Alexander gives the example of a heated metal to illustrate the strongest intensity of the earth's fire. Likewise, here it is the fire that is manifest to sensation that is in question.

[99] *Yuẓannu bihā*. *Ẓann* is 'opinion' in the sense of *doxa*, so *ẓanna* would best be rendered 'to have an opinion' or 'to opine'; but as this is rather awkward in English I have usually translated *ẓanna* 'to believe', belief *(pistis)* being a part of the *doxa*.

[100] cf. *Meteor*. 1.4, 341b21-2 where flame is defined as 'the incandescence of a hot pneuma' and 4.9, 388a2-3, where it is described as the smoke which burns, the latter having been produced through exhalation from wood (*xulôn ... hê thumiasis kapnos*) which is a combustible made of earth and air. Concerning this topic, see M.L. Gill (1989), 78 n. 52.

[101] The definition of smoke given by Philoponus at this place provides additional precision: 'for the exhalation from moisture having something earthy mixed with it constitutes smoke' (235,25-6, trans. C.J.F. Williams (2000)). The exhalation which results from moisture produces smoke in so far as it is mixed with something terrestrial, thus dry. The definition given by Alexander here is less precise, and thus potentially in conflict with Aristotle's canonical description of smoke; cf. *Meteor*. 2.3, 359b32. Smoke is produced by the hot and dry exhalation which emanates from the earth, and constitutes a part of the air, and not by the vapor which constitutes the other part of the air. Cf. *Meteor*. 1.3, 340b24-9 for the composition of the air.

[102] Concerning this paragraph, cf. Philoponus *in GC* 235,22-8, who brings forth almost the same argument.

[103] This difficulty is also raised by Philoponus *in GC* 235,6-18.

in'iqād) and cooling (*al-tabrīd*)}[104] and in each of the two [elements] the difference, which belongs only to one of the two, remains. So when fire is generated out of air and earth, the heat of the air remains, {and this begins to cool if the coldness of earth does not perish. When the dryness of earth remains only the moisture of air perishes completely and does not cool, for earth has, as they say, more dryness than all of the other remaining elements}.

62 Then Aristotle said: **as for those [the elements] that are consecutive, no change into any of the bodies can take place when, in each of the elements, one of the two—i.e. one of the two qualities[105]—perishes. For either identical or contrary [qualities] will be left in the two [elements], and a body cannot <be generated> out of neither of these two [sc. neither from identical qualities nor from contrary qualities]: for example that the dryness of fire and the moisture of air perish, for heat will be left from both of them. But, if the heat of both perishes, the two contraries will be left, I mean moisture and dryness. So likewise with the other parts (*al-ajzā' al-ukhar*): for in all consecutive [elements] there exists one identical thing, and some contrary things.** (*GC* 2.4, 331b27-34)

63 You should know that when he talked about the third way of changing, namely that in which each of the two bodies changes in respect of each of its two differences, so that a third body is generated out of these two, and he explained <that> some bodies are generated in the same manner as earth and air are generated out of water and fire, and water and fire out of air and earth, and these [bodies] are not consecutive but separated in position (*fī al-waḍ'i*), he started explaining that generation cannot take place in this way out of bodies that are consecutive in position.

64 Some [bodies] are consecutive, such as air which is consecutive to fire and comes after it in position; and after air, water, and after water, earth. So that water and earth will not be generated out of fire and water when one of the two powers in each one of them perishes. Nor will air and fire be generated out of water and earth when the very same affection will reach these. Nor will anything be generated out of water and air in this way, because these two elements [air and water] are interchangeable. Thus, the dryness of fire will remain <but its heat will perish>, and the heat of air will perish but its moisture will remain, so that the dryness of fire will remain and the moisture of air. Since these two qualities are contraries it is impossible for them to get together. But, if the moisture of air were to perish while its heat remains, something hot and dry

[104] I tentatively suggest that the parts in between brackets in the rest of the paragraph are an incursion of Jābir's. The choice of terms is not that of purely mechanical elementary transformation, but of blending, where the qualities actually react upon each other and are affected by one another. The cooling and desiccation processes mean a real action of the coldness and the dryness on the contrary qualities, rather than the destruction of the latter.

[105] This is an addition either by Alexander himself, by the translator Abū Bishr Mattā, or even by Jābir. At any rate, this explanatory clause does not exist in the original text of Aristotle.

would be left, and this is the condition of fire. Analogically nothing will come to be, but what was generated will remain as it is. If the dryness of fire were to perish, and its heat were to remain, and if the heat of air were to remain and its moisture were to perish, then two heats would get together, out of which nothing would be generated. On the other hand, if the dryness of fire were to perish, and its heat were to remain, and if the heat of air were to perish while its moisture were to remain, something hot and moist would be left, and this is air. The same arguments hold good of water and the rest [of the elements].

65 Then he said: **'for consecutive [elements] have one identical thing and <one> that is contrary'.**[106] [Aristotle] explains here the reason why it is not possible that a certain body be generated out of consecutive [bodies], when in each of these a single power (*quwwa*) perishes. For the [elements] which are consecutive and finite [in number] have, in relation to the two differences that are prior to them, one identical difference and another contrary one. Therefore, if the two contrary differences perish, those which remain will be identical. And if the difference which is identical in the two perishes, the two remaining differences will be <contrary> and nothing will be generated out of them.[107]

66 [Aristotle] said: **it is manifest then that [the elements] that change from one into one, will be generated when one single thing perishes. As [for the elements] that change from two into one, they will be generated when more than one thing perishes.** (*GC* 2.4, 331b35-6)

67 By saying this, he does not mean that, when the change is <from> one [element] into one, [there is no generation] in actuality when one single thing perishes. But, he means that it is possible, when there is a change of one [element] into one, that only one of the two differences perishes, as in the case of the elements that have [something] in common. When elements change into one, it is necessary that perishes more than one <quality>; <so likewise> when they change into their contraries.[108]

68 Then [Aristotle said]: **that all [the elements] are generated out of all, and the way in which their change into one another takes place, has now been stated. Moreover, we have to examine them in this way.** (*GC* 2.4-5, 331b36-332a3)

69 By saying that, Aristotle started talking about things previously discussed. Those who use other methods and other arguments have also discussed these things. He first explained that none of the primary bodies is matter or principle and also [that matter] is not the intermediate body among these bodies. But, matter is something else, other than a sensible body insofar as it is not a body. Nevertheless, it is not something separated from bodies and it cannot subsist in isolation.[109] Then he explained that the elements, I mean the primary bodies, are

[106] cf. *GC* 2.4, 331b28.
[107] cf. Philoponus *in GC* 235,32-236,4, who brings forth the same argument referring it to Alexander.
[108] cf. Philoponus *in GC* 236,31-237,3.
[109] cf. *GC* 2.5, 332a33-5.

four and that their change takes place from all into all.[110] In this chapter, he explained that the change of the elements does not go on to infinity, but their change does in a circle among them.[111] As to the reason why he explained that the transformation of the elements in a straight line does not go on to infinity, but he did not explain that the elements are not more than four, we say that, given that this had already been said when he explained that, since the sensible contrarieties by which bodies are given a form and affected by a nature are four, it was impossible that there exist more than the four primary bodies.[112]

70 He furthermore said: **for matter is not one of the natural bodies, either one or two or more.** (*GC* 2.5, 332a5-6)

Alexander said: Aristotle has explained here that it is impossible that any one of the four simple bodies become matter, nor any other, or two or more according to the opinion of the *phusikoi* (*al-ṭabī'iyyūn*).[113]

71 Then Aristotle said: **nevertheless, they cannot all be one element, like for instance that they all be water or air or fire or earth, since change in general only belongs to contraries.**[114] (*GC* 2.5, 332a6-8)

72 We say that it is impossible that one of the primary bodies becomes matter for the rest.

73 Aristotle said: **there will be then a certain difference or a contrariety**[115] **of which one of the parts (*aḥad juz'ayhā*) not belonging to it [sc. air], will belong to fire: heat <for example>. Nevertheless, fire will not be hot air, because that would be an alteration, which is not observed [to happen].** (*GC* 2.5, 332a10-13)

74 With this statement, he makes clear that it is impossible that air exist before [sc. before the qualities change]. For if the element is what changes, it will remain as it was. Now, that into which it changes is the contrary of that out of which it changes, for change does not take place except into contraries. [This element] will then have a certain contrariety, of which one of the members will

[110] cf. *GC* 2.5, 332b1-30. Here Aristotle disagrees with the opinion of Plato in the *Timaeus*; see below, §82.

[111] cf. *GC* 2.5, 332b30-333a15.

[112] This introduction is exemplary: Alexander situates the text he is going to comment, articulates it with what preceded it, and briefly recapitulates the outline of the chapter by bringing out three distinct parts. He even goes so as far as to highlight, for pedagogical reasons, what might be interpreted by the reader as a lacuna, for instance the very quick recapitulation of the demonstration of the number of elements: Aristotle had already demonstrated this in 2.3, 330b1-3. See P. Moraux (1979), 53, 'Après une présentation schématisée des arguments, Alexandre passait, dans son commentaire, à l'examen de la *lexis*, pour interpréter morceau par morceau le texte même d'Aristote'.

[113] *Al-ṭabī'iyyūn* is a literal translation of *phusikoi* which traditionally designates the Presocratics. It is usually rendered (not very accurately) as 'Natural philosophers', but it seems less misleading simply to provide the Greek term in transliteration, as I do here.

[114] cf. *Phys.* 1.5, 188a36-b11; 21-6; and 1.7, 190a18-21.

[115] According to H.H. Joachim (1922), 224, *diaphora* ('difference') is 'parenthetical and explanatory'. The Arabic text reverses the order of the Greek text, which has *enantiôsis kai diaphora* ('contrariety and difference'), to facilitate comprehension.

be the generated thing towards which the change has taken place. For instance, if fire is that which is generated and has heat as one of the two members of a contrariety, since the element which is the matter is equivalent to air, it will change into fire. Moreover, if fire is not hot air, fire will be generated out of air and will keep [the nature] of air preserved within its nature. For such a change is, as we have previously said, an alteration, not a generation, for the generation of things from other things is not observed to take place in that way. That this is impossible was also made clear by what he said afterwards.

75 Then Aristotle said: **but one of the two contraries is a privation.** (*GC* 2.5, 332a23-4)

76 He explained in another passage that in all contrarieties, one of the two contraries is the one (*al-maqūl 'alayhi*) called privation,[116] like whiteness which, in the same way as blackness in relation to it, is privation. If [black] cannot belong to [the substratum] at the same time [as white], I mean the privation and the possession, then it is impossible for the <members of> the contrariety to be generated at the same time. For, of these two [white and black], the former is the privation, and the latter the possession.

77 Aristotle said: **if, therefore, there is nothing sensible prior to these [elements], these themselves will be all that there are.** (*GC* 2.5, 332a26-7)

78 We say that **'if there is nothing sensible prior'** thus any one of all these [elements] is related to the others in the same manner, I mean that all four are elements.

79 Aristotle said: **it follows necessarily, therefore, that they either always remain and are unable to change, or they change into one another, either all of them or some of them and some not, as Plato established in the *Timaeus*.**[117] (*GC* 2.5, 332a27-9)

80 As he explained, saying that none of the four simple bodies, I mean fire, air, water and earth, which are elements, is a primary principle or matter for the rest of the parts. But they all are equal as to their essence and existence, in so far as they are primary in the same manner.

[116] cf. *GC* 1.3, 318b14-18 and 2.1, 329a8-13. This lemma and its *commentum* (or what Jābir selected from it) is placed after an argument intended to demonstrate that no body distinct from the elements can be their principle. For example the Infinite of Anaximander might be considered as an intermediary between air and water, or air and fire, from which every thing could be generated. Being a principle and not being characterised by any of the contrarieties which characterise the elements, it would thus be distinct from them. But this, Aristotle claims, is impossible: as soon as one of these contrarieties is added to it, it automatically becomes one of the elements. Among the contrarieties which characterise the elements, each opposite is contrary to the other, as privation to positive condition (*sterêsis* to *hexis*). In the case of the primary contrarieties, the law of excluded middle is applied to this opposition. The Infinite, being a body, could by hypothesis be hot. However, if it is not, then it is necessarily cold, for the cold is the privation of the hot. Not being able to exist without the opposites, it thus cannot be indeterminable, for if it is not hot, it is necessarily cold. Thus, it is necessarily one or the other of the elements, or nothing at all.

[117] cf. *Timaeus*, 54B-D and above, n. 85.

81 Next he started inquiring about these four [simple bodies]: though they are bodies they are primary principles. Therefore <do> they <not> change into one another according to the opinion of Empedocles? For Empedocles considers that all the other primary bodies are generated out of these four, yet these four do not change and are eternal.[118] Or do these [bodies] change into one another as he has explained previously? For one <of> these two cases must necessarily take place. In fact, his enquiry about [the elements] is as I have already explained. Since it was mentioned above, and since some others had already said <this>, this implies that we resume regarding [the elements] in another way. Thus, he said: **'furthermore, we must examine in this manner'**.[119]

82 We say: if these four elements happen to be primary and principles, in the same manner for the rest of the parts (*al-ajzā' al-bāqiya*), either they change into one another <or not>. And if they do, either all of them change into one another or some do and the others do not, as Plato thought. For, in his opinion, earth does not change into the rest of the parts, nor do any of the other three change into it. As for the other three, they do change into one another. He only thought that and believed it owing to the difference between the primary triangles which, in his opinion, constitute [the elements]. We have previously explained that [elements] must necessarily change into one another. Likewise, [we have also explained] that they do not change into one another in <the same> manner <but that they differ> according to the greater or lesser difficulty [of the change].[120]

83 Someone said that the four elements are not eternal, ungenerated and incorruptible, but generated: this is what Aristotle made clear in Book 3 of the book *On the Heavens*. We have mentioned it in several passages of our books, and this is not a convenient place for [this demonstration], thus we put it off.[121] [Here] Aristotle provides a different explanation, because for him [elements] are generated not out of something else, but their generation is out of one another. He also showed this in the book *On Generation and Corruption* in the passage where he showed that [elements] come from contrarieties.[122] For he said that fire, water, air, and earth are compound, and that they are compounded

[118] cf. *GC* 1.1, 314a25 ff. and 314b7-8, where Aristotle attributes this quotation to Empedocles (Diels fr. 8); cf. also 1.8, 325b19-25. In fact, Empedocles recognises four elements, or 'roots', which are at the origin of all things: fire, air, water, and earth. None of them is primary, they are all equally eternal and they are not a result of one another, but everything comes from their union or their separation.

[119] cf. *GC* 2.5, 332a3, first phrase of the chapter. As a matter of fact, Aristotle demonstrated in chapter 4 of Book 2 that the elements transform one into the other. On the other hand, he should demonstrate now (*GC* 2.5, 332b5-30) that, given the transformation of the elements one into the other, it is impossible for one to be the principle of the others.

[120] All of §82 is a paraphrase of *GC* 2.5, 332a26-33.

[121] I am tempted to attribute this sentence to Jābir, but it does happen that Alexander also refers the reader to other places in his exegesis.

[122] cf. *GC* 2.1, 329a24-329b2.

from heat, coldness, moisture and dryness. He then said: **'that [these contrarieties] accompany [the elements] and are not separable from them'.**[123] He refuted the claim that heat is something separate.

84 We have already mentioned the things he said about this and this is not the right place to recall it, for we hasten to let you know what you need to know about the sciences of Natures. If Aristotle had not been an eminent figure of the science of Natures, I would not have mentioned a word of what he said. But the study of morphology (*taṣrīf*) has to be given preference over all the philosophers; this is why I brought forward in this book what he said by quoting him.

85 Aristotle then said: **moreover, their change into one another does not take place in the same manner. But the change is quicker and easier for some and slower and more difficult for others.** (*GC* 2.5, 332a30-2)

86 Then the reason for this was made clear. He reminds us of it now once again, saying that **among the elements, those which have [something] in common**[124] **are generated out of one another quickly. But those which have nothing in common are generated out of one another with more difficulty and more slowly.** (*GC* 2.5, 332a32-3)

87 Those among the elements that have [something] in common are generated out of one another more quickly and more easily, for their change takes place in respect of one thing [sc. a quality] only. As for those that do not have [something] in common, their change is slower and more difficult. [The elements] whose change into one another is quicker and easier relate to one another as earth does to water – for coldness is common for both of them – or water [changing] into air – for they have moisture in common – or air into fire – both being hot – and vice versa; also fire changes into earth and earth into fire in the same manner, for dryness is common to both of them. Moreover, the change of water into fire, of fire into water, of air into earth and of earth into air does not take place in this manner, for the thing whose essence (*huwiyya*) is to belong to them, is not common to both of them.

88 Aristotle said: **if the contrariety according to which <elements> change is one, then [the elements] should necessarily be two.** (*GC* 2.5, 332a34-5)

89 In the same way as he explained and certified that the change of primary bodies takes place through contrariety, and that they all change into all, he also started reminding us that primary bodies are four and that they are neither one nor two nor three, and with respect to this he uses what he has already made clear.

[123] cf. *GC* 2.1, 329a24-6. If this is indeed the intended Greek text, then the Arabic *thumma yaqūlu: innahā ma'ahā ghayr mufāriqa lahā* is no more precise than Aristotle's Greek – the understanding of which remains contested. The grammar of the passage as it stands is that the pronoun *hā* in *innahā* must refer back to the elements which have just been listed. But the quotation is given out of context, so it is not impossible that in its original context the pronoun referred instead to prime matter.

[124] *GC* 2.5, 332a33, *hoti ta men ekhonta sumbolon.*

He said: **'If the contrariety, in respect of which the elements change into one another, is one'** – he means [the contrariety] in respect of which primary and simple bodies reach their contraries (*yaṣīru ... ilā al-aḍdād*), for he has shown that they change into one another – **'the elements will be two'**.[125] Nevertheless, it is rare that the differences, in respect of which the change of primary and simple bodies takes place, be not <more than> two only, and that the contrariety be one, since we observe that the change takes place in respect of more than two differences. There might exist more than one contrariety in respect of which primary bodies exist, just as elements are <more than> two only. If the contrarieties that originate (*al-muḥditha*) the species (*al-anwā'*)[126] are more than one, it is impossible that elements be two. For, just as if the contrariety had been one, the elements would have been two, likewise if the contrarieties are two, the elements will be four. For when he said: **'since they are observed to be more'**,[127] he did not say it regarding bodies, but regarding the thing in respect of which these bodies change into one another. Since the differences out of which the species of the primary body (*anwā' al-jism al-awwal*) originate are more than two, and they change into one another – this being manifest to the senses –[128] nor are they observed to be opposed to one another in respect of heat or coldness or moisture or dryness only, but in respect of all [these differences], the contrariety will not be one.

And he previously said that **'the bodies cannot be three'**.[129] Therefore, elements will be neither two nor three nor one. For as he already explained, the thing cannot change into its contrary while remaining as it is.

[125] cf. *GC* 2.5, 332a34-5.

[126] The terminology used here is somewhat curious, for when it refers to the form of the elements, *eidos* ('form') is generally rendered by *ṣūra*, and *naw'* is reserved for *eidos* in the sense of 'species'. However, the translators did not consistently differentiate between the two: Ḥunayn b. Isḥāq, for example, uses the term *naw'* (pl. *anwā'*) with both meanings in his revision of the first book of the *De Caelo*, whereas Ibn al-Biṭrīq always used *ṣūra*, without distinguishing between form and species; see G. Endress (1973), 134-5 and references there. On the other hand, Abū 'Uthmān al-Dimashqī translates *eidos* by *naw'* where it refers to species, and by *ṣūra* where it refers to form (cf. G. Endress (1973), 137). Abū Bishr Mattā follows the same rule, and in his translation of the commentary of Alexander in *Metaph.* 12, reproduced in the Long Commentary of Ibn Rushd on Aristotle's *Metaphysics*, he invariably translates *eidos* by *ṣūra* when it concerns form, cf. for instance *Metaph.* 12.3, 1069b35; 1070a2; 1070a14 and M. Bouyges (1938-52), vol. 3, 1452,6.8; 1466,6; etc. Could this mean that in the present translation *anwā'* might refer not to the form of the first bodies, but to the elements considered as species of a single genus? See my analysis, above, Introduction, p. 67.

[127] cf. *GC* 2.5, 332b1, *epei de pleiô horâtai onta* (*duo an eien hai elakhistai*). The interpretation of Alexander contradicts in this instance the modern translations of *GC*. For instance both the French translation of J. Tricot (Vrin) and the English version of E.S. Forster (Loeb) consider that this clause refers to the elements, and translate as follows: 'because we observe that <the elements> are more than two, the contrarieties should be at least two'.

[128] cf. *GC* 2.4, 331a9 ff.

[129] cf. *GC* 2.3, 330b16.

90 Aristotle then said: for the matter is intermediate in so far as it is not sensible and inseparable. Since they are observed to be more than two, the contrarieties would be at least two. Since they are two, they [sc. the elements] cannot be three, but they must be four, just as we observe. For this is the number of pairs. Actually they are six, but two of these cannot come to be because they are contrary to one another. (*GC* 2.5, 332a35-332b1)

91 When he said that **'if the contrariety in respect of which primary bodies change into one another is one, the primary bodies will then be two'** – one for each of the contraries and two principles – <he showed> that this matter is a third principle, other than these, which does not necessarily imply that it be a third body. He said: **'for the matter is intermediate'**[130] and it is a substrate (*mawḍū'*) for these [sc. the contrarieties] in respect of which change takes place, in so far as it is not sensible by nature. Furthermore, the change of elements into one another takes place in respect of sensible differences only, for change takes place in respect of a tangible difference. As for what he added: **'inseparable'**,[131] it is due to the fact that it [sc. the matter] is always accompanied by one of these differences, that it does not exist in actuality without being accompanied by these, and that it is not a body separated from these [differences].

92 Aristotle then said: There will be no **<such principle> at the end, since they will all be fire or earth, and this is the same as saying that all phenomena (*āthār*)**[132] **are derived from fire or earth.** (*GC* 2.5, 332b7-9)

93 It has been shown that neither of the elements posited at the end is matter for the rest, because according to this reasoning, they will all be either fire or earth, <as> some claimed. I mean that we can gather from this description that all the elements become either fire or earth. If they claim that [the elements] are generated out of earth or out of fire or out of those [sc. the two extremes] into one of these two [intermediates], then the change will be stable. For saying that all the elements are fire, owing to the fact that fire underlies (*mawḍū'atun*) all the elements, is exactly the same as saying that all are generated out of fire.

[130] cf. *GC* 2.5, 332a35.
[131] cf. *GC* 2.5, 332a35.
[132] *Āthār* is used here in the same way as in the title of the Arabic version of Aristotle's *Meteorologica*, *Kitāb al-āthār al-'ulwiyya*, lit. 'the upper traces' or 'the upper affections'. The Arabic title, which is not a literal translation of the Greek *Meteôrologia*, has not, as far as we know, be discussed or explained by any of the Arabic translators or commentators of the Aristotelian treatise. However, it is worth noting that Samuel Ibn Tibbon, who translated Ibn al-Biṭrīq's version into Hebrew under the title *Otot ha-Shamayim*, pondered the adequate rendering of the Arabic word *āthār* ('traces', 'affections') for which he could hardly find an appropriate Hebrew term that could cover its meaning (see R. Fontaine (1995), xiii ff.). We have translated *āthār* by 'phenomena' according to the definition given by Ḥunayn b. Isḥāq at the end of his compendium of Aristotle's *Meteorology*: '*tamma jawāmi' kitāb al-āthār al-'ulwiyya wa hiya al-aḥdāth allatī taẓhar fī al-jaww* (the events that are manifest in the atmosphere)'. See H. Daiber (1975), 63.

94 Having spoken briefly about the end, he started explaining that it is impossible for someone to claim that either of the two middles between the extremes could be matter for the rest [of the elements], insofar as he explained, at the same time, that neither of the two extremes can be matter for the rest of the parts (*al-ajzā' al-bāqiya*). He said that **'<no> one <of> the elements is principle or matter for the rest of the elements; it is as I already stated in another way',**[133] that is, he did not say it in the same way as he previously did. For he had then posited what is a principle as being unchanging and being preserved in its proper nature. This is why this view has been established in the sense mentioned above. Now, let us take it that [this element] is principle and matter for the the rest of the elements, and is accompanied by <a difference> so that it changes [into them]: for example [if we suppose] that fire is the principle or matter, then each of the remaining bodies will be generated out of it when it changes.[134] This is what the Stoics (*Ahl al-riwāq*)[135] hold: in fact, they resolve the rest of the bodies into fire and generate them again out of fire. But that this is not the case is evident, owing to the fact that all [elements] change into all.

95 Aristotle said: **let the earth be indicated by *A* and water by *M*,**[136] **air by *P* and fire by *R*. Then, if *P* changes into *M* and *R*, there will be a contrariety for *PR*. Let this contrariety be whiteness and blackness. Also, owing to the fact that *P* changes into *M*, there will be another contrariety, for *M* and *R* are not identical. Let this contrariety be dryness and moisture. Let dryness be indicated by *I* and moisture by *L*. If then whiteness remains, water will be white and moist, and if it does not, water will be black, for the change only takes place into contraries. It follows then necessarily that water be**

[133] cf. *GC* 2.5, 332b5. H.H. Joachim (1922), 226, refers to *Phys.* 1.6, 189b16 ff. It is in *Phys.* 1 that Aristotle establishes the principles of change, matter, form and privation. In 189a20, he reminds us that being principles, they should be eternal.

[134] As H.H. Joachim (1922), 227, put it, to consider one of the extreme elements as a principle is tantamount to saying that they all arise by alteration of Fire or Earth. However, whereas Aristotle confines this argument to the extreme elements, Alexander extends it to all elements.

[135] This obviously concerns the Stoics whose name derives from the porch (*stoa*, *stoikoi*) where Zeno used to teach. This explains also their Arabic names. In addition to *ahl al-riwāq*, which we also find in Shahrastānī (*K. al-Milal wa al-niḥal*, ed. W. Cureton (1923), vol. 2, 253), they are also designated by *aṣḥāb al-miẓall* which is also a literal translation of porch, or *aṣḥāb al-usṭuwān* which is simply a transliteration of *stoa*. See O. Amine (1959), 79-97, 82 and references there. Stoic physics says that the world is generated from a primitive fire out of which are produced the four elements through a series of transmutations. Thus, against Aristotle, the point of departure of the transmutation of the elements is fire, and it is not circular, as Aristotle says, but rectilinear, because when it ends at earth, it is only by inverting its course and going back the same path that the transmutation into fire is possible. Hence, fire is the principle *par excellence* for the Stoics; through its condensation, fire produces all the other elements, and in it, all elements are resolved. See E. Bréhier (1951), 134-41.

[136] The letters do not always correspond to the Arabic, since the designation of the elements by the letters in the three Arabic manuscripts on which the text was established was inconsistent and too confusing.

either white or black. Let it then be *J* [black] first; similarly *I* will then belong to *R* – I mean the dryness – so that the change will then occur also to *R* – I mean fire – into water, for they are contraries, since fire was first black and then dry, and water was first moist and then white. (*GC* 2.5, 332b14-27)

96 Alexander said: he wanted to show that change does not take place only from the middle to the two extremes, but that change takes place for the last two extremes also, into one another. For the change of all [the elements] into all annuls [the possibility] that either one of them be their principle. It is believed in this regard that what [Aristotle] explained is not that both extremes change into those that are between them, though he did indeed admit this. Yet this is not so, rather this [sc. that both extremes change into those that are between them] was also shown, *modo continuo* and according to the necessity of the change of all into all, through which both extremes change also into one another.

It is possible that he [sc. Aristotle] might have meant by 'the extremes' that there are very many contrarieties in between them, as for water and fire, air and earth. If someone who believes that it is evident that by 'the extremes', he [sc. Aristotle] meant 'those which are on both sides of the middle which has been posited as the principle', observes that these [change] into one another and do not change only into all of what is between them, then he annuls the principle that has been posited and that we just stated. For he makes clear that fire changes into water and not only into air, which was posited as a principle.[137]

97 The demonstration is as follows:[138] since he[139] had posited one of the intermediates from the four primary bodies, namely air, as a principle, and he

[137] §96 introduces an important point of the Aristotelian demonstration, which Alexander will attempt to analyse in the rest of his *commentum*. Aristotle is not trying to demonstrate that transformation takes place from the two extremes (fire and earth) towards the middle elements (air and water). Rather he wants to show that both extremes can transform into one another. If we only showed that the two extremes transform into the two middle elements, elemental transformation could be rectilinear, albeit reversible. But the transformation of the two extremes into one another requires cyclical transformation, which by itself excludes the existence of a single principle for all the elements.

[138] The point of what follows is to show that neither of the middle elements could be the principle of the other elements. Some think that air is transformed upwards into fire, and downwards into water, and that water is transformed upwards into air, and downwards into earth. However, fire and earth are not transformed one into the other (*GC* 2.5, 332b10-12). Thus, they deny the cyclical transformation of elements. Aristotle is going to demonstrate that the transformation that this theory implies (air into water on one hand, and into fire on the other), means also the possibility of the inverse transformation (fire into water), which ultimately leads to the transformation of all the elements one into another.

[139] Though one might think that Alexander here ascribes the theory in question to Aristotle, he is merely paraphrasing Aristotle's demonstration. Hence the use of the third

had posited that it changes into each of the two [elements] that are on either side of it, namely fire and water, [but also] into earth – he also admitted this – and since each time it [sc. air] changes into something, it does so in respect of a contrariety, <and> since air changes into fire, it is then manifest that it will do so in respect of a certain contrariety. He takes here, as the contrariety in respect of which air changes into fire, whiteness and blackness, and he posits that air is white and fire is black. So when air changes from whiteness into blackness, what is generated will be fire. Or again, when it changes into water, it does so in respect of a contrariety which is however different from the one he had posited, I mean the contrariety of whiteness and blackness. For otherwise, according to this reasoning, water and fire would be one and the same thing, be it water or fire, since both would be generated out of one and the same change. Air will then change into water in respect of another contrariety, namely dryness and moisture,[140] and he posited that air is dry and water is moist. If air changes into water in respect of moisture, then water should necessarily be either white or black. Let it be white since he had posited in the beginning that it is white-dry and that the change of air into fire takes place in respect of whiteness, and into water in respect of dryness. It follows then necessarily that both of these [sc. water and fire] have in common with air the other difference, and that it is contrary to it in respect of the difference in respect of which air changes into each of the two. So then if fire is dry, and this is something common to fire and air, water will be white, and this is what it has in common with air. For, <if someone> posits that water is not white but black, the change of air into water will then take place in respect of the two differences at the same time, not in respect of dryness only. And if the change of air into water takes place in respect of the two differences, the change of air into fire will then take place in respect of two differences also, for these things follow necessarily in the same manner. But, according to this, water and fire will be one and the same thing, for fire will be, according to this, black and moist, just like water. Therefore it is necessary to posit that water is white, and this is what it has in common with air. Since we have posited these things, it has become evident that [elements] on both sides of the middle, that some have posited as principle, change into one another.[141]

person: someone might hold the theory that air is the principle, and this will be refuted in what follows.

[140] According to the theory that Aristotle criticises, when one of the intermediary elements, like air, is transformed, it is transformed upwards into fire according to one contrariety, and downwards into water according to another contrariety.

[141] Before reaching the conclusion, Alexander or Jābir failed to mention the last argument which leads to precisely this conclusion: suppose water is white and moist, as it keeps the whiteness of the air. According to the same principle, fire would be dry and black, the dryness of the air persisting when it transforms into fire. Fire is thus dry and black and water moist and white. Having contrary qualities, they can therefore transform into each other.

98 If someone posits that air changes in respect of the two differences at the same time, this same demonstration will follow necessarily, for the demonstration will follow from the association of the two contrary [differences], because water being moist, air will change into water in respect of both of them. As for its change into fire, [it will take place] in respect of the moisture only or the blackness into one of these two.

99 Furthermore, he explained that earth changes into fire and water, not only into air, and that it is generated out of these two.[142] He has also shown *modo continuo* with the things that have been posited, that earth is generated not only out of air. When explaining this in this way, he said that: 'since air was posited as being a principle, it is manifest that, just like fire and water are generated out of it, likewise earth will also be generated out of them'. If that is so, air will become earth by the change of one of the two differences that are in it, or by the change of both. But by the change of one of the two differences that are in it, it will become either fire or water, but not earth. Earth will not be [generated] by <the change> of only one of those two remaining [differences] since both must change for air to change into earth. Earth will then be black and moist, and water <white> and moist, so that it changes into its contraries, for the contraries are those which change into one another. It is in respect of these that change occurs for fire, air, water and earth, for earth changes into air when it changes and perishes in respect of both its differences at the same time. This is a matter he already admitted. But it changes in respect of one of its two differences into the remaining elements. Its change in respect of one of its two differences is easier than that in respect of both its differences at the same time, as we have already described.

If that is so, earth will change from moisture into dryness, and as to blackness it will keep it, so that fire will then be generated out of it. For he posited that fire is dry and black so that when it changes from blackness into whiteness, water is produced, for he has posited that water is white and moist. Earth changes then into water, which changes into earth, so that fire changes into earth and all [the elements] into all, and neither one of the two intermediate bodies will be a principle for the rest as Anaximenes and Diogenes [of Apollonia] held. For they posited that this is the condition of air. Similarly, Thales posited that this principle was water. According to what he says now it has been shown not only that neither of the two intermediates is a principle, but also that neither of the two extremes is a principle, for you should demonstrate this in one and the same way for all [the elements].

100 Aristotle said: **it is manifest then that the change will take place from all into all, and that moreover *A*, I mean earth, will possess the two remaining common [differences],[143] I mean blackness and moisture, for those two have not been paired yet.** (*GC* 2.5, 332b27-30)

[142] Following the same reasoning, Alexander will show that earth also transforms into all the other elements.
[143] cf. 332b29, *duo sumbola*.

101 Having explained the change of fire and water into one another, he <started> expounding to us that it is in these two directions and that all [the elements] are generated out of all. To this statement he added: **'the remaining contrarieties we previously described as an example'**, I mean whiteness, blackness, dryness and <moisture> which can subsist when we separate them from each other, **'belong to earth, namely moisture and blackness'**.[144] For it was posited that air is white and dry <...> that is moisture and blackness and that the pairing (*izdiwāj*) of the four, every two together, is such. When he said that earth possesses blackness and moisture, then what he said become evident, so he finished with it, since he had now made this known, namely that [earth] changes also into all the elements and that all change into all in the way we have described above.

102 That it is impossible that [the change of the elements into one another] goes on to infinity – which was the idea that we had decided to make clear, when we were led to this idea – is manifest from these things: if the fire that is indicated by the sign *R* is to change into another thing without reverting, like for instance that it changes into *D*, then another contrariety than those already mentioned will belong to *R* – I mean fire – and to *D*, for *D* has not been posited as the same as any of the [four, *AMPR*]. Let <*T*> belong to *R* only and <*B*> to *D*; then *T* will join these, *MARP*. Aristotle said: for they change into one another. (*GC* 2.5, 332b30-333a1)

103 To understand that this [new contrariety] comes from adding one more thing, it is evident and manifest that if ***D*** changes into another thing, another contrariety will belong to ***D*** and ***R***, I mean fire. Thus, the first [element] will have a contrariety, when this is added to it. So, if those [added elements] are infinite in number, the contrarieties in the [first element] will be infinite in number.[145]

104 If that is so, it will be impossible to define any thing, or for any thing to be generated. For if it is generated <out of> something else, it will need to pass and cross through as many as these contrarieties, indeed through even more. (*GC* 2.5, 333a7-10)

105 Alexander said: he repeats what has been already concluded, as I said, as if it had not yet been explained. For the fact that all [the elements] change into one another has been explained already, in the manner we have

[144] cf. *GC* 2.5, 332b28-9.

[145] It is because the transformation is rectilinear that each new transformation implies a new contrariety, and that the previous element must possess contrary qualities. If fire were to transform upwards into a new element, then it must do so on the basis of a new contrariety. We must assume that this new contrariety had been passed on to fire from air and from all the previous elements. Hence, if the transformation continues to infinity, there should be an infinite number of contrarieties in each element. See H.H. Joachim (1922), 229.

mentioned.[146] For if all [the elements] changed into one another, without having ***T*** as a common cause, and if [***T***] belonged to these remaining bodies but not to their contrary, which is ***D***, neither would fire be generated out of one of these bodies, nor would any of these bodies be generated out of fire. For [the contrarieties] will be numerous in that other one [sc. ***D***] in so far as they also attach to it at this moment. So no one will make use of this or that given that it is manifest to the senses.

106 As for what he said, namely **'that they [sc. the elements] might change into one another, and having the possibility [of proceeding] to infinity would not revert in their change such that [the process] would be reversed'**[147] – but they have been described as being generated out of the first element into the next one only, and this [process] is not reversible – he said **'one should not make use of this statement'**,[148] for the change takes place from one <into another>, and this does not happen if it is possible that [it proceed] to infinity. However, he did not stick to that statement.[149] For if change does not revert and reverse, but takes place in a straight line, then the added differences that are in the body before fire will not resolve (*lā tadhūbu*)[150] when they are in the body that comes after fire.

Also, regarding the action [of these differences] in fire, he explained that if it was possible for the change [to proceed] to infinity, when one thing changes into another one, it will follow then necessarily that the contrariety in respect of which they change is also infinite in number. It will follow then necessarily that all these contrarieties are in fire and also in the body prior to it, if fire changes in a straight line into another body juxtaposed to it, and if its change does not revert into that body out of which it was generated. What it [sc. fire] changes into is ***D***, and that also changes into another [body]. Owing to the fact that ***R*** – I mean fire – changes into ***D***, the contrariety ***T B*** and all the other remaining differences will be common to ***R*** and ***D***, so that ***R*** will then contain the contrariety in respect of which ***D*** changes into the next one. Also, just as the change of ***R*** into ***D*** takes place in respect of the contrariety ***B T***, it follows then necessarily that the other body [into which ***D*** changes] contains what is said of

[146] An allusion to *GC* 2.5, 333a3, where Aristotle reconsiders his previous demonstration with a new argument to prove that all elements are transformed into each other. However, Aristotle had already demonstrated that those who placed a principle in the middle were finally forced to accept the cyclical transformation of the elements (332b12-30).

[147] cf. *GC* 2.5, 333a2.

[148] cf. *GC* 2.5, 333a3.

[149] The point of this remark is that Aristotle is only temporarily refraining from assuming the cyclical transformation of the elements ('one should not make use of this statement'), since it would beg the question against his opponents, who claim that the elements are transformed rectilinearly. In the rest of the *commentum*, Alexander describes the way the rectilinear transformation, which continues infinitely would have to take place, and the consequences it would imply.

[150] The choice of the term is probably that of Jābir.

fire, because fire and this other body do not differ with respect to this contrariety. Likewise the differences also in respect of which it changes again into one of the other things that comes after it, will be in ***R*** also – I mean fire – owing to the fact that ***R*** and ***D*** do not differ in any of these respects. This is what some imagined and claimed to be the case in the things that come after these, for the definition of the modes of contrariety, in respect of which the primary [body] is opposed to the one after it, always holds good for all the things prior to this one, since it is not their [own] opposite which is added, so that exists <...> and neither out of one another.[151]

107 If bodies that are consecutive to each other, and through which change is possible, possess the contrarieties in respect of which change takes place in infinite number, then in that case, each of these bodies would contain an infinite number of contrarieties and differences, so that it cannot be neither defined nor generated, since it would need to be generated <out of> things that change <into one another> and the generation of this thing cannot go on to infinity. For, if another thing is added, contrarieties will exist in the preceding things, and it will not be possible for all bodies to exist, since the contrarieties will be infinite in number. It will then be impossible to define the contrarieties of any of [these bodies], and from the beginning there will be no generation at all. For if one had to be generated out of another, it would need to pass through this number of contrarieties and through even more, for this is the proper characteristic of what is infinite, namely that if there exist any amount of it, a greater amount can be taken.

If the contrarieties that are in each [of the bodies] were infinite in number, there would always be another body generated out of a body in a straight line to infinity, so that [these bodies] would be indeterminate and could not be generated. For that [body] has to be generated out of something that always possesses contrarieties whose definition is, somehow, required, and contrarieties whose extremity has come to be and still more others, for they are infinite [in number]. And the contrarieties that have been taken will always be separated from other contrarieties in respect of which the changes belonging to the things that are generated further to infinity take place, and these are the [contrarieties] from which one member of each must necessarily belong to the body that has been generated before. So, none of the bodies will then be generated at all, for the one that exists will always lack something.

108 Aristotle said: **therefore, change into some [elements] will never take place. For instance, if the intermediates are infinite [in number] and it is necessary that they be so, since the elements are infinite [in number].** (*GC* 2.5, 333a10-12)

109 He has explained that if the contrarieties, in respect of which the forms of each of the bodies are affected by a nature, are infinite in number, it will be impossible to define any of these bodies and for any of these to be generated, owing to the fact that all the differences that still exist in the generation of this

[151] See above, n. 145.

body, will benefit, from other proper differences, concerning its existence. Now he starts to explain that it is also impossible for any of [these bodies] to change into one another. For bodies that are infinite [in number] also never change into one <another>, for change into one another must take place by the change of the intermediate bodies. But these cannot be traversed or form a series, and they are countless, because they are infinite. For, if the elements are infinite [in number], and if the contrarieties in respect of which change into one another takes place are infinite [in number], then the intermediate bodies will be infinite in [number].

110 When he said **that the bodies between which there are infinitely many bodies do not change into one another,**[152] he said *modo continuo*: **and further [there will not be a change] from air into fire since there exist infinitely many contrarieties.** (*GC* 2.5, 333a12-13)

111 What he said is just like saying that elements that [change] into one another, or that are juxtaposed to one another, do <not> change into one another, for air and fire are consecutive, and one is next to the other so that there is <no> body between them. We say that the reason why these two do not change into one another <...>.[153]

[152] cf. *GC* 2.5, 333a10-11.

[153] The commentary ends, in the middle of a sentence, as abruptly as it started.

Appendix

Treatise of Ya‘qūb b. Isḥāq al-Isrā’īlī al-Maḥallī

For the author and the manuscript see above, Introduction, **I B**. Ya‘qūb b. Isḥāq's treatise is of interest for the history of textual transmission, especially in that it provides us with another fragment of Alexander's *GC* commentary missing in the *Book of Morphology* and mentioned neither by Philoponus nor by Ibn Rushd in his *Middle Commentary*. He includes also a fragment of Olympiodorus' commentary on *GC* which is otherwise lost.

This translation is based on MS Istanbul, Nuruosmaniye 3589, dated 1269/1270, fols 47b13-48b7.

[47b 13] In the name of God the Merciful, the Compassionate

When the meeting took place at the *majlis* of al-Ra'īs Muhadhdhabaddīn, and [all those present] began to outdo one another,/ I thought that such a [competition] was grounded on principles. However <the meeting> was dominated by an excess of words and gossip. **[l. 15]** When the *majlis* was dispersed and I did not possess the words of Alexander, I obtained them that very night and perused them./ These did not add anything to that which I already knew. This is the wording of what he said:

Aristotle said: since the simple/ bodies are four, each two belong to each of the first two. (*GC* 2.3, 330b30-2 and *Morphology*, §36)

Alexander said:/ he divides the relation they have with places, and because of this they are heavy or light./ (*Morphology*, §37)

Know, may God give you success, that if you consider this statement, you will observe that it designates the efficient cause of lightness **[l. 20]** and heaviness, not lightness and heaviness [themselves]. For he said: 'he divides the relation they have with/ places, and because of this they are heavy or light'. He had in mind the efficient cause of lightness/ and heaviness, not lightness and heaviness [themselves]. We must therefore investigate the relation in virtue of which lightness and heaviness are generated;/ for it is evident from what he said that the phrase 'the first' applies to [this relation] and is the cause.

Then he (Alexander) said, prior to this chapter,/ that: heat is the agent for rarefaction and lightness, while coldness is the agent for condensation and heaviness.

Then he (Alexander) said, again in a chapter **[l. 25]** previous to this one, when talking about roughness and smoothness: or it is more appropriate and adequate to say **[48a1]** that these two qualities are neither active nor passive, just as heaviness and lightness are not. It is therefore manifest/ that all the other tangible differences* which he names contrarieties, can be reduced to/ these four primary ones that were previously described, namely heat, coldness, moisture and dryness./ (*Morphology*, §37) Thus it has been shown that the primary qualities are these four.

As for what he said, namely that the first two are hot **[l. 5]** and cold, it is according to the fact that those two are the active ones. This was made clear through what he said, namely that heat is the agent for rarefaction/ and lightness and coldness the agent for condensation and heaviness. He did not mention, in connection with that, dryness/ and moisture. He has shown in the foregoing that the first two are not lightness and heaviness.

Aristotle said/ in the book *On Generation and Corruption*: of these, heavy and light are neither active nor passive. (*GC* 2.2, 329b20-21)

Olympiodorus said: we say that these qualities are neither active nor acted upon by **[l. 10]** one another, but rather are moving [forces] (*muḥarrika*) and this is the reason why <they are not> primary qualities. It is necessary to seek the qualities that act and are acted upon by/ one another. For it is from these that sublunary things are generated, because they act and are acted upon by one another./

Aristotle said: as for hot and cold, <moist and dry>, one [pair] is said to be active and the other to be acted upon by something./ (*GC* 2.2, 329b25)

Aristotle said: It is then manifest that all the other kinds can be reduced to these four kinds./ (*GC* 2.2, 330a24-5)

Alexander said, in that chapter, about roughness and smoothness that: they are not active nor passive **[l. 15]** just as heaviness and lightness are not. Manifestly then all the other remaining tangible kinds that/ <Aristotle> names contrarieties, are reduced to the first four that were previously described, namely heat, coldness,/ dryness and moisture.

Then Alexander also said, commenting on what Aristotle said/ in order to refute the claim of those who said that the elements are <not> generated from one another: in this chapter he mentions/ that heat is the agent for rarefaction and lightness, while coldness is the agent for condensation and heaviness.

When Aristotle said: **[l. 20]** since the simple bodies are four, each two belong to each of the /first two (*GC* 2.3, 330b30-2 and *Morphology*, §36), Alexander said: he divides the relation they have with places, and/ because of this they are heavy or light. (*Morphology*, §37)

* Here we follow the text given in the margin; the main text has instead 'kinds (*aṣnāf*)'.

It is evident to me from what Alexander has said that he was aiming for the cause of lightness/ and heaviness, not for lightness and heaviness <themselves>. The proof for that is what he said, namely 'because of which they are heavy and light'./ He made clear in the foregoing that the primary qualities are heat, coldness, moisture and dryness. He also made clear **[l. 25]** that heat and coldness are worthier of primacy since they are the active ones. When saying 'the relation they have **[48b1]** to places' he must have meant through that that the relation of simple hot to the upper [place] is by nature, and that lightness/ is subsequent to it, and that the movement of simple cold toward the lower [place] is by nature and heaviness follows it./

When Aristotle said in the book *On Generation and Corruption* 'that the primary qualities of all the sublunary <things> are heat,/ coldness, dryness and moisture'; then he said 'the first two of them' he was meaning that, among these four, heat and coldness **[l. 5]** are worthier of primacy because they are the active ones – the meaning of 'active' is that they act more and are acted upon/ less, and dryness and moisture are passive because they act less and are acted upon more – and because rarefaction and condensation,/ lightness and heaviness are produced by heat and coldness. That is why lightness and heaviness are not said to be primary.

Bibliography

Abū Ridā, M.A., ed., 1950-3, *Rasā'il al-Kindī al-falsafiyya*, 2 vols, Cairo.

Afshār, I. and Dānesh-Pazūh, M.T., with the collaboration of M.B. Ḥojjati and A. Monzawi, 1992, *Fehrest-e Noskhehā-ye khaṭṭī-ye Ketābkhāne-ye mellī-ye Malek, vābeste be Āstān-e Qods*, vol. 9, Teheran.

al-'Alawī, J., ed., 1994, *Talkhīṣ al-āthār al-'ulwiyya li-Abī al-Walīd Muḥammad b. Rushd al-ḥafīd*, Beirut.

____ ed., 1995, *Talkhīṣ al-kawn wa al-fasād li-Abī al-Walīd Muḥammad b. Rushd*, Beirut.

Algra, K., 1995, *Concepts of Space in Greek Thought*, Leiden-New York-Köln.

Amine, O., 1959, 'Le stoïcisme et la pensée islamique', *Revue thomiste* 59, 79-97.

Anawati, G.C., 1997, 'L'alchimie arabe', in R. Rashed, ed., *Histoire des sciences arabes*, vol. 3: *Technologie, alchimie et sciences de la vie*, Paris, 111-41.

Aouad, M., and Goulet, R., 1989, 'Alexandros d'Aphrodisias', in R. Goulet (1989), 125-39.

Aouad, M., 1996, 'Définition par Averroès du concept de "point de vue immédiat" dans le commentaire moyen de la Rhétorique', *Bulletin d'Etudes Orientales* 48, 115-30.

Badawī, A. 1947, *Arisṭū 'inda al-'Arab*, Cairo.

____ 1948, *Manṭiq Arisṭū* (Dirāsāt islāmiyya, 6), Cairo.

____ 1953, *Arisṭūṭālīs, fann al-shi'r*, Cairo.

____ 1961, *Arisṭūṭālīs fī al-samā' wa al-āthār al-'ulwiyya* (Dirāsāt islāmiyya, 28), Cairo.

____ 1980², *Arisṭūṭālīs fī al-nafs*, Koweit-Beirut.

____ 1987², *La transmission de la philosophie grecque au monde arabe*, Paris.

Baffioni, C., 1986, 'Filosofia della natura e alchimia nei commenti ad Aristotele della Scuola di Alessandria', *Gli interscambi culturali e socio-economici fra l'Africa settentrionale e l'Europa mediterranea, Atti del Congresso Internazionale di Amalfi, 5-8 dicembre 1983*, Naples, 403-31.

al-Baghdādī, Abū al-Barakāt, 1939, *Al-Kitāb al-mu'tabar fī al-ḥikma*, Hyderabad.

Bouyges, M., ed., 1938-52, Ibn Rushd, *Averroès, Tafsīr mā ba'd aṭ-ṭabī'at*, (Bibliotheca Arabica Scholasticorum), Beirut.

____ ed., 1983², Averroès, *Talkhīṣ kitāb al-maqūlāt*, Beirut.

Bréhier, E., 1951, *Chrysippe et l'ancien stoïcisme*, Paris.

Brisson, L., 1974, *Le même et l'autre dans la structure ontologique du Timée de Platon: un commentaire systématique du Timée de Platon*, Paris.

Burgman, J., and Drossaart Lulofs, H.J., eds, 1971, *Aristotle Generation of Animals. The Arabic translation commonly ascribed to Yaḥyā b. al-Biṭrīq* (De Goeje Fund, XXIII), Leiden.

Burkert, W., 1959, '*Stoicheion*. Eine semasiologische Studie', *Philologus* 103, 167-97.

Busse, A., ed., 1887, Porphyry, *Isagoge*, Berlin.

Butterworth, C.E., 1978, 'La valeur philosophique des commentaires d'Averroès sur Aristote', *Multiple Averroès*. Actes du Colloque International organisé à l'occasion du 850ème anniversaire de la naissance d'Averroès. Paris 20-23 sept. 1976, Paris, 117-26.

Charlton, W., 1992², *Aristotle Physics, Books I and II*, Oxford.

Chaniotis, A., 2004a, 'New inscriptions from Aphrodisias 1995-2001', *American Journal of Archeology*, 108.3, 377-416.

____ 2004b, 'Epigraphic evidence for the philosopher Alexander of Aphrodisias', *Bulletin of the Institute of Classical Studies* 47, 79-81.

Crombie, A.C., ed., 1961, *Scientific Change. Historical studies in the intellectual, social and technical conditions for scientific discovery and technical invention, from antiquity to the present*, London.

Coutant, V.C.B., ed. and trans., 1971, *Theophrastus De Igne. A post-Aristotelian view of the nature of fire*, Assen.

Cureton, W., ed., 1923, Shahrastānī, *K. al-Milal wa al-niḥal* (*Book of the Religious and Philosophical Sects*), Leipzig.

Daiber, H., 1975, *Ein Kompendium der Aristotelischen Meteorologie in der Fassung des Hunain ibn Ishaq*, Amsterdam, Oxford.

____ 1980, *Aetius Arabus, Die Vorsokratiker in arabischer Überlieferung*, Wiesbaden.

Dānesh-Pazūh, M.T., 1953, *Fehrest-e Ketāb-khāna-ye ehdā'ī-e āqā-ye Sayyed Muḥammad Meshkāt be Ketāb-khāna-ye dāneshgāh-e Tehrān*, vol. 4, Teheran.

Delamarre, A. J.-L., 1980, 'La notion de *ptôsis* chez Aristote et les stoïciens', in P. Aubenque, ed., *Concepts et catégories dans la pensée antique*, Paris, 321-45.

Diels, H., 1899, *Elementum*, Leipzig.

Dieterici, F., ed., 1892, *Alfārābī's philosophische Abhandlungen*, Leiden.

Dietrich, A., 1964, 'Die arabische Version einer unbekannten Schrift des Alexander von Aphrodisias über die Differentia specifica', *Nachrichten der Akademie der Wissenschaften in Göttingen* I, Philologische-Historische Klasse, Göttingen, 85-148.

____ 1966, *Medicinalia Arabica*, Studien über arabische medizinische Handschriften in türkischen und syrischen Bibliotheken, *AAWG* III. Folge, no. 66, Göttingen.

Dooley, W.E., 1989, *Alexander of Aphrodisias, On Aristotle Metaphysics 1*, London.

____ 1993, *Alexander of Aphrodisias, On Aristotle Metaphysics 5*, London.

Dozy, R., 1927, *Supplément aux Dictionnaires arabes*, 2nd edn, Paris-Leiden.

Elamrani-Jamal, A., 1983, *Logique aristotélicienne et grammaire arabe*, Paris.

Endress, G., 1973, *Proclus Arabus. Zwanzig Abschnitte aus der Institutio Theologica in arabischer Übersetzung*, eingeleitet, herausgegeben und erklärt (Beiruter Texte und Studien herausgegeben vom Orient-Institut der deutschen morgenländischen Gesellschaft 10), Beirut.

van Ess, J., 1965, 'Über einige neue Fragmente des Alexander von Aphrodisias und des Proklos in arabischer Übersetzung', *Der Islam*, Band 42, Heft 1, 148-168.

Fazzo, S. and Wiesner, H., 1993, 'Alexander of Aphrodisias in the Kindī-circle and in al-Kindī's Cosmology', *Arabic Sciences and Philosophy* 3, 119-53.

Fazzo, S., 1997, 'L'Alexandre Arabe et la génération à partir du néant', in Hasnawi et al., eds, 1997, 277-87.

____ 2002, 'Alexandre d'Aphrodise contre Galien?', *Philosophie Antique. Problèmes, Renaissances, Usages* 2, 109-44.

____ 2003, 'Alexandros d'Aphrodisias', in R. Goulet (dir.), 2003, 61-70.

Festugière, A.J., 1971, 'Modes de composition des commentaires de Proclus', *Etudes de Philosophie grecque*, Paris, 551-74.

Flügel, G., ed., 1872, Ibn al-Nadīm, *Kitāb al-Fihrist*, 2 vols, Leipzig: Vogel.

Fobes, F.H., ed., 1956, *Averrois Cordubensis commentarium medium in Aristotelis De Generatione et Corruptione libros* (Medieval Academy of America), Cambridge, MA.

Fontaine, R., ed. and trans., 1995, *Otot ha-shamayim. Samuel Ibn Tibbon's Hebrew version of Aristotle's Meteorology*, Leiden.

Forster, E.S., 1955, *Aristotle on Coming-to-Be and Passing Away* (Loeb Classical Library), London.

Frank, R.M., 1974, 'Notes and remarks on the *ṭabā'i'* in the teaching of al-Māturīdī', in P. Salmon (ed.), *Mélanges d'Islamologie*. Volume dédié à la mémoire d'Armand Abel, Leiden, 138-149

Frede, M., 1994, 'The Stoic notion of a *lekton*', in S. Everson, ed., *Companions to Ancient Thought*, 3: *Language*, Cambridge, 109-28.

Furlani, G., 1923, 'Il Trattato di Rêsh'ayna sull'Universo', *Rivista Trimestrale di Studi Filosofici e Religiosi* 4, 1-22.

Garel, M., 1991, *D'une main forte. Manuscrits hébreux des collections françaises*, Paris.

Gätje, H., 1966, 'Zur arabischen Überlieferung des Alexander von Aphrodisias', *Zeitschrift der Deutschen Morgenländischen Gesellschaft* (*ZDMG*), 116, 255-78.

Genequand, C., 1997, 'Vers une nouvelle édition de la *Maqāla fī mabādi' al-kull* d'Alexandre d'Aphrodise', in Hasnawi et al., eds, 1997, 271-6.

____ 2001, *Alexander of Aphrodisias on the Cosmos* (Islamic Philosophy Theology and Science, 44), Leiden-Boston-Köln.

Georr, K., 1948, *Les Catégories d'Aristote dans leurs versions syro-arabes*, Beirut.

Ghorab, A.A., 1972, 'The Greek commentators on Aristotle quoted in al-'Āmirī's *al-Sa'ada wa al-is'ād*', in S.M. Stern, A. Hourani, and V. Brown, eds, *Islamic Philosophy and the Classical Tradition*, London, 77-88.

Giannakis, E., 1996, 'Fragments from Alexander's lost commentary on Aristotle's *Physics*', *Zeitschrift für Geschichte der arabisch-islamischen Wissenschaften* 10, 157-87.

Gibb, H.A.R. et al., eds., 1960-, *Encyclopedia of Islam*, 2nd ed., 11 vols, Leiden.

Gill, M.L., 1989, *Aristotle on Substance. The Paradox of Unity*, Princeton, NJ.

Gimaret, D., and Monot, G., trans., 1986, *Shahrastani, Livre des Religions et des Sectes*. Traduction avec introduction et notes, Louvain/ Paris.

Goichon, A.M., 1938, *Lexique de la langue philosophique d'Ibn Sīnā*, Paris.

Goldschmidt, V., 1956, 'La théorie aristotélicienne du lieu', in *Mélanges de philosophie grecque offerts à Mgr Diès*, Paris, 79-119.

Goulet, R., ed., 1989, *Dictionnaire des philosophes antiques*, Paris.

____ ed., 2003, *Dictionnaire des philosophes antiques, Supplément*, Paris.

Gutas, D., 1988, *Avicenna and the Aristotelian Tradition*, Leiden.

____ 1993, 'Aspects of literary form and genre in Arabic logical works' in C. Burnet, ed., *Glosses and Commentaries on Aristotelian Logical Texts. The Syriac, Arabic and medieval Latin traditions* (Warburg Institute Surveys and Texts, XXIII), London, 29-76.

Gyekye, K., 1971, 'The terms "prima intentio" and "secunda intentio" in Arabic logic', *Speculum*, 32-8.

de Haas, F.A.J., 1997, *John Philoponus' New Definition of Prime Matter. Aspects of its background in Neoplatonism & the ancient commentary tradition*, Leiden.

Hajji-Athanasiou, M., 1982, *Le Traité de Némésius d'Emèse, De Natura Hominis, dans la tradition arabe*, Thèse pour le doctorat d'Etat, Paris (unpublished).

Hasnawi, A., Elamrani-Jamal, A., and Aouad, M., eds, 1997, *Perspectives arabes et médiévales sur la tradition scientifique et philosophique grecque*. Actes du colloque de la *SIHSPAI*, Paris, 31 mars-3 avril 1993, Paris-Louvain.

Hasnawi, A., 1994, 'Alexandre d'Aphrodise vs Jean Philoponus: notes sur quelques traités d'Alexandre "perdus" en grec, conservés en arabe', *Arabic Sciences and Philosophy* 4, 53-109.

Hugonnard-Roche, H., 1985, 'L'Epitomé du *De caelo* d'Aristote par Averroès: questions de méthode et de doctrine', *Archives d'Histoire doctrinale et littéraire du Moyen Âge* 51, 7-39.

Joachim, H.H., 1904, 'Aristotle's conception of chemical combination', *Journal of Philology* 29, 72-86.

____ 1922, *Aristotle on Coming-to-Be and Passing Away*, Oxford.

Kahn, C.H., 1960, *Anaximander and the Origins of Greek Cosmology*, New York.

King, H., 1956, 'Aristotle without materia prima', *Journal of the History of Ideas* 17, 370-89.

Kraus, P., 1935, *Jābir b. Ḥayyān. Essai sur l'histoire des idées scientifiques dans l'Islam*, vol. 3, *Textes choisis* (*Mukhtār rasā'il Jābir b. Ḥayyān*), Paris-Cairo.

____ 1943, *Contribution à l'histoire des idées scientifiques dans l'Islam*, vol. I, *Le Corpus des Ecrits jābiriens*, *Mémoires de l'Institut d'Egypte*, Cairo.

____ 1986[2], *Contribution à l'histoire des idées scientifiques dans l'Islam*, vol. II: *Jābir et la science grecque*, Paris.

Kurland, S., trans., 1958, *Averroes on Aristotle's De generatione et Corruptione. Middle Commentary and Epitome* (Corpus Commentariorum Averrois in Aristotelem, Versio Anglica, IV 2), Cambridge, MA.

Lacey, A.R., 1965, 'The Eleatics and Aristotle on some problems of change', *Journal of the History of Ideas* 26, 451-68.

Lane, W., 1893, *Arabic-English Lexicon*, 8 vols, London-Edinburgh.

Lang, H., 1992, *Aristotle's Physics and its Medieval Varieties*, Albany, NY.

Lewis, E., 1996, *Alexander of Aphrodisias on Aristotle Meteorology 4*, London.

Liddell, H.G., Scott, R., Jones, H.S., 1968, *Greek-English Lexicon*, Oxford.

Lippert, J., ed., 1903, Al-Qifṭī, *Ta'rīkh al-Ḥukamā'*, Leipzig.

Lory, P., 1985, 'La science des lettres en terre d'Islam: le chiffre, la lettre, l'œuvre', *Cahiers de l'Université St. Jean de Jérusalem* 11, 89-101.

____ 1996, 'La mystique des Lettres en terre d'Islam', *Annales de Philosophie, Université St-Joseph* 17, 101-9.

____ 1996[2], *Jābir ibn Hayyān, Dix traités d'alchimie. Les dix premiers traités du Livre des Soixante-dix*, Paris.

Merlan, P., 1963, *Monopsychism, Mysticism, Metaconsciousness*, La Haye.

Moraux, P., 1965, *Aristote, Du ciel*, Paris.

____ 1979, *Le commentaire d'Alexandre d'Aphrodise aux 'Seconds Analytiques' d'Aristote* (Peripatoi 13), Berlin/New York.

Moreau, J., 1962, *Aristote et son école*, Paris.

Morrow, G., 1969, 'Qualitative change in Aristotle's *Physics*', in I. Düring, ed., *Naturphilosophie bei Aristoteles und Theophrast*. Verhandlungen des 4. Symposium Aristotelicum veranstaltet in Göteborg. August 1966, Heidelberg, 154-67.

Mugler, C., 1966, *Aristote, De la génération et de la corruption*, Paris.

Muḥammad, 'A., ed., n.d., Fakhruddīn al-Rāzī, *Mafātīḥ al-ghayb*, Cairo.

Müller, A., ed., 1884, Ibn Abī Uṣaybi'a, *'Uyūn al-anbā' fī ṭabaqāt al-aṭṭibā'*, Königsberg.

Muntasar, A.H. et al., eds, 1965, Ibn Sīnā, *Al-Shifā'*, *al-Ṭabī'īyyāt*, t. 5: *al-ma'ādin wa al-āthār al-'ulwiyya*, Cairo.

O'Brien, D., 1981, *Theories of Weight in the Ancient World. Four essays on Democritus, Plato and Aristotle. A study in the development of ideas*. Vol. 1, *Democritus, Weight and Size. An exercise in the reconstruction of early Greek philosophy*, Paris-Leiden.

Oliver, J.H., 1977, 'The didadochè at Athens under the humanistic emperors', *American Journal of Philology* 98, 160-78.

Petraitis, C., 1967, *The Arabic Version of Aristotle's Meteorology*, Beirut.

Pilla, S., ed., al-Mas'ūdī, *Murūj al-dhabab wa ma'ādin al-jawhar*, 7 vols, Beirut.

Pines, S., 1979, 'De la composition et de la méthode du *Kitāb al-mu'tabar*. L'appel aux évidences', *The Collected Works of Shlomo Pines*, vol. 1, Leiden, 96-108.

____ 1986a, *Studies in Arabic versions of Greek Texts and in Medieval Science, The collected works of Shlomo Pines*, vol. 2, Jerusalem-Leiden.

____ 1986b, '*Omne quod movetur necesse est ab aliquo moveri*: a refutation of Galen by Alexander of Aphrodisias and the theory of motion', in Pines 1986a, 218-51.

____ 1986c, 'The spiritual force permeating the Cosmos according to a passage in the treatise on the principles of the all by Alexander of Aphrodisias and the theory of motion', in Pines 1986a, 252-5.

____ 1986d, 'Un texte inconnu d'Aristote en version arabe', in Pines 1986a, 157-95.

Puig Montada, J., 1996, 'Aristotle and Averroes on *Coming-to-be and Passing away*', *Oriens* 35, 1-34.

Qāsim, M. and Madkour, I., eds, 1969, *Ibn Sīnā, Al-Shifā', al-Ṭabī'iyyāt, al-Kawn wa al-fasād*, Cairo.

Rashed, M., 1995, 'Alexandre d'Aphrodise et la "Magna Quaestio". Rôle et indépendance des scholies dans la tradition byzantine du corpus aristotélicien', *Les Etudes Classiques* 63, 296-351.

____ 2003, 'Aristote de Stagire. *De generatione et corruptione*. Tradition arabe', in R. Goulet (2003), 304-14.

Rescher, N., and Marmura, M.E., 1965 (1971²), *The Refutation by Alexander of Aphrodisias of Galen's Treatise on the Theory of Motion*, Islamabad (London²).

Robinson, H.M., 1974, 'Prime matter in Aristotle', *Phronesis* 19, 168-88.

Ruland, H.J., 1976, *Die arabischen Fassungen von zwei Schriften des Alexander von Aphrodisias. Über die Vorsehung und über das liberum arbitrium*, Diss. Saarbrücken.

Ryding, K.C., 1990, 'Alchemy and linguistics: connections in Early Islam', in Z.R.W.M. von Martels, ed., *Alchemy Revisited*. Proceedings of the International Conference on the History of Alchemy at the University of Gronigen, 17-19 April 1989, Leiden, 117-20.

____ 1997, 'The heritage of Arabic alchemy: the multicultural matrix', in Hasnawi et al., eds, 1997, 235-48.

Sambursky, S., 1961, 'Conceptual developments and modes of explanation in later Greek scientific thought', in Crombie 1961, 61-78.

____ 1962, *The Physical World of Late Antiquity*, London.

Seeck, G., 1964, *Über die Elemente in der Kosmologie des Aristoteles*, Munich.

Serra, G., 1973, 'Note sulla traduzione arabo-latina del *De gen. corr.* di Aristotele', *Giornale critico della filosofia italiana* 4, serie 4, anno 52, 383-427.

____ 1997, 'La traduzione araba del *De generatione et corruptione* di Aristotele citata nel *Kitāb al-Taṣrīf* attribuito a Jābir', *La diffusione dell'eredità classica nell'età tardoantica e medievale. Forme e modi di transmissione.* Atti del Seminario Nazionale (Trieste, 19-20 settembre 1996), Torino, 177-88.

Sharples, R.W., 1975, 'Responsibility, chance and not being (Alexander of Aphrodisias, *Mantissa* 169-172)', *Bulletin of the Institute of Classical Studies* 22, 37-64.

____ 1987, 'Alexander of Aphrodisias: scholasticism and innovation', *Aufstieg und Niedergang der Römischen Welt (ANRW)* II 36, 2, Berlin, 1176-1243.

____ 1990a, 'The school of Alexander?', in R. Sorabji, ed., 1990, 84-111.

____ 1990b, *Alexander of Aphrodisias, Ethical Problems*, London.

____ 1992, *Alexander of Aphrodisias, Quaestiones 1.1-2.15*, London.

____ 1994, *Alexander of Aphrodisias, Quaestiones 2.16-3.15*, London.

Sokolowski, R., 1970, 'Matter, elements and substance in Aristotle', *Journal of the History of Philosophy* 8, 263-88.

Solmsen, F., 1958, 'Aristotle and prime matter: a reply to Hugh R. King', *Journal of the History of Ideas* 19, 243-52.

____ 1960, *Aristotle's System of the Natural World. A Comparison with his predecessors*, New York.

Sorabji, R., 1988, *Matter, Space and Motion: Theories in antiquity and their sequel*, London.

____ ed., 1990a, *Aristotle Transformed: The ancient commentators and their influence*, London.

____ 1990b, 'The ancient commentators on Aristotle', in Sorabji 1990a, 1-31.

Sorabji, R., ed., 2004, *The Philosophy of the Commentators, 200-600 AD: A Sourcebook in Three Volumes*, London.

Stuart Crawford, F., ed., 1953, *Averrois Cordubensis Commentarium Magnum in Aristotelis De anima libros*, Cambridge, MA.

al-Taftazānī, A.W. and Zāyid, S., eds, 1994, *Jawāmi' al-kawn wa al-fasād*, Cairo.

Tessier, A., 1979, 'Note alla traduzione Arabo-Ebraica del *De generatione et corruptione* di Aristotele', *Annali della Facoltà di Lettere e Filosofia*, Università di Padova, vol. IV, 263-8.

____ 1984, *La Traduzione Arabo-Ebraica del De Generatione et Corruptione di Aristotele, Atti della Academia Nazionale dei Lincei*, Anno 1984, Memorie, Classe di Scienze morali, storiche e filologiche, serie 8, vol. 28, fasc. 1, Rome.

Thillet, P., 1980, *Alexandre d'Aphrodise*, Thèse pour le docorat d'Etat, Paris 1979 (Bibl. de la Sorbonne: W 1980 [10^{1-7}] 40), vol. 4-5: *Traité de la Providence. Version arabe de Abū Bishr Mattā b. Yūnus.*

____ 1984, *Alexandre d'Aphrodise, Traité du Destin*, Paris.

Todd, R.B., 1972a, 'Alexander of Aphrodisias and the Alexandrian *Quaestiones* 2.12', *Philologus* 116, 293-305.

____ 1972b, '*Epitedeiotes* in philosophical literature: towards an analysis', *Acta classica* 15, 25-35.

____ 1976, *Alexander of Aphrodisias on Stoic Physics. A study of the* De Mixtione *with preliminary essays, text, translation and commentary*, Leiden.

Vajda, G., 1953, *Index général des manuscrits arabes musulmans de la Bibliothèque Nationale de Paris*, Paris.

Verdenius, W.J. and Waszink, J.H., 1946, *Aristotle on Coming-to-Be and Passing-Away, Some Comments* (Philosophia Antiqua, 1), Leiden.

Versteegh, C.H.M., 1977, *Greek Elements in Arabic Linguistic Thinking*, Leiden.

Walzer, R., 1976, 'Philosophical terms in medieval Arabic', in A. Dietrich (ed.), *Akten des VII. Kongresses für Arabistik und Islamwissenschaft*, Göttingen, 15 bis 22 August 1974, Göttingen, 385-9.

Waterlow, S., 1982, *Nature, Change and Agency in Aristotle's Physics*, Oxford.

Williams, C.J.F., 2000, *Philoponus On Aristotle On Coming-to-Be and Perishing 1.6-2.4*, London.

Zimmermann, F.W. and Brown, H.V., 1973, 'Neue arabische Übersetzungstexte aus dem Bereich der spätantiken griechischen Philosophie', *Der Islam*, Band 50, Heft 1, 313-24.

Zimmermann, F.W., 1987, 'Philoponus' impetus theory in the Arabic tradition', in R. Sorabji, ed., *Philoponus and the Rejection of the Aristotelian Science*, London, 121-9.

____ 1994a, 'Proclus Arabus rides again', *Arabic Sciences and Philosophy*, 4, 9-51.

____ 1994b, '*Topics* and the misnamed *Book of Poetic Gleanings* attributed to Aristotle and Alexander of Aphrodisias in a medieval Arabic manuscript', in Fortenbaugh, W.W., and Mirhady, D.C., eds, *Peripatetic Rhetoric after Aristotle* (Rutgers University Studies in Classical Humanities, 6) New Brunswick, 314-19.

English-Arabic Glossary

about: *(fī) (min) amr*
above, to have described above: *qaddama waṣfuhā*; to be mentioned above: *taqaddama fa-khabbara*
accomplishment: *tamām*
achieve, how to achieve: *kayfa al-wuṣūl*
action: *fi'l*; active: *fā'il*
actual, in actuality: *bi-al-fi'l, fa''āl*
add: *aḍāfa, zāda, ziyāda fī al-qawl*; to be added: *ukhidha ziyādatan*
adjacent: *muttaṣil*; to be adjacent: *waliya*
admit: *sarra, muqirr bi-*
adulterate: *shāba*
affection: *athar, ta'thīr*
afterwards; to say afterwards: *atba'a bi-kalām*
again: *thāniyan*
aim: *qaṣd*
air: *hawā'*
all: *jamī', ajma', bi-ajma'ihim*; all the other: *sā'ir*
almighty: *ta'āla*
alphabet: *mu'jam*
already: *taqaddama*
alter: *istaḥāla*; alteration: *istiḥāla*
always: *dā'iman*
amount: *miqdār*
analogy, by analogy: *'alā hādhā al-qiyās*
analyse: *taḥlīl*
animal: *ḥayawān*
annul: *mubṭil*
answer: *jawāb*
any: *shay', wāḥid, wa lā fī wāḥid*; any one: *ayy shay', kull wāḥid*; anything: *kull shay' ayy shay', lā ... shay'*
apply to: *waqa'a fī*
appropriate: *aḥrā*; better and more appropriate: *al-awwal wa al-aḥrā*
Arabic: *'arabiyya*
argument: *ḥujja*; arguments: *qawl*
arrange, to be arranged: *tarattaba*
as: *'alā al- ṭarīq*; as many as: *mithl*; such as: *bi-manzila*
aspect: *wajh*
assimilate: *shabbaha*
association: *iqtirān*
at least: *aqall mā yakūn*
attach: *waḍa'a ma'*
attainment: *tanāhi*
balance: *mīzān*; science of Balances: *'ilm al-mawāzīn*
be: *ṣāra, wujida*; to be in: *wujida fī*; *mawjūd fī*
become: *kāna, ṣāra*
before: *qablu, qadama, taqaddama qablu*
begin to: *akhadha*; beginning: *awwal, ibtidā'*; the beginning: *awwal al-amr*
believe: *ẓanna*
belong: *wujida li-, mawjūd li-*
benefit: *fā'ida, maḥsana*; to benefit: *intafa'a*
better, better and more appropriate: *al-awwal wa al-aḥrā*
black: *aswad*; blackness: *sawād*
body: *jism*; the simple bodies: *al-ajsām al-basīṭa*; the primary bodies: *al-ajsām al-uwwal*; the natural bodies: *al-ajsām al-ṭabī'iyya*
boiling: *ghalayān*
book: *kitāb*; *maqāla*
both: *jamī'an*

boundary: *ḥadd*
briefly: *bi-ikhtiṣār*
bring forward: *awrada*; bring up: *atā bi-*
brittle, the brittle: *al-qaḥal*
burn: *sha'ala*
call: *qāla*; *sammā*; to be called: *maqūl 'alayhi*
can, cannot: *(lā) (laysa) yumkin, lam yajuz*
carry, carry on: *tabi'a*; to be carried along: *ṣāra*
case: *mawḍi', qism*; as in the case of: *bi-manzila*
cause: *'illa, sabab*
centre: *wasaṭ*
certify: *akkada*
change: *al-ghayr, taghayyur*; to change: *taghayyara, mutaghayyir*; changing: *taghayyur*; do not change: *ghayr mutaghayyir*; unchanging: *ghayr mutaghayyir*; to be unable to change: *lā takūn mutaghayyira*
chapter: *bāb*
circle, to do in circle: *dāra*
claim: *kalām*; to claim: *anzala, qāla, za'ama*
clear: *wāḍiḥ*; to make clear: *bayyana, awḍaḥa, bayān dhālika*; to be made clear: *tabayyana*
close to: *qarīb*
cold: *al-bard, bārid*; coldness: *burūda*, cooling: *tabrīd*
combination: *ta'līf*; to combine: *allafa*
come to be: *kāna*
common, to have something in common, to be common: *shāraka, ishtaraka, shirka, mushāraka, mushtarak, mushārak li-, ishtirāk*; to be held in common: *'āmm*
compassionate: *raḥīm*
compound: *murakkab*
comprehensible: *mustaw'ab*
concerning: *fī bāb*
conclude: *antaja*
condition: *ḥāl*
configuration: *tashakkul*
confine, to be confined: *inḥāza, inḥiyāz*; confines: *ḥayyiz*
connection: *ittiṣāl*; to be connected with: *lahu munāsaba ilā*
consecutive, to be consecutive: *talā ba'ḍuhā al-ba'ḍ*
consider: *naẓara, ra'ā*
constitute: *qiwām*
consume, to be consumed: *nafada*
contact, to come into contact: *massa*
contain: *wujida li-, fī*
contemplate: *ta'ammala*
contemplation: *naẓar*
contrary: *ḍidd, muḍādd*; *mutaḍādd*; to be contrary: *ḍādda*; contrariety: *taḍādd, muḍādda*; contrarieties: *mutaḍāddāt*
convenient: *lā'iq*
correspond: *munāsib*
counterpart: *ghāya*; differences which are their counterpart in relation to each other: *fuṣūl hiya ghāyātuhā ba'ḍuhā 'inda ba'ḍ*
countless: *lā yublagh 'adaduhu*
cross through: *jāza*
cyclical: *bi-al-dawr*
damp: *mablūl*; the damp: *al-mablūl*; *al-mubtall*
decide: *'āzim*
defect: *'illa*
define: *ḥadda, taḥdīd*; to be defined: *taḥaddada*; definition: *ḥadd*
demonstrate: *barhana*; demonstration: *burhān*
depth: *qa'r*
describe: *dhakara, rasama, waṣafa*;
description: *waṣf*
designate: *dalla 'alā*
desiccation: *in'iqād*
differ: *ikhtalafa, mukhālif*; to differ from: *takhālafa*; to be different: *khālafa*; difference: *faṣl, khilāf, ikhtilāf, farq*: <they> do not differ with respect to this contrariety: *laysa al-farq alladhī baynahu wa baynahā bi-hādhihi al-muḍādda*
difficult: *ṣa'ib*; most difficult, more difficult: *aṣ'ab*; to be difficult: *'asr al-naẓar*; with greater, more difficulty: *a'sar*; which is hard or difficult: *madda bi-'usr wa ṣu'ūba*; someone can raise a difficulty: *tashakkaka al-mutashakkik*
direction: *naḥw*
discourse: *kalām*
discuss: *takallama*
divide, to be divided: *inqasama*; the part divided: *qāsim*
do: *fa'ala*

domestic: *li-al-khidma*
dominate: *ghalaba, ghālib*
dry: *yābis*; the dry: *al-yābis*; dryness: *yubūsa*
each: *aḥad*; each one: *kull wāḥid*
earth: *arḍ*
easy: *sahl*; to be easy to, easily: *bi-suhūla*; to become easier: *sahula*; more easily, easier, with lesser difficulty: *ashal*
either: *lā ... shay'*
element: *'usṭuquss*
else: *ākhar*
enclose: *iṭār*
encrust, to become encrusted: *laḥaja*
end: *nihāya*
enquire: *ṭalaba*; enquiry: *baḥth*
equal: *mutasāwī*
equivalent, to be equivalent: *bi-manzila*
essence: *dhāt*
essentially: *'alā al-qaṣd al-awwal*
establish: *thabata, athbata, waḍa'a*
eternal: *sarmadiyy*
evident: *bayyin*; to make evident: *bayyana*; evidently: *min bayān*, to become evident: *tabayyana*
exactly the same: *nafsihi bi-'aynihi*
exalt, to be exalted: *ta'āla*
examine: *baḥatha*
example: *mithāl*; for example: *mathalan*; *mithāl dhālika*; like for example: *mithāl*
excel: *jawwada*; excellent: *fāḍil*
excess: *ghalaba*
exhalation: *bukhār*
exhaustively, to deal exhaustively: *ṭawwala*
exist: *ḥaṣala, wujida, mawjūd*; existence: *wujūd*
explain: *fassara, khabbara*; to be explained: *tabayyana*; explanation: *basṭ, sharḥ*; the explanation of this: *bayān dhālika*; providing an explanation: *mukhbir, bayyana*; by way of explaining: *tafsīr*
expound: *khabbara*
extend further: *akthar min*
extreme: *akhīr, nihāya, ṭaraf*; extremely: *fī al-ghāya*; extremity: *ākhir*
eye: *'ayn*; to observe with one's own eyes: *yarā 'ayānan*
fair: *ḥaqīq*
far: *ba'īd*
favour: *minna*
few, fewer: *aqall*
figure: *wajh*; to be an eminent figure: *akhadha al-wujūh*
fill up: *mala'a*; capacity for filling up: *imtilā'*
find: *wajada*
fine: *laṭīf*; the fine: *al-laṭīf*; fineness: *laṭāfa*
finish with: *farigha min*
finite (in number): *mutanāhī*
fire: *nār*
first: *awwal, awwalan*; the first one: *awwal*; say first: *qaddama*
five: *khamsa*
flame: *lahīb*
fluid: *munṣabb*
follow: *tabi'a*; *tābi'*
foregoing, the foregoing: *taqaddama qabl*; in the foregoing: *fī-mā salafa*
foreign: *gharīb*
form: *ṣūra*; to be given a form: *taṣawwara*
former times: *sālif al-zamān*
formulation: *lafẓ*
four: *arba'a*
freezing: *jumūd*
frequent use: *kathura*
fruitful: *muthmir*
gather, to be gathered from: *ijtama'a min*
general: *'āmm*; in general: *bi-al-kulliyya*
generate: *awlada*
generation: *kawn, takwīn*; to be generated: *kāna, kawn, kā'in, mukawwan, kāna al-kawn li-*; generative: *muwallid*; ungenerated: *ghayr mukawwan*
get: *ḥaṣala li-*; get together: *ijtama'a ma'*
glue: *dibq*
go on: *marra*
God: *Allāh*
grammarian: *naḥawiyy*
great: *'aẓīm*; greater: *akthar*
guard: *ḥafaẓa*
hard: *'usr*; harder: *a'sar*; hardness: *al-ṣalāba*; the hard: *al-ṣalb*
hasten to: *mubādir*
have to: *inbaghā*
have: *wujida li-*; *wujida fī*
health, to keep in good health: *'āfa*
heat: *ḥarāra*; hot: *ḥārr*; the hot: *al-ḥārr*;

hotter: *akthar ḥarāra*
heavy: *thaqīl*; heaviness: *thiql*
hold: *qāla*; hold good for: *shabīh bi-*
how many: *kamm*
ice: *jalīd*
idea: *ma'nā*
identical: *bi-'aynihi*, *wāḥid bi-'aynihi*
illustration: *dalīl 'alā*
imagine: *tawwahama*
imply: *taḍammana*
impossible, to be impossible: *lā yajūz*, *lā yalta'im*
incline: *'aṭafa*
incorruptible: *ghayr fāsid*
increase in number: *yakūn akthar*
indeterminate: *ghayr ma'lūm*
indicate: *dalla*; to be indicated: *marsūm 'alayhi*, *'alayhi 'alāma*
infinity, infinite, infinitely many: *lā nihāya*; *ghayr mutanāhī*
insert, to be inserted: *dākhil*
instance, for instance: *mithl anna*; *mithāl dhālika*; like for instance: *mithāl*
instruction: *ta'līm*
intellect: *'aql*
intend: *arāda*
interaction: *ta'thīr*
interchangeable: *mutabādil*
intermediate: *mutawassiṭ*
interpretation: *taṣrīf*
isolation: *infirād*; isolated: *wāḥid*, *munfarid*
join: *ijtama'a min*
juxtapose, to be juxtaposed: *mawḍū' ilā jānibihi*
keep: *baqiya*, *ḥafaẓa*
kind: *jins*, *ṣinf*
know: *'alima*, *'arafa*; to make known: *'arrafa*; to be known: *ma'rūf*; to let you know: *ta'rīfuka*
lack: *yasīr*; to lack: *naqaṣa*; lack of: *qilla*
language: *kalām*
large quantity: *kathra*
last: *ākhir*, *akhīr*; latter: *akhīr*
lead, to be led: *ṣāra ilā*
leave off: *'adala bi-*; to be left: *baqiya*
letter: *ḥarf*
light: *khafīf*; lightness: *khiffa*
like: *musāwī*
limit: *ṭaraf*; extreme limit: *tanāhī*
link, to be linked: *maqrūn*
liquid: *sayyāl*; liquid pitch: *zift*
long: *ṭawīl*; to take longer: *ṭūl midda*
Lord: *Rabb*
low, lower <place>: *asfal*
man: *insān*
manifest, manifestly: *ẓāhir*
manipulate: *al-'amal (fī) (bī-)*
manner, in the manner: *mithāl dhālika*; in the same manner: *'alā mithāl*, *'alā mithāl wāḥid*, *bi-manzila*; in this manner: *'alā hādhā al-naḥw*
many: *kathīr*
mass: *razāna*
matter: *mādda*, *amr*
mean: *'anā*, *qāla*
member: *juz'*
mention: *dhakara*, *qāla*
merciful: *raḥmān*; to be merciful: *raḥama*
method: *sabīl*
middle: *wasaṭ*, *awsaṭ*, *mutawassiṭ*
mixture: *ikhtilāṭ*
mode: *wajh*; *modo continuo*: *'alā al-ittiṣāl*
moisture: *ruṭūba*; the moist: *al-raṭb*; moist: *raṭb*
moment, at the moment: *al-sā'a*
more: *akthar*, *fawq*, *mā zāda*; more prevalent: *akthar*; more than: *akthar min*
morphology: *taṣrīf*
move: *intaqala*; move on to: *'aṭafa*
must: *wajaba*
name: *ism*; to name; *sammā*, *ja'ala ism 'alā*; namely: *ya'nī*
nature: *ṭabī'a*; Natures: *ṭabā'i'*; science of Natures: *'ilm al-ṭabā'i'*; the natural bodies: *al-ajsām al-ṭabī'iyya*; to be affected by a nature: *inṭaba'a*, *munṭabi'*; by nature: *min sha'n*
necessary, necessarily: *ḍarūratan*; must necessarily, to imply necessarily, to follow necessarily: *lazima*, *lazima ḍarūratan*, *yajibu ḍarūratan*; to be necessary: *min al-iḍṭirār*, *(bi-) (fī) al-wājib*; according to the necessity: *bi-iḍṭirār*; to become necessary: *lam yakun budd min*
need: *ḥāja*; to need: *iḥtāja*
neither: *lā ... shay'*, *lā min wāḥid*
never: *wa lā fī waqt min al-awqāt*
next: *ilā jānib*; to be next: *atā ba'd*, *waliya*

none: *wa lā min wāḥid*; *laysa wāḥid*
nothing: *lā ... shay'*
now: *al-ān*
number: *'adad*, *mablagh*
numerous, to be numerous: *kathura*
observe: *ra'ā*
occur: *ḥaṣala*
oil: *dihn*
one, *shay'*; someone: *insān*; any one: *aḥad*; one more: *ākhar*; one single: *wāḥid*; only one: *wāḥid wāḥid*; one identical, one and the same: *wāḥid bi-'aynihi*
opinion: *ra'y*; according to the opinion: *kamā ẓanna*
opposite: *mukhālif*; *muqābil*; to be opposite to: *qābala*; to be opposed to: *mawḍū' qubāl*, *wuḍi'a qubālata*, *'alā qubālata*, *mawḍū' 'alā qubālata*, *muqābil*, *khālafa*, *khilāf*; things are opposed to: *mawḍū' lahu muqābalāt*; the one opposite to: *mutaqābil*
orally: *ḥikāya*
order: *ḥāl*
originate, which originate: *muḥdith*
other: *ākhar*, *sā'ir*; the other: *bāqī*; another: *aḥad*, *ākhar*; any other: *ākhar*
owing to: *sabab*
own, of its own: *khāṣṣ*
pair; pairing: *izdiwāj*; to be paired: *izdawaja*
part: *juz'*
pass: *marra*
passage: *mawḍi'*
passive: *munfa'il*
peace, peace be upon (him): *sallama taslīman*
penetrate: *dākhala*
perish: *fasada*; *kāna fasād*
persevere: *dāma*
petrify: *istaḥjara*; to be petrified: *mutaḥajjir*; petrified: *mustaḥjir*
phenomenon: *athar*
philosopher: *faylasūf*
phusikoi: *al-ṭabī'iyyūn*
place: *makān*, *mawḍi'*
posit: *waḍa'a*; to be posited: *mawḍū'*; position: *waḍ'*, *mawḍi'*
possess: *wujida li-*; possession: *malaka*
possible: *mumkin*; to be possible: *amkana*, *imkān*, *jāza*; possibility: *imkān* impossible: *ghayr mumkin*; to be impossible: *(lā) (laysa) yumkin*, *lam yakun mumkin*
posteriority: *ta'akhkhur*
power: *quwwa*
praise: *ḥamd*
pray: *ṣallā*
precede, preceding: *awwal*; what is preceding: *mā qabl*
preference, to be given preference: *muqaddam*
present: *mawjūd*; to present: *qaddama*, *ātā*; to be present in: *mawjūd fī*
preserve, to be preserved: *maḥfūẓ*
pressure, that whose mass sinks into itself due to pressure: *mā ṭubi'a wa inghamara fīhī razānatuhu*; to be impressed, impressed: *inṭaba'a*
previously: *qablu*, *qaddama*, *taqaddama*, *mutaqaddim*, *fī-mā maḍā*
primary: *awwal*; the primary bodies: *al-ajsām al-uwwal*
principle: *aṣl*, *mabda'*
prior: *qablu*; *muqaddam li-*; priority: *taqaddum*
privation: *'adam*; to be deprived of: *'ādim li-*
produce: *takwīn*
prolongation: *imtidād*
pronounce: *naṭaqa*
proof: *dalīl 'alā*
proper; in the proper sense: *khāṣṣ*; the proper characteristic: *khāṣṣa*, *khāṣṣiya*; properly, most properly: *khāṣṣatan*
prophet: *nabiyy*
pure: *maḥḍ*
put off: *awrada*
quality: *kayfiyya*
quantity: *kammiyya*
quickly: *sur'a*; more quickly, quicker: *asra'*
quote, quoting: *mustashhid*
rather than: *akthar min*
reach: *aṣāba*, *waṣala*, *ṣāra ilā*, *nāla*
reaction: *infi'āl*
reality, in reality: *('alā) (bi-) al-taḥqīq*
reason: *sabab*
reasoning: *kalām*; according to this reasoning: *'alā hādhā al-qiyās*
recall: *dhakara*
reduce, to be reduced to: *ijtama'a 'alā*,

irtaqā
refer to: *dalla ʿalā*
refute: *dafaʿa*
regarding: *(fī) (min) amr*
relate: *aḍāfa, nasaba*; relation: *tanāsub*
remain: *baqiya*; remaining: *bāqī*
remind: *dhakkara*
repeat: *aʿāda*
reply: *radda*
require, to be required: *iqtaḍā*
resolve: *dhawb, ḥalla*; to be resolved: *inḥalla*
rest, the rest: *bāqī*
resume: *ʿaṭafa, ista'nafa*
reverse, to be reversible, to be reversed: *inʿakasa*
revert: *rajiʿa*
rich, richest in science: *akthar ʿulūman*
rise up: *samā*
root: *aṣl*
rough: *khashin*; roughness: *khushūna*
same: *wāḥid*; very same: *bi-ʿaynihi*; one and the same: *wāḥid bi-ʿaynihi*
say: *qāla*; *qawl*; saying: *qawl*; what was said: *kalām*
science: *ʿilm*; science of Balances: *ʿilm al-mawāzīn*; science of Natures: *ʿilm al-ṭabāʾiʿ*
seal: *khātim*
second: *thānī*
self: *nafs*
sense: *maʿnā, naḥw, ḥiss*; to sense: *ḥassa*; sensation: *ḥiss*; sensible: *maḥsūs*; not sensible: *ghayr maḥsūs*
separate: *faṣala*; separate: *munfarid, muftariq*; to be separated: *mufāriq, ʿalā infirād, iftirāq*; separable: *mufāriq*; inseparable: *(lā) (ghayr) mufāriq*
series, to form series: *salsala*
several: *kathīr*
share with: *shāraka*; to be shared: *mushtarak*
should: *wajaba, inbaghā*
show: *dalla ʿalā, bayyana*; to be shown: *tabayyana*
shrink: *inghamara, inghimār*
side: *janb*
sign: *ʿalāma*
simple: *mufrad, basīṭ*; the simples: *al-basīṭa, al-basāʾiṭ*; the simple bodies: *al-ajsām al-basīṭa*
single: *wāḥid*
sink: *inghamara*; sink into: *rasaba*
six: *sitta*
slide: *ẓaliqa*
slowly: *baṭī'*; more slowly; slower: *abṭa'*
small: *ṣaghīr*; smaller: *aqall*
smoke: *dukhān*
smoothness: *malāsa*; the smooth: *al-amlas*
snow: *thalj*
soaked: *muntaqaʿ*; the soaked: *al-muntaqaʿ*
soft, the soft: *al-layyin*
solid: *jāmid*; the solid: *al-jāmid*; solidify: *inʿaqada*; to be solidified: *munʿaqid*; the solidified: *al-munʿaqid*
some others: *qawm*
somehow: *nawʿ mā*
sometimes: *aḥyānan*
speak: *khabbara*
species: *nawʿ*
stable: *thābit*
start: *akhadha*
state: *ḥāl*
statement: *kalām, qawl*; to state: *qāla, waḍaʿa*
stick: *taʿallaqa*
stoikheia: *ḥarf*
straight, in a straight line: *(ʿalā) (bi-) al-istiqāma*
strict, strictly speaking: *yuqāl (ʿalā) (bi-) al-taḥqīq*
study: *taʿallum*
subject: *mawḍūʿ*
sublime: *khaṭīr*
subsist: *lahu qiwām*; to cannot subsist: *lā qiwām li-*
substrate: *mawḍūʿ*
subsume, to be subsumed under: *inḥaṣara taḥta, maḥṣūr taḥta*
subtlety: *diqqa*
such: *mithl*
surface: *ẓāhir*
surround: *ḥawla*
syllogism: *qiyās*
take: *akhadha*
talk: *takallama*
tangible: *malmūs*
teach: *ʿallama*
thickness: *ghalaẓ*
thing: *amr*
thing, something: *shay'*

think: *ra'ā*
this: *amr*
this sort: *mithl*
three: *thalātha*; third: *thālith*
time: *waqt*, *zamān*
together: *jamī'an, jamī'ihimā*
topic: *ma'nā*
totality: *jumla*
transmit, to be transmitted: *manqūl naql*
transmutation: *taṣrīf*; to become transmuted: *inqalaba*
traverse: *qaṭa'a*
triangle: *muthallath*
true: *ṣaḥīḥ*; to prove true, to be true: *ṣaḥḥa*
two: *ithnān*; every two: *ithnān ithnān*
ultimate: *ākhir*
underlie: *mawḍū'*
understand: *adraka, fahima*
union: *jam'*
upper: *fawq*; upper place: *al-fawq*
use: *isti'māl*; to make use: *ista'mala, istanfa'a*
uttermost: *al-akhīr jiddan*
very: *jiddan*
vice versa: *'aks, bi-al-'aks*
view: *madhhab*
viscous: *lazij*; the viscous: *al-lazij*; viscosity: *luzūja*
vocalisation: *taḥrīk*; to become vocalised by a *fatḥa*: *infitāḥ*
vowel, to become unvowelled: *sakana, sukūn*
want: *arāda*
water: *mā'*
way: *sabīl, ṭarīq, wajh, jiha*; in the same way: *'alā hādhā al-naḥw*; *bi-manzila*; in this way: *bi-hādhā al-naḥw*
weak, the weak letters: *dhawāt al-'ilal*
what it is about: *al-ḥāl fī*
white: *abyaḍ*; whiteness, *bayāḍ*
will: *shā'a*
without qualification: *'alā al-iṭlāq*
wondrous: *'ajīb*
word: *kalām, lafẓ*; words: *qawl*
work: *ta'līf, al-'amal (fī) (bī-)*
world: *'ālam*
write: *kataba*

Arabic-English Index

References are to the paragraph numbers of the translation. Numbers between brackets indicate the occurrence of a term within the same paragraph. Under a given root the sequence of entries is as follows: the verb in the perfect comes first. It is followed by the verbal forms, then the *maṣdar*. Then come nominal forms arranged according to their length and followed by verbal nouns. Adjectives, and all active and passive participles follow at the end. Particles, as well as pronouns, have been disregarded. The article and the plural have been selected only when it was significant.

'-t-y

atā bi-, to bring up, 25
atā ba'd, to be next, 55
ātā, to present, 11; 44

'-th-r

athar, affection, 16 (2); 64; phenomenon, 92
ta'thīr, interaction, 5; affection 13; 14; 43; 44; 46

'-ḥ-d

aḥad, each, 55; 111; any one, 70; one, 19; 72; 73; 74 (2); 75; 76; 94; 97; 99 (6); 105; 107; 111; another, 107

'-kh-dh

akhadha, to begin, 61; to start, 18; 44; 50; 63; 69; 81; 89; 94; 101; 109; to take, 20 (2); 22 (2); 94; 97; 107 (2); *akhadha al-wujūh*, to be an eminent figure, 84; *ukhidha ziyādatan*, to be added, 107

'-kh-r

ākhir, last, 27; ultimate, 96; extremity, 107
ākhar, another, 3 (2); 12; 18; 19; 65; 76; 81; 94; 95; 97; 102 (2); 103 (2); 106 (5); 107 (2); else, 20; 69; 83; 104; other, 44; 52; 56 (2); 62; 69 (2); 97; 105; 107; 109; 111 (2); any other, 70; one more, 106
akhīr, extreme, 37; 38 (2); 40; last, 37; latter, 37; *al-akhīr jiddan*, uttermost, 40
ta'akhkhur, posteriority, 45

'usṭuquss

'usṭuquss, element, 35; 37; 38 (2); 42; 47; 48 (3); 50 (2); 52 (2); 54; 55 (5); 56; 61; 62; 67 (2); 69; 74 (2); 78; 80; 82; 83; 87; <88>; 89 (7); 91; 93 (3); 94 (2); 99; 101; 108; 109; 111

'-r-ḍ

arḍ, earth, 37; 39; 41; 42; 51 (6); 53 (4); 56 (3); 57 (6); 59; 60 (4); 61 (3); 63 (2); 64 (3); 71; 80; 82; 83; 87 (5); 92 (2); 93 (3); 95; 96; 97; 99 (14); 100; 101 (2)

'-ṣ-l

aṣl, principle, 3; 96; root, 6

'-ṭ-r
iṭār, *ashal iṭāran*, easier to enclose, 42

'-k-d
akkada, to certify, 89

'-l-f
allafa, to combine, 6
ta'līf, work, 1; combination, 4; 5; 7

'-l-h
Allāh, God, 1; 2 (3); 8; 20, 22

'-m-r
amr, matter, 24; this, 49; thing, 87; *(fī) (min) amr*, about, 42; 55; 81 (2); regarding, 81; *awwal al-amr*, the beginning, 107

'-m-l
ta'ammala, to contemplate, 54

'-n-s
insān, man, 12; one, 24; someone, 94

'-n-f
ista'nafa, to resume, 81

'-w-l
awwal, first, 19; 24; 36; 37; 38 (2); 40; 52; 103; 106; the first one, 55 (2); beginning, 55; primary, 80 (2); 81; 82 (2); 106; preceding, 107; *awwal al-amr*, the beginning, 107; *al-awwal wa al-aḥrā*, better and more appropriate, 24; *al-ajsām al-uwwal*, the primary bodies, 42; 44; 69 (3); 72; 81; 89 (6); 91 (2); 97
awwalan, first, 19; 46; 69; 95 (3)

'-w-n
al-ān, now, 56; 86; 94; 109

B-ḥ-th
baḥatha, to examine, 68; 81
baḥth, enquiry, 50

B-kh-r
bukhār, exhalation, 60

B-d-'
mabda', principle, 69; 80; 81; 82; 91 (2); 94 (4); 96 (3); 97 (2); 99 (4)
ibtidā', beginning, 97

B-d-d
budd, *lam yakun budd min*, it has become necessary, 4 (2); 7

B-d-r
mubādir, to hasten to, 84

B-d-l
mutabādil, interchangeable, 64

B-r-d
al-bard, cold, 30; 31
burūda, coldness, 3; 24; 32; 33; 35; 41 (2); 42 (5); 51 (2); 53 (2); 56 (3); 57 (3); 60; 61; 83; 87; 89
tabrīd, cooling, 61 (3)
bārid, cold, 32; 33 (2); 35; 44; 47 (2); 51 (4)

B-r-h-n
barhana, to demonstrate, 22
burhān, demonstration, 44; 48; 96; 98 (2); *akhadha burhān*, to demonstrate, 99

B-s-ṭ
basṭ, explanation, 11
basīṭ, simple, *al-basīṭa*, *al-basā'iṭ*, the simples, 4 (2); 5 (2); 25; *al-ajsām al-basīṭa*, the simple bodies, 36; 43; 44 (3); 51; 70; 80; 89

B-ṭ-'
abṭa', more slowly, 51; 86; slower, 51; 85; 87

B-ṭ-l
mubṭil, to annul, 96 (2)

B-'-d
Only the entries related to *bu'd* were selected.
ba'īd, far, 55

B-gh-y
inbaghā, should, 9; 11; 21; 24; 27; 43; 63; 106; to have to, 68

B-q-ā
baqiya, to remain, 56; 57 (3); 61 (3); 64 (9); 65 (2); 74; 79; 89; 95 (2); to be left, 62 (3); 64 (2); to keep, 74
bāqī, remaining, 24; 25; 61; 94; 99 (2); 100; 101; 105; 106; the rest, 44; 64; 72; 80; 82 (2); 93; 94 (5); 99; the other, 82

B-l-gh
balagha, *lā yublagh 'adaduhu*, to be countless, 109
mablagh, number, 90

B-l-l
al-mablūl, the damp, 20 (3); 22 (3)

mablūl, damp, 19
al-mubtall, the damp, 17

B-w-b
bāb, chapter, 69; *fī bāb*, concerning, 109

B-y-ḍ
bayāḍ, whiteness, 76; 95 (2); 97 (4); 99; 101
abyaḍ, white, 95 (3); 97 (7); 99; 101

B-y-n
bayyana, to show, 7; 12; 18; 19; 20 (3); 27; 44; 55; 83 (2); 89; 91; 96; 99; to provide explanations, 8; to explain, 19 (2); 44; 48 (2); 69 (4); 70; 76; 80; 89 (2); 99 (2); 94 (2); 96; 101; 105; to make clear, 44; 56; 74; 83; 89; 96; to make evident, 52
tabayyana, to become evident, 22; 97; 101; to be made clear, 74; 86; to explain, 82; to be shown, 93; 96; 99; to be explained, 105; *tabayyana bayānan*, to be explained, 58
bayān dhālika, the explanation of this, 14; 18; 33; to make clear, 102; *min bayān*, evidently, 47
bayyin, evident, 14; 44 (3); 51; 52; 58; 59; 94; 96; 103

T-b-ʻ
tabiʻa, to follow, 44; to carry on, 59; *atbaʻa bi-kalām*, to say afterwards, 74
tābiʼ, to follow, 46

T-m-m
tamām, accomplishment, 8

Th-b-t
thabata, to establish, 94
athbata, to establish, 79
thābit, stable, 93

Th-q-l
thiql, heaviness, 24
thaqīl, heavy, 37 (2); 40 (2)

Th-l-th
thalātha, three, 7; 25; 82 (2); 89 (3); 90
thālith, third, 55; 56; 63 (2); 91 (2); *al-maqāla al-thālitha*, book III, 83
muthallath, triangle, 82

Th-l-j
thalj, snow, 30

Th-m-r
muthmir, fruitful, 35

Th-n-y
ithnān, two, 25; 36; 37 (2); 55 (2); 57 (2); 62; 61 (4); 66; 70 (2); 88; 89 (8); 90 (4); 91; 97; *ithnān ithnān*, every two, 36; 101
thānī, second, 50; 52; 54; 55
thāniyan, again, 94; 106

J-z-ʼ
juzʼ, part, 10 (2); 12 (2); 62; 73; 80; 82 (2); 94; member, 74 (2); 107

J-s-m
jism, body, 37 (2); 40 (3); 42; 44 (2); 62 (2); 63 (4); 65; 69 (5); 81; 89 (2); 91 (2); 94 (2); 99; 105; 106 (4); 107 (7); 109 (5); 110 (2); 111; *al-ajsām al-basīṭa*, the simple bodies, 36; 43; 44 (3); 51; 70; 80; *al-ajsām al-uwwal*, the primary bodies, 42; 44; 69 (3); 72; 81; 89 (6); 91 (2); 97 *al-ajsām al-ṭabīʻiyya*, the natural bodies, 70

J-ʻ-l
jaʻala, jaʻala mā qaddamnā ākhiran fī qawlihi, he said last what we have said first, 27; *hādhihi allatī ʻalayhā khāṣṣatan yujʻalu isma al-nāri*, that which is properly called fire, 36

J-l-d
jalīd, ice, 30; 31; 32; 33 (4); 34; 35

J-m-d
jumūd, freezing, 31; 32 (2); 33 (2)
al-jāmid, the solid, 19; 20 (3); 21 (3); 22; 26
jāmid, solid, 19; 24

J-m-ʻ
ijtamaʻa ʻalā, to be reduced to, 25; *ijtamaʻa maʻ*, to get together, 64 (2); *ijtamaʻa min*, to be gathered from, 93; to join, 102
jamʻ, union, 8
jamīʻ, all, 19; 20 (3); 23; 24; 42; 47; 48 (2); 51 (2); 62; 68 (2); 69 (2); 76; 89 (3); 93 (2); 94 (2); 96

(4); 99 (3); 100 (2); 101 (5); 106 (2); 107; 109 ***jamī'an***, both, 46; together, 61; at the same time, 97; 98; 99 (2); ***jamī'ihimā***, together, 61; ***ajma', bi-ajma'ihim***, all, 43; 80; 92; 106

J-m-l
jumla, totality, 10 (2); 12

J-n-b
janb, side, 96; 97 (2)
jānib, ilā jānib, next, 111; ***mawḍū' ilā jānibihi***, to be juxtaposed, 106; 111

J-n-s
jins, kind, 24; 40

J-w-b
jawāb, answer, 24; 61

J-w-d
jawwada, to excel, 25
jiddan, very, 35; 51; 55; 96

J-w-z
jāza, to be possible, 40; to cross through, 104; ***lā yajūz***, to be impossible, 25; ***lam yajuz***, could not, 5

Ḥ-j-j
ḥujja, argument, 69

Ḥ-j-r
istaḥjara, to petrify, 13
mutaḥajjir, to be petrified, 15; 16 (2)
mustaḥjir, petrified, 19

Ḥ-d-th
muḥdith, which originate, 89 (2)

Ḥ-d-d
ḥadda, to define, 18; 19; 22; 44; 55; 104; ***taḥaddada***, to be defined, 107 (2)
ḥadd, definition, 20; 106; 107; boundary, 39; 40
taḥdīd, laysa yumkin… taḥdīd, it is impossible to define, 109

Ḥ-r-r
ḥarāra, heat, 3; 24; 28; 29 (2); 31; 32; 33; 35 (2); 41 (2); 42 (2); 51 (2); 56; 57 (2); 60; 61; 62 (2); 64 (8); 73; 74; 83 (2); 89; ***akthar ḥarāra***, hotter, 42
al-ḥārr, the hot, 32; 33 (2)
ḥārr, hot, 29 (2); 33; 42; 44; 47 (2); 51 (4); 64 (2); 73; 74; 87

Ḥ-r-f
ḥarf, letter, 3; 4 (3); 5; 6; 7 (3); *stoikheia*, 20; 23

Ḥ-r-k
taḥrīk, vocalisation, 6

Ḥ-r-y
aḥrā, al-awwal wa al-aḥrā, better and more appropriate, 24

Ḥ-s-s
ḥassa, to sense, 43
ḥiss, sensation, 44 (5); 46; 59; sense, 89; 105
maḥsūs, sensible, 69 (2); 77; 78; 90; ***ghayr maḥsūs***, not sensible, 90; 91

Ḥ-s-n
maḥsana, benefit, 22

Ḥ-ṣ-r
inḥaṣara taḥta, to be subsumed under, 18
maḥṣūr taḥta, to be subsumed under, 12; 14 (2); 16 (3); 19 (3); 24; 40

Ḥ-ṣ-l
ḥaṣala, to occur, 42 (2); to exist, 69; to be put, 45; ***ḥaṣala li-***, to get, 42 (2)

Ḥ-f-ẓ
ḥafaẓa, to guard, 8; to keep, 56; 99
maḥfūẓ, preserved, 74; 94

Ḥ-q-q
ḥaqīq, fair, 7
taḥqīq, ('alā) (bi-) al-taḥqīq, strictly speaking, 18; 44 (2); in reality, 42; ***yuqāl 'alā al-taḥqīq***, strictly speaking, 21; 22

Ḥ-k-y
ḥikāya, orally, 31

Ḥ-l-l
ḥalla, to resolve, 94
inḥalla, to be resolved, 56
taḥlīl, to analyse, 11

Ḥ-m-d
ḥamd, praise, 2

Ḥ-w-j
iḥtāja, to need, 84; 104; 107 (2)
ḥāja, need, 8 (2)

Ḥ-w-z
inḥāza, to be confined, 10 (2); 12 (3); 18 (2)

ḥayyiz, confines, 10 (2); 12; 18 (4);
inḥiyāz, to be confined, 18 (2)
Ḥ-w-l
istaḥāla, to alter, 44
ḥāl, state, 8; 22; 35; condition, 12; 21; 35; 64; 99; order, 45; *al-ḥāl fī*, what it is about, 55
ḥawla, to surround, 40
istiḥāla, alteration, 43; 44 (9); 46; 73; 74
Ḥ-y-n
ḥīn, aḥyānan, sometimes, 20 (4)
Ḥ-y-y
ḥayawān, animal, 12
Kh-b-r
khabbara, to explain, 43 (2); 46; 50 (2); 55; 56; 63; 65; 69 (2); 63; 81 (2); 106; 109 (2); to speak, 94; to expound, 101
mukhbir, providing an explanation, 83
Kh-t-m
khātim, seal, 2
Kh-d-m
khidma, li-al-khidma, domestic, 35
Kh-sh-n
khushūna, roughness, 24 (2)
khashin, rough, 24
Kh-ṣ-r
ikhtiṣār, bi-ikhtiṣār, briefly, 94
Kh-ṣ-ṣ
khāṣṣ, of its own, 12; 18 (2); 21; 22 (3); proper, 94; 109; in the proper sense, 60
khāṣṣa, the proper characteristic, 42; *khāṣṣatan*, properly, 10; 29; 35; 42 (2); 60; most properly, 59
khāṣṣiya, the proper characteristic, 107
Kh-ṭ-r
khaṭīr, sublime, 4
Kh-f-f
khiffa, lightness, 24
khafīf, light, 37 (2); 40 (2)
Kh-l-ṭ
ikhtilāṭ, mixture, 60
Kh-l-f
khālafa, to be different, 19; 22 (2); 83; to be opposed to, 106
takhālafa, to differ from, 56
ikhtalafa, to differ, 82
khilāf, difference, 33; 51; to be opposed to, 89
mukhālif, to differ, 106; the opposite, 106
ikhtilāf, difference, 82
Kh-m-s
khamsa, five, 25
D-b-q
dibq, glue, 14
D-kh-l
dākhala, to penetrate, 12
dākhil, to be inserted, 44
D-kh-n
dukhān, smoke, 59 (2); 60 (3)
D-r-k
adraka, to understand, 103
D-f-ʻ
dafaʻa, to refute, 83
D-q-q
diqqa, subtlety, 54
D-l-l
dalla, to indicate, 3; *dalla ʻalā*, to refer to, 3; to show, 4 (3); to designate, 19
dalīl ʻalā, to show, 3; illustration, 6; proof, 35
D-h-n
dihn, oil, 13; 14
D-w-r
dāra, to do in circle, 69
dawr, bi-al-dawr, cyclical, 51
D-w-m
dāma, to persevere, 8
dā'iman, always, 79; 91; 107 (4)
Dh-k-r
dhakara, to describe, 4; 8; to mention, 83; 84 (2); 105; to recall, 84, *dhakkara*, to remind, 44; 86; 89
Dh-h-b
madhhab, view, 94
Dh-ū
dhāt, essence, 80
Dh-w-b
dhawb, laysa wujūd al-fuṣūl … bi-al-dhawb, the differences … will not resolve, 106

R-'-y
ra'ā, to observe, 43; 44 (6); 46; 60; 73; 74; 89 (3); 90 (2); 96; to think, 46; 82 (2); to consider, 81
ra'y, opinion, 82 (2)
R-b-b
Rabb, Lord, 2
R-b-'
arba'a, four, 23; 24; 25; 36; 40; 42; 69 (4); 70; 78; 80; 81 (2); 82; 83; 89 (2); 90; 97; 101
R-t-b
tarattaba, to be arranged, 18
R-j-'
raji'a, to revert, 102; 106 (3)
R-ḥ-m
raḥama, to be merciful, 1
raḥīm, compassionate, 2
raḥmān, merciful, 2
R-d-d
radda, to reply, 44
R-z-n
razāna, mass, 15; 16
R-s-b
rasaba, to sink into, 12 (2)
R-s-m
rasama, to describe, 5
marsūm 'alayhi, to be indicated, 102
R-ṭ-b
ruṭūba, moisture, 3; 10 (2); 12 (2); 13 (3); 14 (3); 15 (3); 16; 18; 20 (2); 21 (3); 22 (10); 24 (2); 41 (2); 42 (5); 51 (2); 53; 56; 57 (3); 60 (2); 61; 62 (2); 64 (5); 83; 87; 89; 95 (2); 97 (2); 98; 99; 100; 101 (4)
al-raṭb, the moist, 12 (2); 14; 15; 16 (4); 17 (3); 18 (2); 19 (3); 20 (8); 21 (2); 22 (7); 24; 26; 27; 42
raṭb, moist 14; 16 (2); 19; 22; 32; 33 (2); 42; 47 (3); 51 (4); 64; 95 (2); 97 (2); 98; 99 (3)
R-q-ā
irtaqā, to be reduced, 20; 23; 24; 25 (2)
R-k-b
murakkab, compound, 4 (2); 83
R-w-d
arāda, to intend, 11; to want, 19; 25; 96
Z-'-m
za'ama, to claim, 93 (2)
Z-f-t
zift, liquid pitch, 14
Z-l-q
zaliqa, to slide, 14
Z-m-n
zamān, 'alā sālif al-zamān, in the former times, 31
Z-w-d
zāda, to add, 103; 106 (2), ***mā zāda***, more, 25
ziyāda, ziyāda fī al-qawl, to add, 91; ***ukhidha ziyāda***, to be added, 107
Z-w-j
izdawaja, to be paired, 100
izdiwāj, pair, 90; pairing, 101
S-b-b
sabab, cause, 9; reason, 12; 35; 42 (4); 65; 69; 86; 111; owing to, 82
S-b-l
sabīl, way, 8; method, 69
S-t-t
sitta, six, 25; 90
S-r-r
sarra, to admit, 46
S-r-'
sur'a, quickly, 86
asra', more quickly, 51 (2); 87; quicker, 85; 87
S-r-m-d
sarmadiyy, eternal, 81; 83
S-f-l
asfal, lower <place>, 37 (2); 38 (3)
S-l-f
salafa, fī-mā salafa, in the foregoing, 48
sālif, 'alā sālif al-zamān, in the former times, 31
S-l-s-l
salsala, to form series, 109
S-l-m
sallama taslīman, peace be upon (him), 2
S-m-m
sammā, to name, 5 (2); 24; 35 (2); 40; to call, 44
ism, name, 2; 5; ***ja'ala ism 'alā***, to name, 35

S-m-w
samā, to rise up, 39
S-k-n
sakana, to become unvowelled, 6
sukūn, to become unvowelled, 6
S-h-l
sahula, to become easier, 11; to be easily, 18
suhūla, bi-suhūla, to be easy to, 12; easily, 14, 18; 50
sahl, easy, 50; 51; 55
ashal, more easily, 42; 51 (2); 87; easier, 55; 57; 61; 85; 87; 99; with lesser difficulty, 82
S-w-d
sawād, blackness, 76; 95; 97 (3); 98; 99 (2); 100; 101 (4)
aswad, black, 95 (3); 97 (4); 99 (3)
S-w-ʻ
al-sāʻa, at the moment, 105
S-w-y
musāwī, like, 111
mutasāwī, equal, 80
S-y-r
sā'ir, other, 23; all, 45; all the other, 18; 25; 61; 81
S-y-l
sayyāl, liquid, 24
Sh-'-n
sha'n, min sha'n, by nature, 47
Sh-b-h
shabbaha, to assimilate, 40;
shabīh bi-, to hold good for, 64
Sh-r-ḥ
sharḥ, explanation, 22
Sh-r-k
shāraka, to share with, 42; to have something in common, 42 (2); 51; 97 (3)
ishtaraka, to have in common, 22; 55; to be common, 87
shirka, something in common, 86
mushāraka, something in common, 51 (2); 86
ishtirāk, to have something in common, 67; common, 100
mushārak li-, to have something in common, 3
mushtarak, to be shared, 50; to have something in common, 87 (2); common, 105
Sh-ʻ-l
shaʻala, to burn, 60
Sh-k-k
tashakkaka al-mutashakkik, someone can raise a difficulty, 42
Sh-k-l
tashakkul, configuration, 42
Sh-h-d
mustashhid, quoting, 84
Sh-w-b
shāba, to adulterate, 13; 16 (2)
Sh-y-'
shā'a, to will, 20; 22
shay', thing, 3; 10; 12 (2); 14 (2); 15; 19 (5); 20 (4); 33; 41; 43; 44; 51 (3); 53; 55; 60; 61; 62 (2); 65; 66 (2); 67; 69; 74 (3); 87; 89 (2); 97 (2); 106 (3); 107 (6); something, 24; 55; 64 (2); 69 (2); 83 (2); 84; 97 (2); 99; 102 (2); 103 (2); 104 (2); 107; one, 70; 91; 93; 106; any, 106; ***ayy shay'***, any one, 78; ***shay' wāḥid bi-ʻaynihi***, one and the same thing, 97 (2); ***kull shay' ayy shay'***, anything, 48 (2); ***lā … shay'***, nothing, 34; 35 (2); 64 (2); 65; 77; 78; anything, 35; 64; either, 94; neither, 94; ***shay' min kalāmihi***, a word, 84
Ṣ-b-b
munṣabb, fluid, 24
Ṣ-ḥ-ḥ
ṣaḥḥa, to prove true, 22; to be true, 33
ṣaḥīḥ, true, 25
Ṣ-r-f
taṣrīf, morphology, 1; 5 (4); 7 (2); 8; 9; 84; transmutation, 5 (1); interpretation, 11
Ṣ-ʻ-b
ṣaʻib, difficult, 27; 53; 55
ṣuʻūba, lā yamudduhā bi-ʻusr wa ṣuʻūba, whose <changing> is not hard or difficult, 50
aṣʻab, most difficult, 27; more difficult, 55; 85; 87
Ṣ-gh-r
ṣaghīr, small, 10; 12 (2)

Ṣ-l-w
ṣallā, to pray, 2
Ṣ-l-b
al-ṣalāba, hardness, 16
al-ṣalb, the hard, 15 (2); 16 (2); 19 (2)
Ṣ-n-f
ṣinf, kind, 22; 23
Ṣ-w-b
aṣāba, to reach, 22
Ṣ-w-r
ṣāra, to become, 6 (2); 40; to be, 16; 24; 37; 42 (5); 97; to be carried along, 39; 40; *ṣāra ilā*, to reach, 89; to be led, 102
taṣawwara, to be given a form, 69
ṣūra, form, 29; 42 (4); 44 (2); 56; 61; 109
Ḍ-d-d
ḍādda, to be contrary, 90; 97
ḍidd, contrary, 13; 14; 33; 47 (2); 48 (3); 50; 55; 61 (3); 62 (3); 64; 65 (2); 67; 71; 74 (2); 75; 76; 89 (2); 90; 95 (2); 99 (2); 105
taḍādd, contrariety, 33; 47; 48; 89
muḍādda, contrariety, 73; 74 (2); 76; 88; 89 (5); 95 (4); 96; 97 (7); 102; 103 (2); 106 (6); 107 (8); 109
muḍādd, contrary, 22; 65
mutaḍādd, contrary, 12 (2); 18 (2); 48; 61; 65; 98; contrary <to one another>, 47 (3); 55
mutaḍāddāt, contrarieties, 24; 69; 76; 83; 89; 90; 101; 103; 104; 107; 109; 110
Ḍ-r-r
ḍarūratan, necessarily, 79; 81; 82; 88; 97 (2); necessary, 108; *lazima ḍarūratan*, must necessarily, 53 (3); 107; to imply necessarily, 91; to follow necessarily, 95; 97; 106 (2)
iḍṭirār, *min al-iḍṭirār*, to be necessary, 67; *bi-iḍṭirār*, according to the necessity, 96
Ḍ-m-n
taḍammana, to imply, 46; 81
Ḍ-y-f
aḍāfa, to relate, 27; to add, 101
Ṭ-b-ʻ
ṭabaʻa, *mā ṭubiʻa wa inghamara fīhī razānatuhu*, that whose mass sinks into itself due to pressure, 15
inṭabaʻa, to be impressed, 16 (2); to be affected by a nature, 42; 61; 69; 109
ṭabīʻa, nature, 74; 91; 94; *ṭabāʼiʻ*, Natures, 7 (2); 8; 9; *ʻilm al-ṭabāʼiʻ*, science of Natures, 84 (2)
ṭabīʻī, *al-ajsām al-ṭabīʻiyya*, the natural bodies, 70; *al-ṭabīʻiyyūn*, *phusikoi*, 70
munṭabiʻ, affected by a nature, 44
Ṭ-r-f
ṭaraf, extreme, 7; 96 (6); 99; limit, 40
Ṭ-r-q
ṭarīq, way, 81; *ʻalā al-ṭarīq*, as, 20
Ṭ-l-b
ṭalaba, to enquire, 24; 61; 81 (2)
Ṭ-l-q
iṭlāq, *ʻalā al-iṭlāq*, without qualification, 41
Ṭ-w-l
ṭawwala, to deal exhaustively, 25
ṭūl, *ṭūl midda*, to take longer, 53
ṭawīl, long, 27
Ẓ-n-n
ẓanna, to believe, 60; 82; 96 (2); *kamā ẓanna*, according to the opinion, 70; 81
Ẓ-h-r
ẓāhir, manifest, 10; 22 (2); 25; 42 (2); 44 (2); 47 (2); 50; 58; 66; 89; 97; 99; 100; 102; 103; 105; manifestly, 23; 24; surface, 22
ʻ-b-ʼ
mustawʻab, comprehensible, 4
ʻ-j-b
ʻajīb, wondrous, 42
ʻ-j-m
muʻjam, alphabet, 46
ʻ-d-d
ʻadad, number, 25; 107; *lā yublagh ʻadaduhu*, to be countless, 109
ʻ-d-m
ʻadam, privation, 75; 76 (4)

'ādim li-, to be deprived of, 21; 22

'-d-l

'adala bi-, to leave off, 3

'-r-b

'arabiyya, Arabic, 6

'-r-f

'arafa, to know, 22; 27; ***'arrafa***, to make known, 101

ta'rīf, mubādirūn ilā ta'rīfika, we hasten to let you know, 84

ma'rūf, to be known, 44

'-z-m

'āzim, to decide, 102

'-s-r

'asura, to be not easily …, 18

'usr, hard, 50; 53; 55

'asr al-naẓar, to be difficult, 49

a'sar, with greater difficulty, 51; 82; harder, 55; with more difficulty, 86

'-ṭ-f

'aṭafa, to resume, 26; to incline, 44; to move on to, 50

'-ẓ-m

'aẓīm, great, 4

'-f-w

'āfa, to keep in a good health, 8

'-q-d

in'aqada, to solidify, 14

in'iqād, dessication, 61

mun'aqid, to be solidified, 15; 16 (2); ***al-mun'aqid***, the solidified, 17

'-q-l

'aql, intellect, 54

'-k-s

in'akasa, the other way round, 16; to be reversed, 106; to be reversible, 106; to reverse, 106

'aks, bi-al-'aks, vice versa, 44; 87

'-l-ā

ta'āla, to be exalted, 1; almighty, 20; 22

'-l-q

ta'allaqa, to stick, 106

'-l-l

'illa, defect, 25; cause, 105

dhawāt al-'ilal, the weak letters, 46

'-l-m

'alima, to know, 7; 9; 21; 24; 27; 31; 63

'allama, to teach, 3 (2)

'ilm, science, 3; 27 (2); ***'ilm al-mawāzīn***, science of Balances, 3; ***'ilm al-ṭabā'i'***, science of Natures, 84 (2)

'ālam, world, 2; 40 (2)

'alāma, sign, 102; ***'alayhi 'alāma***, to be indicated, 95 (4)

ta'līm, instruction, 8

ta'allum, study, 84

ma'lūm, min al-ma'lūm anna, we know that, 10; ***ghayr ma'lūm***, indeterminate, 107

'-m-m

'āmm, general, 20; held in common, 50; common, 55; 87 (3); 97; 106

'-m-l

ista'mala, to use, 19; 69; 89; to make use, 105; 106

'amal, al-'amal (fī) (bī-), to work, 3; to manipulate, 4 (2)

isti'māl, use, 4

'-n-y

'anā, to mean, 20; 29; 38; 40 (2); 42 (2); 56; 67 (2); 76; 78; 89; 93; 95; 96 (2); 100 (2); 101 (2); 102; 103; 106 (2); namely, 37 (3); 97 (3)

ma'nā, idea, 44; 102 (2); sense, 19; 42; 94; topic, 22

'-w-d

a'āda, to repeat, 105

'-y-n

'ayn, eye, 54; ***bi-'aynihi***, identical, 62; 65; very same, 64; the same, 92; 93; 98; ***wāḥid bi-'aynihi***, one and the same, 38; 42; 97 (3); 99; identical, 62; 65 (3); ***yarā 'ayānan***, to observe with one's own eyes, 43

Gh-r-b

gharīb, foreign, 18 (2); 21; 22 (4)

Gh-l-b

ghalaba, to dominate, 42; 51 (3)

ghalaba, excess, 28; 29; 30; 31 (3); 32 (3); 33 (4); 35 (4)

ghālib, to dominate, 42 (5)

Gh-l-ẓ
ghalaẓ, thickness, 10, 12
Gh-l-ā
ghalayān, boiling, 29; 31; 32 (2); 33 (3); 35
Gh-m-r
inghamara, to sink, 15; to shrink, 16 (2)
inghimār, to shrink, 16
Gh-y-r
Only the entries related to change were selected.
taghayyara, to change, 44 (4); 46 (2); 47; 48 (3); 50; 51; 56 (2); 60; 61 (5); 63; 66 (2); 67 (2); 74 (4); 79; 81; 82 (9); 87; 88; 89 (5); 91; 95 (2); 96 (5); 97 (12); 98 (2); 99 (12); 101 (2); 102 (3); 105 (2); 106 (9); 107; 109 (2); 110; 111 (2)
al-ghayr, change, 69
taghayyur, change, 43; 44 (3); 46; 50; 51 (6); 53; 55 (5); 56 (3); 57; 62; 69 (2); 74 (3); 85; 87 (4); 89 (3); 91 (2); 93; 94 (3); 95 (2); 96 (5); 97 (5); 98; 99 (7); 100; 101; 103; 106 (6); 107 (3); 108; 109 (3); changing, 52 (3); 54; 55; 56; 61 (5); 63; 67 (2); 68; 69; 71; *kāna al-taghayyur li-*, to change, 48; 50; 89
mutaghayyir, to change, 82, *ghayr mutaghayyir*, do not change, 46; 81 (2); unchanging, 94; *lā takūn mutaghayyira*, to be unable to change, 79
Gh-y-y
ghāya, fuṣūl hiya ghāyātuhā ba'ḍuhā 'inda ba'ḍ, differences which are their counterpart in relation to each other, 50; *fī al-ghāya*, extremely, 13; extreme, 33
F-t-ḥ
infitāḥ, to become vocalised by a *fatḥa*, 6
F-r-d
mufrad, simple, 4
infirād, isolation, 69; *'alā infirād*, to be separated, 91
munfarid, isolated, 6; separate, 83
F-r-q
farq, laysa al-farq alladhī baynahu wa baynahā bi-hādhihi al-muḍādda, <they> do not differ with respect to this contrariety, 106
mufāriq, separated, 69; separable, 83; *(lā) (ghayr) mufāriq*, inseparable, 90
iftirāq, to be separated, 101
muftariq, separate, 63
F-r-gh
farigha min, to finish with, 22; 101; *qad farightu minhu fīmā taqaddama min al-kutub*, I have dealt with it in previous books, 25
F-s-d
fasada, to perish, 51; 53 (3); 55 (2); 57 (4); 61 (4); 62 (3); 64 (8); 65 (3); 66 (2); 67 (3); 99
fasād, kāna fasād, to perish, 61
fasid, ghayr fāsid, incorruptible, 83
F-s-r
fassara, to explain, 27
tafsīr, by way of explaining, 31 (2)
F-ṣ-l
faṣala, to separate, 107
faṣl, difference, 24; 42; 44 (3); 47 (4); 48; 50 (2); 52 (2); 55 (2); 56 (4); 61 (7); 63; 65 (6); 67; 73; 89 (4); 91 (3); 94; 97 (5); 98; 99 (6); 106 (4); 107; 109 (2)
F-ḍ-l
fāḍil, excellent, 27
F-'-l
fa'ala, to do, 15
fi'l, action, 12; 106; *bi-al-fi'l*, in actuality, 91
fa''āl, in actuality, 67
infi'āl, reaction, 3
fā'il, active, 24
munfa'il, passive, 24
Falsafa
faylasūf, philosopher, 5; 27; 84
F-h-m
fahima, to understand, 11

F-w-q
fawq, more, 8; upper, 38; upper place, 38; ***al-fawq***, the upper <place>, 37 (2); 38
F-y-d
fā'ida, benefit, 4; 27
Q-b-l
qābala, to be opposite to, 19
qablu, previously, 44; before, 74; 106; prior, 77; 78; 106 (2); ***mā qabl***, what is preceding, 6
qubālata, wuḍi'a qubālata, to be opposed to, 20 (5); ***'alā qubālata***, to be opposed to, 20; ***mawḍū' 'alā qubālata***, to be opposed to, 20
muqābil, opposite, 19; 20; 22; to be opposed to, 33; ***mawḍū' lahu***
muqābalāt, things are opposed to, 19
mutaqābil, the one opposite to, 19; opposite, 20
Q-ḥ-l
al-qaḥal, the brittle, 14
Q-d-r
miqdār, amount, 107 (2)
Q-d-m
qadama, al-jismu alladhī qadama an yakūn, the body that has been generated before, 107
qaddama, to present, 22; to say first, 27; to say previously, 74; ***qaddama waṣfuhā***, to have described above, 101
taqaddama, previous, 25; 44; previously, 43; 44; 69; 81; 82; 89; 94; 101; already, 81; 94; 99; to be already, 69; ***taqaddama fa-khabbara***, to be mentioned above, 81; ***taqaddama qabl***, before, 3; the foregoing, 3; ***taqaddama waḍ'uhā***, to be previously posited, 20
taqaddum, priority, 45
muqaddam, to be given preference, 84; ***muqaddam li-***, prior, 65
mutaqaddim waṣfuhā, that we have previously described, 24
Q-r-b
qarīb, close to, 55
Q-r-r
muqirr bi-, to admit, 96; 97; 99
Q-r-n
iqtirān, association, 98
maqrūn, to be linked, 42
Q-ṣ-d
qaṣd, aim, 22; ***'alā al-qaṣd al-awwal***, essentially, 29
Q-s-m
inqasama, to be divided, 14; 37
qism, case, 81
qāsim, the part divided, 14
Q-ḍ-y
iqtaḍā, to be required, 107
Q-ṭ-'
qaṭa'a, to traverse, 109
Q-'-r
qa'r, depth, 21 (2); 22 (6)
Q-l-b
inqalaba, to become transmuted, 6
Q-l-l
qilla, lack of, 14
aqall, smaller, 25; fewer, 25; ***aqall mā yakūn***, at least, 90
Q-w-l
qāla, to say, 9 (2); 17 (2); 18 (2); 19 (5); 20 (4); 21; 22 (5); 23; 24 (2); 25 (2); 26; 28; 29; 30; 31 (3); 32; 34; 36; 39; 42; 43 (2); 44 (8); 45 (2); 47; 48; 49; 50 (2); 51; 53; 55 (2); 57; 59; 60; 61 (2); 62; 65; 66; 68; 69; 70 (2); 71; 72; 73; 75; 77; 78; 79; 80; 81 (2); 82, 83 (2); 84; 85; 86; 88; 89 (4); 90; 91; 92; 94; 95; 99 (2); 100; 101 (2); 102; 104; 105 (2); 106 (2); 108; 110 (2); 111 (2); to call, 14; to mean, 40 (2); to claim, 94; to hold, 94; 99; to state, 68; 94; 96; to mention, 102
qawl, statement, 19; 46 (2); 106 (2); the same as saying, 25; 92 (2); 93; as saying, 111; saying, 44; 93; to say, 27; 35; 89; 94; 106; by saying, 38; 40; 67 (2); in saying, 46; words, 44; arguments, 64 (2); what has been said, 69; ***qīla qawl***, someone said, 83
maqāla, book, 83
maqūl 'alayhi, to be called, 76

Q-w-m
qawm, some others, 81
qiwām, to constitute, 82; *lā qiwām li-*, to cannot subsist, 69; *kāna lahu qiwām*, to subsist, 101
istiqāma, ('alā) (bi-) al-istiqāma, in a straight line, 69; 106 (2); 107

Q-w-y
quwwa, power, 42; 64; 65

Q-y-s
qiyās, syllogism, 7; *'alā hādhā al-qiyās*, by analogy, 31; analogically, 64; according to this reasoning, 93; 97

K-t-b
kataba, to write, 3
kitāb, book, 1; 3 (2); 4; 5 (2); 8 (3); 11 (2); 17; 25; 27 (2); 44 (3); 47; 48; 79; 83 (3); 84

K-th-r
kathura, frequent use, 6; to be numerous, 105
kathra, large quantity, 42
kathīr, many, 3; 51; 96; several, 17; 19 (4); 20; 83
akthar, more prevalent, 42; more, 70 (2); 89; 107 (2); greater, 107; *akthar min*, to extend further, 16; more than, 20 (2); 42; 53; 61; 67; 69 (2); 89 (6); 90; 104; rather than, 41 (4); 66; *yakūn akthar*, increase in number, 25; *akthar 'ulūman*, the richest in science, 27; *akthar ḥarāratan*, hotter, 42

K-l-l
kulliyy, *bi-al-kulliyya*, in general, 71

K-l-m
takallama, to talk, 63; to discuss, 69
kalām, language, 4; 7 (3); statement, 18; 25; 52; 55 (2); 56; 58 (2); 74; 101; reasoning, 27; what was said, 31 (2); 42; 74; 84 (2); claim, 43; discourse, 45; *bi-hādhā al-kalām*, by saying that, 69; *akhadha fī al-kalām*, started talking, 69

K-m-m
kamm, how many, 20
kammiyya, quantity, 3 (2); 8

K-w-n
Only the entries related to generation and change were selected.
kāna, to be generated, 44 (6); 46 (3), 47; 48 (2); 51 (12); 53 (5); 56 (3); 57 (5); 59; 60; 61 (4); 62; 63 (3); 64 (5); 65 (2); 66 (2); 68; 74 (3); 76; 81; 86; 93 (2); 97; 99 (5); 101; 104 (2); 105 (2); 106 (2); 107 (7); 109; to come to be, 64; 107; to become, 93; 99 (2)
kawn, generation, 44 (5); 47; 50; 53; 60; 61; 63; 74 (2); 83; 107 (3); 109; to be generated, 83; 86; 87; *kāna al-kawn li-*, to be generated, 48
makān, place, 37 (4); 38 (2); 40
takwīn, to produce, 11; generation, 56
kā'in, to be generated, 74; 107
mukawwan, generated, 83; *ghayr mukawwan*, ungenerated, 83

K-y-f
kayfiyya, quality, 3; 12 (2); 24; 62

L-'-m
ilta'ama, lā yalta'im, to be impossible, 104

L-ḥ-j
laḥaja, to become encrusted, 12

L-z-j
luzūja, viscosity, 13 (2); 14 (2)
lazij, viscous, 14; *al-lazij*, the viscous, 14; 16 (2)

L-z-m
lazima, to be necessarily, 7; 12; to follow necessarily, 10; 97; 98; 106; *lazima ḍarūratan*, must necessarily, 53 (3); 107; to imply necessarily, 91; to follow necessarily, 95; 97; 106 (2)

L-ṭ-f
laṭāfa, fineness, 10; 12 (2)
laṭīf, fine, 10 (3); 12; *al-laṭīf*, the fine, 12

L-f-ẓ
lafẓ, word, 31; formulation, 44

L-m-s
malmūs, tangible, 24; 43; 44 (3); 46; 91

L-h-b
lahīb, flame, 59; 60 (4)
L-y-q
lā'iq, convenient, 83
L-y-n
al-layyin, the soft, 15 (4); 16 (7); 19
M-th-l
mithl, this, 7; like, 16; like for instance, 102; such, 22; 74; this sort, 60; 61; as many as, 104
mithl anna, for instance, 108
mathalan, for example, 73
mithāl, like for example, 46; like for instance, 71; example, 101
mithāl dhālika, for example, 51; for instance, 74; in the manner, 105; *'alā mithāl*, in the same manner, 78; *'alā mithāl wāḥid*, in the same manner, 14; 80; 82 (2); 85; 87; 97
M-ḥ-ḍ
maḥḍ, pure, 54
M-d-d
mudda, *ṭūl mudda*, to take longer, 53
mādda, matter, 29; 69 (2); 70 (2); 72; 74; 80; 89; 93; 94 (5)
imtidād, prolongation, 30
M-r-r
marra, to go on, 102; to pass, 104; 107
M-s-s
massa, to come into contact, 10 (2); 12 (4)
M-ḍ-y
maḍā, *kamā bayyanāhu fī-mā maḍā*, as we have previously made evident, 27
M-k-n
amkana, can, 43 (2); 94 (2); to be possible, 67; 96; *yukhabbir ayumkin an yakūn al-kalām*, explain the possibility of the claim, 43; *(lā) (laysa) yumkin*, cannot, 4; 25; 62 (2); 63; 71; 76; 89 (2); 90 (2); 107; to be impossible, 64; 65; 69; 70; 72; 74; 76; 89; 94; 102; 109 (2)
imkān, possibility, 106 (2); to be possible, 106; 107
mumkin, possible, 53; *ghayr mumkin*, impossible, 73; *lam yakun mumkin*, to be impossible, 107
M-l-'
mala'a, to fill up, 10 (2); 12 (2)
imtilā', capacity for filling up, 10
M-l-s
malāsa, smoothness, 24
al-amlas, the smooth, 24 (2)
M-l-k
malaka, possession, 76 (2)
M-n-n
minna, favour, 8
M-w-h
mā', water, 37; 39; 40; 41; 42 (7); 47 (4); 51 (5); 53 (4); 56 (5); 57 (8); 61 (2); 63 (2); 64 (6); 71; 80; 83; 87 (4); 95 (6); 96 (2); 97 (16); 98 (2); 99 (8); 101
N-b-'
nabiyy, prophet, 2
N-t-j
antaja, to conclude, 105
N-ḥ-w
naḥw, sense, 20; direction, 101; *'alā hādhā al-naḥw*, in this manner, 81; in the same way, 51; *bi-hādhā al-naḥw*, in this way; 56, 68; *'alā anḥā' kathīra*, in several senses, 17; 19 (4); 2
naḥawiyy, grammarian, 5; 46
N-z-l
anzala, to claim, 106
manzila, *bi-manzila*, as in the case of, 13; 67; such as, 14; 47 (2); in the same manner, 63; to be equivalent, 74; in the same way, 76; as, 87; 96
N-s-b
nasaba, to relate, 27
munāsaba, *lahu munāsaba ilā*, to be connected with, 38
tanāsub, relation, 37
munāsib, to correspond, 37 (2)
N-ṭ-q
naṭaqa, to pronounce, 4
N-ẓ-r
naẓara, to consider, 8; 54
naẓar, contemplation, 8; *'asr al-naẓar*, to be difficult, 49

N-f-d
nafada, to be consumed, 60
N-f-s
nafs, self, 8; 31; 52; 77; ***nafsihi bi-'aynihi***, exactly the same, 93
N-f-'
intafa'a, to benefit, 109
istanfa'a, to make use of something, 46
N-q-ṣ
naqaṣa, to lack, 107
N-q-'
muntaqa', soaked, 22; 27; ***al-muntaqa'***, the soaked, 21; 22 (7)
N-q-l
intaqala, to move, 15; 16 (5)
manqūl naql, to be transmitted, 31
N-h-y
nihāya, end, 39; 40; 92; 93; 94; extreme 94 (2); ***lā nihāya***, infinity, 69 (2); 102; 103 (2); 106 (4); 107 (2); infinite, 107; 109; infinite in number, 107 (5); 108 (2); 109 (5); infinitely many, 110 (2)
tanāhi, attainment, 33; extreme limit, 33
mutanāhī, finite (in number), 65; ***ghayr mutanāhī***, infinite, 107
N-w-r
nār, fire, 28; 29 (5); 31; 32; 33 (5); 34; 35 (3); 37; 39; 40; 41; 42 (2); 47 (2); 51 (5); 53 (4); 56 (5); 57 (7); 59 (2); 60 (2); 61; 62; 63 (2); 64 (8); 71; 73 (2); 74 (4); 80; 83; 87 (5); 92 (2); 93 (6); 94 (3); 95 (3); 96 (2); 97 (12); 98; 99 (7); 101; 102 (2); 103; 105 (2); 106 (8); 110; 111
N-w-'
naw', species, 89 (2); ***naw' mā***, somehow, 107
N-y-l
nāla, to reach, 64
H-w-ā
hawā', air, 29; 37; 39; 40; 41; 42 (9); 47 (2); 51 (5); 53 (4); 56 (2); 57 (6); 59; 60 (4); 61 (3); 62; 63 (2); 64 (11); 71; 73; 74 (4); 80; 83; 87 (4); 95; 96 (2); 97 (15); 98 (2); 99 (8); 101; 110; 111
W-j-b
wajaba, must, 24; 81 (2); 82; 109; should, 88; 97; ***yajibu ḍarūratan***, it follows necessarily, 79
wājib, ***(bi-) (fī) al-wājib***, to be necessary, 42 (2); 97
W-j-d
wajada, to find, 7; ***wujida***, to be, 73; 109; happen to be, 82; 106; to exist, 89; 106; 107 (4); 109; 110; ***wujida li-***, to contain, 21 (2); 22 (3); to have, 22 (2); 37; 47; 50; 61; 65 (2); to belong, 73; 76; to possess, 100; 107 (2); ***wujida fī***, to have, 74; to be in, 106 (2); to contain, 107
wujūd, to exist, 43; 89; 91; existence, 80; 109; ***wujūd li-***, to belong to, 87
mawjūd, present, 22; to exist, 48; ***mawjūd fī***, to be true of, 19; to be present in, 33; to be in, 106; to hold good for, 106; ***mawjūd li-***, to belong, 101; 105
W-j-h
wajh, aspect, 3; 8; way, 3; mode, 106; ***akhadha al-wujūh***, to be an eminent figure, 84
jiha, way, 29; 43; 51; 52 (3); 54 (2); 55 (2); 63 (3); 64; 68; 94 (2); 101
W-ḥ-d
wāḥid, isolated, 4; one, 20 (3); 41; 47; 51 (2); 52 (2); 53; 55 (2); 56 (2); 57; 61 (4); 62 (3); 64; 66 (4); 67 (6); 70; 71; 81; 82; 87; 88; 89 (8); 91 (2); 96; 98; 99; 105; one single, 66; 67; single, 55; 65; any, 25; 107; same, 97; ***wāḥid wāḥid***, only one, 67; ***kull wāḥid***, each, 17; 19 (3); 20 (3); 36; 38; 42; 44 (2); 49; 55; 56 (3); 57; 61; 62; 63 (2); 64; 65; 91; 94; 97 (3); 107 (3); 109; each one, 25; 41; any one, 55; ***wāḥid bi-'aynihi***, one and the same, 38; 42; 97 (3); 99; one identical, 62; 65 (2); identical, 65; 95; ***wa lā min wāḥid***, none, 69; 80; any, 82; 105; 109 (3); ***wa lā fī wāḥid***, any, 102; neither, 93; 99; ***lā min***

wāḥid, neither, 62; ***laysa wāḥid***, none, 107

W-r-d

awrada, to put off, 83; to bring forward, 84

W-z-n

mīzān, ***'ilm al-mawāzīn***, science of Balances, 3

W-s-ṭ

wasaṭ, middle, 7; 37; 44; 94; centre, 39; 40
awsaṭ, middle, 96
mutawassiṭ, intermediate, 90; 91; 97 (2); 99 (2); 108; middle, 96

W-ṣ-f

waṣafa, to describe, 99; 106
waṣf, description, 93; ***mutaqaddim waṣfuhā***, that we have previously described, 24; 101; ***qaddamna waṣfuhā***, to previously desribe, 101

W-ṣ-l

waṣala, to reach, 22
wuṣūl, ***kayfa al-wuṣūl***, how to achieve, 4
ittiṣāl, to be connected, 44; ***'alā al-ittiṣāl***, *modo continuo*, 96; 99; 110 ***muttaṣil***, adjacent, 55

W-ḍ-ḥ

awḍaḥa, to make clear, 20
wāḍiḥ, clear, 58

W-ḍ-'

waḍa'a, to establish, 35; 50; to posit, 94; 96 (2); 97 (10); 98; 99 (6); 101; 102; ***waḍa'a ma'***, to attach, 105
waḍ', position, 63 (2); 64
taqaddama waḍ'uhā, to be previously stated, 20
mawḍi', position, 4; case, 5 (3); passage, 44; 76; 83 (2); place, 83; 84
mawḍū', substrate, 91; to be posited, 93; 96; to underlie, 93; subject, 99; ***mawḍū' ilā jānibihi***, to be juxtaposed, 106; 111; ***mawḍū' qubāl***, to be opposed, 17 (2)

W-f-q

ittafaqa, ***ayy shay' ittafaqa***, anything no matter what it is, 48

W-q-t

waqt, time, 44 (2); ***wa lā fī waqt min al-awqāt***, never, 109

W-q-'

waqa'a fī, to apply to, 7

W-l-d

awlada, to generate, 94
muwallid, generative, 35

W-l-y

waliya (***yalī***), to be adjacent, 37 (2); to be next to, 51; ***talā ba'ḍuhā al-ba'ḍ***, to be consecutive, 51; 52; 55 (2); 62 (2); 63 (2); 64 (2); 65 (3); 107; 111

W-h-m

tawwahama, to imagine, 106

Y-b-s

yubūsa, dryness, 3; 10; 12; 13; 14 (2); 15; 16; 18; 20 (2); 21; 24 (3); 29; 41 (2); 42; 51 (4); 53; 56 (3); 57 (4); 60; 61 (2); 62 (2); 64 (4); 83; 87; 89; 95 (3); 97 (3); 99; 101
yābis, dry, 13; 16; 19 (2); 32; 33 (3); 47; 51; 64; 95; 97 (3); 99; 101
al-yābis, the dry, 16; 17 (3); 18 (2); 19 (3); 20 (10); 22; 42

Y-s-r

yasīr, lack, 13

Subject Index

The definite article (al-) is disregarded for purposes of alphabetisation.

Abū Bishr Mattā, 7, 90-2, 94, 110, 116
Alexander of Aphrodisias, life, 2-3
Alexander of Aphrodisias, works
De Anima, 3-4, 81
De Fato, 3
De Mixtione, 3, 6-7, 47, 67, 78-9
De Providentia, 3, 92, 98
in Metaph., 62, 67-8, 71, 76, 93, 96, 99, 116
in Meteor., 47, 49, 51, 54, 58, 62, 69, 76, 103
Mantissa, 4
Quaestiones, 4-5, 7, 14, 30-1, 34, 39, 46-9, 54, 77-81, 99-100, 103, 108
alteration, distinct from generation, 59-63, 104-5, 112
al-ʿĀmirī, 8
Anaxagoras 38
Anaximander, 37-8, 113
Anaximenes, 18, 37, 121
Aristotle, works
Categories, 12, 21-2
De Anima, 4, 12
De Caelo, 12, 27-31, 35, 39, 42-3, 50, 53, 55-6, 58, 61, 64, 71, 96, 102, 104, 114, 116
De Interpretatione, 22
Metaphysics, 31, 37, 43, 58-9, 61, 68, 72, 75, 77, 80, 96, 116
Meteorologica, 1, 27, 38, 41, 44-7, 50-1, 53-4, 73-6, 92-4, 109, 117
On Generation and Corruption, passim
On the Generation of Animals, 73
On the Parts of Animals, 43, 73-4, 96
Physics, 30-1, 35, 37, 53, 55-6, 58-9, 61, 64, 71-3, 80, 91, 100, 112, 118
Rhetoric, 6
Topics, 6, 12
Aristotle of Mytilene, 3
Asṭāth, 7, 41
Averroes, see Ibn Rushd
Avicenna, see Ibn Sīnā
al-Baghdādī, 41, 89, 91, 100
Boethius, 99
al-Dimashqī, 5, 7, 116
'domestic' fire, 46, 101
elements
as matter, 16, 30
number of, 15-16, 103, 112-13, 116, 123-5
reciprocal transformation, 13, 15-19, 43, 60, 63-8, 107-8, 111-12, 114, 119, 121-5
speed or ease of transformation, 64-8, 106-8, 114-15
Diogenes of Appolonia, 121
Empedocles, 104, 114
al-Fārābī, 1, 91
Fihrist, see Ibn al-Nadīm
Galen, 3, 11, 33
fine and thick, 21, 37-8, 91-2
hard, see soft and hard

heavy, see light and heavy
Ḥunayn b. Isḥāq, 7, 94, 116-17
hupekkauma, 47, 49, 55, 100
Ibn al-Biṭrīq, 92, 116-17
Ibn al-Nadīm, 1, 7, 100
Ibn Rushd, works
in De An., *Long*, 99
in Cael., *Short* (*Epitome*), 50-2
in GC, *Middle*, 8, 32-3, 39-41, 46, 49, 51, 93-4
in GC, *Short* (*Epitome*), 8, 101
in Metaph., *Long*, 93, 116
in Meteor., *Middle*, 49-54
Ibn Sīnā, 2, 28, 41-2, 91-2
Ibn Tibbon, 117
ice, 52-3, 100
Isḥāq b. Ḥunayn, 4, 7-8, 91-2, 94
Jābir b. Ḥayyān, 10-14 and passim
balance theory, 10-13, 88, 115
Jāḥiẓ, 89
al-Kindī, 1-2, 5, 77
light and heavy, 20-1, 27-42, 66, 97, 102, 127-9
morphology (*taṣrīf*), 11-12, 88-90, 105, 115
Mu'tazilites, 89
Nemesius, 92
Olympiodorus, 9, 22, 41, 128
Philoponus, works
De aeternitate mundi, 5
in GC, 6-9, 16-21, 25-7, 34, 38-40, 45-6, 48, 63, 95-6, 100-1, 103, 106, 108-9, 111
in Phys. 4, 32
place, natural, 29-32, 34-5, 54, 65, 91, 102, 127
Plato, 96, 100
Timaeus, 32, 49, 55, 57, 76-8, 80, 105, 113-14
Plotinus, 79, 81
Plutarch, 38
Porphyry, 99
Presocratics, 18, 37-8, 62, 112
prime matter, 55-81, 89
Proclus, 5, 79, 81
al-Qifṭī, 7, 26-7
qualities, active and passive, 13, 19-21, 28, 35-6, 38-42, 66-7, 70, 74, 76, 128-9
Qusṭā b. Lūqā, 7
al-Rāzī, Abū Bakr, 1-2
al-Rāzī, Fakhruddīn 12
receptacle, see Plato, *Timaeus*
rough, see smooth and rough
Sergius of Resh'aynā, 6
Sharastānī, 89, 118
Simplicius, 20, 30-2, 42, 47
smooth and rough, 19-21, 39-40, 97, 128
Socrates, 100
soft and hard, 21, 40, 94-5
Stoics, 3, 12, 28, 55, 118
tangibility, 13, 19-20, 39, 59, 60, 62-3, 67, 69-77
Thales, 18
Themistius, 7, 9, 22
Theophrastus, 38, 48, 55
thickness, see fine and thick
Yaḥyā b. 'Adī, 7
Ya'qūb b. Isḥāq, 15, 21-7, 33, 35-9, 41-2